Dear Sw...

In Their

OWN WORDS

Autobiographical Stories from the Lives of the Prophets

Thanks ! You are wonderful
Susan
George
_2016_

SUSAN EASTON BLACK &
MARY JANE WOODGER

Covenant Communications, Inc.

Printed in the United States of America
First Printing: March 2016

21 20 19 18 17 16   10 9 8 7 6 5 4 3 2 1

ISBN 978-1-68047-901-0

INTRODUCTION

IN THEIR OWN WORDS: AUTOBIOGRAPHICAL Stories from the Lives of the Prophets is unique in Latter-day Saint literature. There have been several biographies written on the lives of modern prophets, but no autobiographies have been published. This gap in Latter-day Saint literature has left readers to learn about the lives of prophets from the perspective of biographers, most of whom have written narrative and editorial interpretations sprinkled with occasional firsthand accounts. In each of those biographies, words of the prophets are too often obscured or relegated to secondary status as the life of the prophet unfolds.

As professors, we discovered long ago the power and inspiration that comes from quoting prophetic words. That's why *In Their Own Words* stands alone in Church literature: In this book, readers will find inspirational, humorous, and heart-wrenching stories about the lives of prophets presented in their own words.

For example, our telling the story of Joseph Smith's First Vision pales in comparison to quoting Joseph's words: "I saw two Personages, whose brightness and glory defy all description, standing above me in the air. One of them spake unto me, calling me by name and said, pointing to the other—*This is My Beloved Son. Hear Him!*" (Joseph Smith—History 1:17).

We have learned that the Spirit comes into the classroom with greater intensity when quoting such prophets as Spencer W. Kimball:

> In the hospital one day I was wheeled out of the oper-
> ating room by an attendant who stumbled, and there

issued from his angry lips vicious cursing with a combination of the names of the Savior. Even half-conscious, I recoiled and implored: "Please! Please! That is my Lord whose names you revile." There was a deathly silence, then a subdued voice whispered, "I am sorry." He had forgotten for the moment that the Lord had forcefully commanded all his people, "Thou shalt not take the name of the Lord thy God in vain; for the Lord will not hold him guiltless that taketh his name in vain."[1]

Most teachers of youth and adults have had the occasion to encourage the payment of tithes by telling the story of President Lorenzo Snow speaking in May 1899 in the St. George Tabernacle. How much better their encouragement would be if they quoted his words:

> The word of the Lord to you is not anything new; it is simply this: The time has now come for every Latter-day Saint, who calculates to be prepared for the future and to hold his feet strong upon a proper foundation, to do the will of the Lord and to pay his tithing in full. That is the word of the Lord to you, and it will be the word of the Lord to every settlement throughout the land of Zion. The Lord has blessed at times when we have not done fully His will and this because of our ignorance or lack of education, but after this we shall be held responsible and be without such pleading. We shall not hear the voice of God until we pay full tithing.[2]

Or what about encouraging family, friends, and ward members to participate in humanitarian efforts by quoting President Howard W. Hunter: "I have never been on a gloomy welfare project. I have climbed trees and picked lemons, peeled fruit, tended a boiler, carried boxes, unloaded trucks, cleaned the cannery, and a thousand and one other things, but the things I remember most are the laughing and the singing and the good fellowship of people engaged in the service of the Lord."[3]

There is much emphasis on teachers and parents being able to inspire, encourage, and motivate those whom they love to grasp the iron rod and hold fast to eternal principles. How can teachers improve their lessons? How can parents improve their influence? Quote the words of the prophets! Discover for yourselves the inspiration that comes directly from their words. As authors, we believe *In Their Own Words* serves as a companion to the set of volumes *Teachings of Presidents of the Church*. Imagine having within your grasp not only the teachings of prophets but their life stories in their own words, delivered from their unique perspectives.

TABLE OF CONTENTS

Joseph Smith Jr.

Born: December 23, 1805, Sharon, Vermont
Died: June 27, 1844, Carthage, Illinois
President of the Church: April 6, 1830, to June 27, 1844

Joseph Smith Jr.

Joseph Smith Jr., son of Joseph Smith Sr. and Lucy Mack, was born December 23, 1805, in Sharon, Vermont. As a youth, Joseph heard religious revivalists shout, "Lo here, lo there." The contest that ensued in Palmyra, New York, led young Joseph to ask himself, "What is to be done? Who of all these parties are right; or, are they all wrong together? If any one of them be right, which is it, and how shall I know it?"[4] One day while reading in the Epistle of James, first chapter and fifth verse, Joseph read, "If any of you lack wisdom, let him ask of God, that giveth to all men liberally, and upbraideth not; and it shall be given him." He later wrote, "Never did any passage of scripture come with more power to the heart of man than this did at this time to mine."[5]

On a beautiful clear day in the spring of 1820, Joseph asked God in prayer which church he should join. In answer to his prayer, he saw "two Personages, whose brightness and glory defy all description," and was told to join none of the churches, "for they were all wrong." Despite the ridicule and persecution that followed the relating of his vision to a local minister, Joseph declared, "I had actually seen a light, and in the midst of that light I saw two Personages, and they did in reality speak to me. . . . I knew it, and I knew that God knew it, and I could not deny it."[6]

Three and a half years after Joseph's heavenly manifestation, Moroni, an ancient prophet who had once lived in America, appeared to him as an angel. Moroni told him of a book "written upon gold plates, giving an account of the former inhabitants of this continent."7 In 1829 Joseph received and translated the ancient writings of that book, known today as the Book of Mormon.

On April 6, 1830, in Fayette, New York, Joseph organized a church now known as The Church of Jesus Christ of Latter-day Saints. From small beginnings, the Church grew rapidly despite mounting persecution against Joseph and his followers in New York, Ohio, Missouri, and Illinois. The growth of the Church led Josiah Quincy, a former mayor of Boston, to pen, "It is by no means improbable that some future textbook . . . will contain a question something like this: What historical American of the nineteenth century has exerted the most powerful influence upon the destinies of his countrymen? And it is by no means impossible that the answer to that interrogatory may be thus written: Joseph Smith, the Mormon Prophet."8

Throughout his life, Joseph Smith sought to do the will of God. The Lord blessed him with revelations, translations, covenants, and eternal truths. Joseph sealed his testimony of these truths with his blood on June 27, 1844, at Carthage, Illinois, and in so doing "left a fame and name that cannot be slain."9

The Life Story of Joseph Smith Jr. in His Own Words

"Deprived of the Benefit of an Education"

"Being in indigent circumstances, [we] were obliged to labor hard for the support of a large family. . . . And as it required the exertions of all that were able to render any assistance for the support of the family, therefore we were deprived of the benefit of an education. Suffice it to say, I was merely instructed in reading, writing, and the ground rules of arithmetic."

—Joseph Smith, *History 1832*, 1. Letter Book I, 1829–1835, Joseph Smith Collection.

"I Retired to a Secret Place in a Grove"

"I was born in the town of Sharon, Windsor [County], Vermont, on the 23rd of December, A.D. 1805. When [I was] ten years old, my parents removed to Palmyra, New York, where we resided about four years, and from thence we removed to the town of Manchester. My father was a farmer and taught me the art of husbandry. When about fourteen years of age, I began to reflect upon the importance of being prepared for a future state, and upon enquiring [about] the plan of salvation, I found that there was a great clash in religious sentiment; if I went to one society they referred me to one plan, and another to another; each one pointing to his own particular creed as the *summum bonum* of perfection: considering that all could not be right, and that

God could not be the author of so much confusion I determined to investigate the subject more fully, believing that if God had a Church it would not be split up into factions, and that if He taught one society to worship one way, and administer in one set of ordinances, he would not teach another principles which were diametrically opposed.

"Believing the word of God, I had confidence in the declaration of James—'If any of you lack wisdom, let him ask of God, that giveth to all men liberally, and upbraideth not; and it shall be given him.' [James 1:5] I retired to a secret place in a grove, and began to call upon the Lord, while fervently engaged in supplication, my mind was taken away from the objects with which I was surrounded, and I was enwrapped in a heavenly vision, and saw two glorious personages who exactly resembled each other in features and likeness, surrounded with a brilliant light which eclipsed the sun at noon-day. They told me that all religious denominations were believing in incorrect doctrines, and that none of them was acknowledged of God as his church and kingdom. And I was expressly commanded 'to go not after them,' at the same time receiving a promise that the fulness of the Gospel should at some future time be made known unto me."

—Joseph Smith, "Church History," *Times and Seasons*, Mar. 1, 1842, 706–707; and Joseph Smith, *History of the Church*, 5:36–41.

"A PERSONAGE STOOD BEFORE ME"

"On the evening of the 21st of September, A.D. 1823, while I was praying unto God, and endeavoring to exercise faith in the precious promises of scripture, on a sudden a light like that of day, only of a far purer and more glorious appearance, and brightness, burst into the room; indeed the first sight was as though the house was filled with consuming fire; the appearance produced a shock that affected the whole body; in a moment a personage stood before me surrounded with a glory yet greater than that with which I was already surrounded. This messenger proclaimed himself to be an angel of God, sent to bring the joyful tidings that the covenant which God made with ancient Israel was at hand to be fulfilled, that the preparatory work for the second coming of the Messiah was speedily to commence, that the time was at hand for the gospel in all its fulness to be preached in power, unto all nations that a people might be prepared for the millennial reign. I was informed that I was chosen to be an instrument in the hands of God to bring about some of his purposes in this glorious dispensation."

—Joseph Smith, "Church History," *Times and Seasons*, Nov. 15, 1841, 707; and Joseph Smith, *History of the Church*, 5:36–41.

"By the Power of God"

"By the power of God I translated the Book of Mormon from hieroglyphics, the knowledge of which was lost to the world, in which wonderful event I stood alone, an unlearned youth, to combat the worldly wisdom and multiplied ignorance of eighteen centuries, with a new revelation."

—Joseph Smith, *History of the Church*, 6:74.

"I Was the Very Prophet"

"My grandfather, Asael Smith, long ago predicted that there would be a prophet raised up in his family, and my grandmother was fully satisfied that it was fulfilled in me. My grandfather Asael died in East Stockholm, St. Lawrence county, New York, after having received the Book of Mormon, and read it nearly through; and he declared that I was the very Prophet that he had long known would come in his family."

—Joseph Smith, *History of the Church*, 2:443.

"We Were Filled with the Holy Ghost"

"We [Joseph and Oliver Cowdery] experienced great and glorious blessings from our Heavenly Father. No sooner had I baptized Oliver Cowdery, than the Holy Ghost fell upon him, and he stood up and prophesied many things which should shortly come to pass. And again, so soon as I had been baptized by him. I also had the spirit of prophecy, when, standing up, I prophesied concerning the rise of this Church, and many other things connected with the Church, and this generation of the children of men. We were filled with the Holy Ghost, and rejoiced in the God of our salvation."

—Joseph Smith—History, 1:73.

"THE UPBUILDING OF A 'HOLY CITY'"

"I received, by a heavenly vision, a commandment in June [1831], to take my journey to the western boundaries of the State of Missouri, and there designate the very spot which was to be the central place for the commencement of the gathering together of those who embrace the fullness of the everlasting Gospel. Accordingly I undertook the journey, with certain ones of my brethren, and after a long and tedious journey, suffering many privations and hardships, arrived in Jackson County, Missouri, and after viewing the country, seeking diligently at the hand of God, He manifested Himself unto us, and designated, to me and others, the very spot upon which He designed to commence the work of the gathering, and the upbuilding of an 'holy city,' which should be called Zion—Zion, because it is a place of righteousness, and all who build thereon are to worship the true and living God, and all believe in one doctrine, even the doctrine of our Lord and Savior Jesus Christ. 'Thy watchmen shall lift up the voice, with the voice together shall they sing: for they shall see eye to eye, when the Lord shall bring again Zion' [Isaiah 52:8]."

—Joseph Smith, *History of the Church*, 2:254; Joseph Smith, "To the Elders of the Church of Latter Day Saints," *Messenger and Advocate*, Sept. 1835, 179–180.

"IT WAS A SEASON OF JOY"

"I assisted the Colesville branch of the Church to lay the first log, for a house, as a foundation of Zion in Kaw township, twelve miles west of Independence. The log was carried and placed by twelve men, in honor of the twelve tribes of Israel. At the same time, through prayer, the land of Zion was consecrated and dedicated by Elder Sidney Rigdon for the gathering of the Saints. It was a season of joy to those present, and afforded a glimpse of the future, which time will yet unfold to the satisfaction of the faithful."

—Joseph Smith, *History of the Church*, 1:196.

"The Thoughts of Home"

On October 13, 1832, Smith wrote to his wife Emma from New York City:

"This day I have been walking through the most splendid part of the city of New York. The buildings are truly great and wonderful, to the astonishing of every beholder. . . . After beholding all that I had any desire to behold, I returned to my room to meditate and calm my mind; and behold, the thoughts of home, of Emma and Julia, rush upon my mind like a flood and I could wish for a moment to be with them. My breast is filled with all the feelings and tenderness of a parent and a husband, and could I be with you I would tell you many things."

—Letter from Joseph Smith to Emma Smith, Oct. 13, 1832, New York City, Community of Christ Archives, Independence, MO, cited in *Teachings of Presidents of the Church: Joseph Smith*, 241.

"I Wanted My Brethren to Fare as Well as I Did"

On May 29, 1834, Joseph Smith wrote:

"I discovered that a part of my company [in Zion's Camp] had been served with sour bread, while I had received good, sweet bread from the same cook. I reproved Brother Zebedee Coltrin for this partiality, for I wanted my brethren to fare as well as I did."

—Joseph Smith, *History of the Church*, 2:75.

"God Heard and Answered Our Prayers"

In October 1835, Joseph Smith wrote in his journal in Kirtland:

"Waited on my father again, who was very sick. In secret prayer in the morning, the Lord said, 'My servant, thy father shall live.' I waited on him all this day with my heart raised to God in the name of Jesus Christ, that He would restore him to health, that I might be blessed with his company and advice, esteeming it one of the greatest earthly blessings to be blessed with the society of parents, whose mature years and experience render them capable of administering the most wholesome advice. At evening Brother David Whitmer came in. We called on the Lord in mighty prayer in the name of Jesus Christ, and laid our hands on him, and rebuked the disease. And God heard and answered our prayers—to the great joy and satisfaction of our souls. Our aged father arose and dressed himself, shouted, and praised the Lord."

—Joseph Smith, *History of the Church*, 2:289.

"I Was Nothing but a Man"

On November 6, 1846, Joseph Smith wrote in his journal:

"I was this morning introduced to a man from the east. After hearing my name, he remarked that I was nothing but a man, indicating by this expression, that he had supposed that a person to whom the Lord should see fit to reveal His will, must be something more than a man. He seemed to have forgotten the saying that fell from the lips of St. James, that [Elijah] was a man subject to like passions as we are, yet he had such power with God, that He, in answer to his prayers, shut the heavens that they gave no rain for the space of three years and six months; and again, in answer to his prayer, the heavens gave forth rain, and the earth gave forth fruit [see James 5:17–18]. Indeed, such is the darkness and ignorance of this generation, that they look upon it as incredible that a man should have any [dealings] with his Maker."

—Joseph Smith, *History of the Church*, 2:302.

"My Heart Is Filled with Gratitude to God"

"This being the beginning of a new year [January 1, 1836], my heart is filled with gratitude to God that He has preserved my life, and the lives of my family, while another year has passed away. We have been sustained and upheld in the midst of a wicked and perverse generation, although exposed to all the afflictions, temptations, and misery that are incident to human life; for this I feel to humble myself in dust and ashes, as it were, before the Lord."

—Joseph Smith, *History of the Church*, 2:352.

"We Saw the Lord"

"I retired to the pulpit [in the Kirtland Temple on April 3, 1836], the veils being dropped, and bowed myself, with Oliver Cowdery, in solemn and silent prayer. [While praying,] the veil was taken from our minds, and the eyes of our understanding were opened. We saw the Lord standing upon the breastwork of the pulpit, before us; and under his feet was a paved work of pure gold, in color like amber. His eyes were as a flame of fire; the hair of his head was white like the pure snow; his countenance shone above the brightness of the sun; and his voice was as the sound of the rushing of great waters, even the voice of Jehovah. [The Savior said:] I have accepted this house. . . . And the fame of this house shall spread to foreign lands; and this is the beginning of the blessing which shall be poured out upon the heads of my people."

—Joseph Smith, in D&C 110: Introduction and verses 1–3, 7, 10.

"I Professed to Be Nothing but a Man"

In November 1838, while journeying from Far West to Richmond, Missouri, Joseph Smith wrote:

"We were visited by some ladies and gentlemen. One of the women came up, and very candidly inquired of the troops which of the prisoners was the Lord whom the 'Mormons' worshiped? One of the guards pointed to me with a significant smile, and said, 'This is he.' The woman then turning to me inquired whether I professed to be the Lord and Savior? I replied, that I professed to be nothing but a man, and minister of salvation, sent by Jesus Christ to preach the Gospel.

"This answer so surprised the woman that she began to inquire into our doctrine, and I preached a discourse, both to her and her companions, and to the wondering soldiers, who listened with almost breathless attention while I set forth the doctrine of faith in Jesus Christ, and repentance, and baptism for remission of sins, with the promise of the Holy Ghost, as recorded in the second chapters of the Acts of the Apostles [see Acts 2:38–39].

"The woman was satisfied, and praised God in the hearing of the soldiers, and went away, praying that God would protect and deliver us."

—Joseph Smith, *History of the Church*, 3:200–201.

"ALL WILL TURN OUT FOR THE BEST"

On November 12, 1838, while being held prisoner in Richmond, Missouri, Joseph Smith wrote to his wife Emma:

"I received your letter, which I read over and over again; it was a sweet morsel to me. O God, grant that I may have the privilege of seeing once more my lovely family in the enjoyment of the sweets of liberty and social life. To press them to my bosom and kiss their lovely cheeks would fill my heart with unspeakable gratitude. Tell the children that I am alive and trust I shall come and see them before long. Comfort their hearts all you can, and try to be comforted yourself all you can. . . .

"P.S. Write as often as you can, and if possible come and see me, and bring the children if possible. Act according to your own feelings and best judgment, and endeavor to be comforted, if possible, and I trust that all will turn out for the best."

—Letter from Joseph Smith to Emma Smith, Nov. 12, 1838, Richmond, Missouri, Community of Christ Archives, cited in *Teachings of Presidents of the Church: Joseph Smith*, 241.

"WE GLORY IN OUR TRIBULATION"

On December 16, 1838, Joseph Smith wrote to the Latter-day Saints in Caldwell County, Missouri:

"Dear brethren, do not think that our hearts faint, as though some strange thing had happened unto us, for we have seen and been assured of all these things beforehand, and have an assurance of a better hope than that of our persecutors. Therefore God hath made broad our shoulders for the burden. We glory in our tribulation, because we know that God is with us, that He is our friend, and that He will save our souls. We do not care for them that can kill the body; they cannot harm our souls. We ask no favors at the hands of mobs, nor of the world, nor of the devil, nor of his emissaries the dissenters, and those who love, and make, and swear falsehoods, to take away our lives. We have never dissembled, nor will we for the sake of our lives."

—Joseph Smith, *History of the Church*, 3:227.

"I KNEW MY INNOCENCE"

"During the time I was in the hands of my enemies [while imprisoned in Liberty Jail], I must say, that although I felt great anxiety respecting my family and friends, who were so inhumanly treated and abused. . . . yet as far as I was concerned, I felt perfectly calm, and resigned to the will of my Heavenly Father. I knew my innocence as well as that of the Saints, and that we had done nothing to deserve such treatment from the hands of our oppressors. Consequently, I could look to that God who has the lives of all men in His hands, and who had saved me frequently from the gates of death, for deliverance; and notwithstanding that every avenue of escape seemed to be entirely closed, and death stared me in the face, and that my destruction was determined upon, as far as man was concerned, yet, from my first entrance into the camp, I felt an assurance that I, with my brethren and our families, should be delivered."

—"Extract from the Private Journal of Joseph Smith Jr.," *Times and Seasons*, Nov. 1839, 7–8; Joseph Smith, *History of the Church*, 3:328–329.

"I AM IN PRISON THAT THEIR LIVES MIGHT BE SAVED"

On March 21, 1839, Joseph Smith wrote from Liberty Jail to his wife Emma:

"My dear Emma, I very well know your toils and sympathize with you. If God will spare my life once more to have the privilege of taking care of you, I will ease your care and endeavor to comfort your heart. I want you to take the best care of the family you can. I believe you will do all you can. I was sorry to learn that Frederick was sick, but I trust he is well again and that you are all well. I want you to try to gain time and write to me a long letter and tell me all you can and even if old Major is alive yet and what those little prattlers say that cling around your neck. . . . Tell them I am in prison that their lives might be saved. . . .

"God ruleth all things after the counsel of his own will. My trust is in him. The salvation of my soul is of the most importance to me forasmuch as I know for a certainty of eternal things. If the heavens linger, it is nothing to me. I must steer my [ship] safe, which I intend to do. I want you to do the same. Yours forever."

—"Letter from Joseph Smith to Emma Smith, March 21, 1839, Liberty Jail, Liberty, Missouri," Joseph Smith Collection.

"TRUTH WILL CUT ITS OWN WAY"

"The Saints can testify whether I am willing to lay down my life for my brethren. If it has been demonstrated that I have been willing to die for a 'Mormon,' I am bold to declare before Heaven that I am just as ready to die in defending the rights of a Presbyterian, a Baptist, or a good man of any other denomination; for the same principle which would trample upon the rights of the Latter-day Saints would trample upon the rights of the Roman Catholics, or of any other denomination who may be unpopular and too weak to defend themselves.

"It is a love of liberty which inspires my soul—civil and religious liberty to the whole of the human race. Love of liberty was diffused into my soul by my grandfathers while they dandled me on their knees. . . .

"If I esteem mankind to be in error, shall I bear them down? No. I will lift them up, and in their own way too, if I cannot persuade them my way is better; and I will not seek to compel any man to believe as I do, only by the force of reasoning, for truth will cut its own way."

—Joseph Smith, *History of the Church*, 5:498–499; from a discourse given by Joseph Smith on July 9, 1843, in Nauvoo, Illinois, as reported by Willard Richards.

"The Enemy of Truth Does Not Slumber"

On June 4, 1839, Joseph Smith said:

"My enemies endeavored to take every advantage of me, and heaping up abuse, getting up vexatious lawsuits, and stirring up the minds of the people against me and the people with whom I was connected, although we had done nothing [on our part] to deserve such treatment, but were busily engaged in our several vocations, and desirous to live on peaceable and friendly terms with all men. In consequence of such threats and abuse which I was continually subject to, my family were kept in a continual state of alarm, not knowing any morning what would befall me from day to day, particularly when I went from home. . . . I have learned by experience that the enemy of truth does not slumber, nor cease his exertions to bias the minds of communities against the servants of the Lord, by stirring up the indignation of men upon all matters of importance or interest."

—Joseph Smith, *History of the Church*, 3:368–369; 2:437.

"When the Horses Took Fright"

"While on the mountains some distance from Washington, our coachman stepped into a public house to take his grog, when the horses took fright and ran down the hill at full speed. I persuaded my fellow travelers to be quiet and retain their seats, but had to hold one woman to prevent her from throwing her infant out of the coach. The passengers were exceedingly agitated, but I used every persuasion to calm their feelings; and opening the door, I secured my hold on the side of the coach the best way I could and succeeded in placing myself in the coachman's seat and reining up the horses, after they had run some two or three miles, and neither coach, horses, or passengers received any injury. My course was spoken of in the highest terms of commendation as being one of the most daring and heroic deeds, and no language could express the gratitude of the passengers, when they found themselves safe and the horses quiet. There were some members of Congress with us, who proposed naming the incident to that body, believing they would reward such conduct by some public act; but on inquiring my name to mention as the author of their safety, and finding it to be Joseph Smith the 'Mormon Prophet,' as they called me, I heard no more of their praise, gratitude, or reward."

—Joseph Smith, *History of the Church*, 4:23–24.

"I LOVE TO WAIT UPON THE SAINTS"

On January 5, 1842, Joseph Smith wrote to Bishop Edward Hunter:

"I rejoice that we have been enabled to do as well as we have [with the merchandising business in the Red Brick Store], for the hearts of many of the poor brethren and sisters will be made glad with those comforts which are now within their reach.

"The store has been filled to overflowing, and I have stood behind the counter all day, dealing out goods as steady as any clerk you ever saw, to oblige those who were compelled to go without their usual Christmas and New Year's dinners, for the want of a little sugar, molasses, raisins, &c., &c.; and to please myself also, for I love to wait upon the Saints, and be a servant to all, hoping that I may be exalted in the due time of the Lord."

—"Letter of Joseph Smith to Edward Hunter, Jan. 5, 1842, Nauvoo, Illinois," in *History of the Church*, 4:492.

"The Standard of Truth Has Been Erected"

On March 1, 1842, Joseph Smith wrote to John Wentworth:

"Persecution has not stopped the progress of truth, but has only added fuel to the flame, it has spread with increasing rapidity. . . .

"The Standard of Truth has been erected; no unhallowed hand can stop the work from progressing; persecutions may rage, mobs may combine, armies may assemble, calumny may defame, but the truth of God will go forth boldly, nobly, and independent, till it has penetrated every continent, visited every clime, swept every country, and sounded in every ear, till the purposes of God shall be accomplished, and the Great Jehovah shall say the work is done."

—Joseph Smith, *History of the Church*, 4:540; Joseph Smith, "Church History," *Times and Seasons*, Mar. 1, 1842, 709.

"Deep Water Is What I Am Wont to Swim In"

On September 1, 1842, Joseph Smith wrote to the Latter-day Saints:

"And as for the perils which I am called to pass through, they seem but a small thing to me, as the envy and wrath of man have been my common lot all the days of my life. . . .

"Deep water is what I am wont to swim in. It all has become a second nature to me; and I feel, like Paul, to glory in tribulation; for to this day has the God of my fathers delivered me out of them all, and will deliver me from henceforth; for behold, and lo, I shall triumph over all my enemies, for the Lord God hath spoken it."

—Joseph Smith, in D&C 127:2.

"IT IS MY MEDITATION ALL THE DAY"

On April 15, 1843, Joseph Smith said:

"It is my meditation all the day, and more than my meat and drink, to know how I shall make the Saints of God comprehend the visions that roll like an overflowing surge before my mind."

—Joseph Smith, *History of the Church*, 5:362.

"I AM LIKE A HUGE, ROUGH STONE ROLLING"

In May 1843, Joseph Smith said:

"I am like a huge, rough stone rolling down from a high mountain; and the only polishing I get is when some corner gets rubbed off . . . all hell knocking off a corner here and a corner there. Thus I will become a smooth and polished shaft in the quiver of the Almighty."

—Joseph Smith, *History of the Church*, 5:401.

"I POSSESS THE PRINCIPLE OF LOVE"

"Sectarian priests cry out concerning me, and ask, 'Why is it this babler gains so many followers, and retains them?' I answer, It is because I possess the principle of love. All I can offer the world is a good heart and a good hand."

—Joseph Smith, *History of the Church*, 5:498.

"LIKE A LAMB TO THE SLAUGHTER"

In June 1844, Joseph Smith said:

"I am going like a lamb to the slaughter, but I am calm as a summer's morning. I have a conscience void of offense toward God and toward all men. If they take my life I shall die an innocent man, and my blood shall cry from the ground for vengeance, and it shall be said of me 'He was murdered in cold blood!'"

—Joseph Smith, *History of the Church*, 6:555.

Brigham Young

BORN: JUNE 1, 1801, WHITINGHAM, VERMONT
DIED: AUGUST 29, 1877, SALT LAKE CITY, UTAH
PRESIDENT OF THE CHURCH: DECEMBER 27, 1847, TO AUGUST 29, 1877

BRIGHAM YOUNG

BRIGHAM YOUNG, SON OF JOHN Young and Abigail Howe, was born on June 1, 1801, in Whitingham, Vermont. Reading the Book of Mormon, listening to missionaries, and studying the principle of baptism brought answers to Brigham's search for truth: "When I saw a man without eloquence, or talents for public speaking, who could only say, 'I know, by the power of the Holy Ghost, that the Book of Mormon is true, that Joseph Smith is a Prophet of the Lord,' the Holy Ghost proceeding from that individual illuminated my understanding, and light, glory, and immortality were before me."[10]

Brigham journeyed to Kirtland, Ohio, to meet the Prophet Joseph Smith. He recalled, "Here my joy was full at the privilege of shaking the hand of the Prophet of God, and receiving the sure testimony, by the spirit of prophecy, that he was all that any man could believe him to be as a true Prophet."[11] Brigham was zealous in defense of the Prophet. One evening, after overhearing a man loudly rail against Joseph Smith in Kirtland, he reacted: "I put my pants and shoes on, took my cowhide, went out, and laying hold on him, jerked him round, and assured him that if he did not stop his noise and let the people enjoy their sleep without interruption, I would cowhide him on the spot, for we had the Lord's Prophet right here, and we did not want the devil's prophet yelling round the streets. The nuisance was forthwith abated."[12]

The darkest day of Brigham's life was June 27, 1844, when the Prophet Joseph Smith was martyred. Of that day, Brigham wrote before learning of the martyrdom, "I felt a heavy depression of Spirit, and [was] so melancholy I could not converse with any degree of pleasure. . . . I could not assign my reasons for my peculiar feelings."[13] Twelve days later in Massachusetts, he learned of the tragic deaths of Joseph and his brother Hyrum. "The first thing that I thought of . . . was, whether Joseph had taken the keys of the kingdom with him from the earth," wrote Brigham. "Bringing my hand down on my knee, I said, the keys of the kingdom are right here with the Church."[14]

Brigham declared to the Latter-day Saints, "The Twelve are appointed by the finger of God . . . an independent body who have the keys of the priesthood—the keys of the kingdom of God to deliver to all the world."[15] Determined to carry forward the Lord's work, Brigham encouraged the completion of the Nauvoo Temple. "We want to build the Temple in this place," he said, "if we have to build it as the Jews built the walls of the Temple in Jerusalem, with a sword in one hand and the trowel in the other."[16] As the temple neared completion in February 1846, Brigham advised the Saints to flee from Illinois to safety in Iowa. Thousands responded and fled to the rigors of Iowa's wilderness and from there to the Rocky Mountains.

In December 1847 Brigham was sustained as President of The Church of Jesus Christ of Latter-day Saints, fulfilling a prophecy uttered by Joseph Smith many years before in Kirtland: "The time will come when Brigham Young will preside over this church."[17] Brigham served faithfully as president for nearly thirty years. During his administration, he oversaw the migration of thousands to the Salt Lake Valley and the settlement of communities in the West. When asked in 1877 if he intended to settle more valleys, he said, "Why certainly we expect to fill the next valley and then the next, and then the next, and so on. . . . We intend to hold our own here, and also penetrate the north and the south, the east and the west, there to make others and to raise the ensign of truth. . . . We will continue to grow, to increase and spread abroad, and the powers of earth and hell combined cannot hinder it."[18] Brigham died on August 29, 1877, in Salt Lake City.

The Life Story of Brigham Young in His Own Words

"It Is Nonsense to Me"

"I has appeared to me, from my childhood to this day, as a piece of complete nonsense, to talk about the inhabitants of the earth being thus irretrievably lost—to talk of my father and mother, and yours, or our ancestors, who have lived faithfully according to the best light they had; but because they had not the everlasting covenant and the holy Priesthood in their midst, that they should go to hell and roast there to all eternity. It is nonsense to me; it always was, and is yet."

—Brigham Young, in Widtsoe, *Discourses of Brigham Young*, 384.

"If I Could See the Face of a Prophet"

"I felt in those days [before joining the Church], that if I could see the face of a prophet, such as had lived on the earth in former times, a man that had revelations, to whom the heavens were opened, who knew God and his character, I would freely circumscribe the earth on my hands and knees; I thought that there was no hardship but what I would undergo, if I could see one person that knew what God is and where he is, what was his character, and what eternity was."

—Brigham Young, in *Deseret News Weekly*, Oct. 8, 1856.

"WE WOULD WORK FROM SUNRISE TO SUNSET"

Elder Heber C. Kimball wrote:

"Brigham and myself used to work hard, side by side, for fifty cents a day and board ourselves; we had seventy-five cents a day when we worked in the hayfield; we would work from sunrise to sunset, and until nine o'clock at night if there was no sign of rain. We would rake and bind after a cradler for a bushel of wheat a day, and chop wood, with snow to our waist for eighteen cents a cord, and take our pay in corn at seventy-five cents a bushel."

—Heber C. Kimball, in *Deseret News Weekly*, July 30, 1862.

"I EXAMINED THE MATTER STUDIOUSLY, FOR TWO YEARS"

Brigham Young said:

"'Hold on,' says I. . . . Wait a little while; what is the doctrine of the book [of Mormon], and of the revelations the Lord has given? Let me apply my heart to them.' . . . I examined the matter studiously, for two years, before I made up my mind to receive that book. I knew it was true, as well as I knew that I could see with my eyes, or feel by the touch of my fingers, or be sensible of the demonstration of any sense. Had not this been the case, I never would have embraced it to this day."

—Brigham Young, "Cultivate Forbearance," *Millennial Star*, July 11, 1892, 441–442.

"NOT A SHOE TO MY FOOT"

"When we arrived in Kirtland [September 1833], if any man that ever did gather with the Saints was any poorer than I was—it was because he had nothing. . . . I had two children to take care of—that was all. I was a widower. 'Brother Brigham, had you any shoes?' No; not a shoe to my foot, except a pair of borrowed boots. I had no winter clothing, except a homemade coat that I had had three or four years. 'Any pantaloons?' No. 'What did you do? Did you go without?' No; I borrowed a pair to wear till I could get another pair. I had travelled and preached and given away every dollar of my property. I was worth a little property when I started to preach. . . . I had traveled and preached until I had nothing left to gather with; but Joseph said: 'come up'; and I went up the best I could."

—Brigham Young, in *Deseret News: Semi-Weekly*, Mar. 9, 1867.

"In My Prayer I Spoke in Tongues"

"We found the Prophet, and two or three of his brothers, chopping and hauling wood. Here my joy was full at the privilege of shaking the hand of the prophet of God, and receiving the sure testimony, by the spirit of prophecy, that he was all that any man could believe him to be, as a true Prophet. He was happy to see us, and bid us welcome. We soon returned to his house, he accompanying us.

"In the evening a few of the brethren came in, and we conversed together upon the things of the kingdom. He called upon me to pray, in my prayer I spoke in tongues. As soon as we arose from our knees the brethren flocked around him, and asked his opinion concerning the gift of tongues that was upon me. He told them it was the pure Adamic language. Some said to him they expected he would condemn the gift brother Brigham had, but he said, 'No, it is of God, and the time will come when brother Brigham Young will preside over this Church.' The latter part of this conversation was in my absence."

—Brigham Young, in "History of Brigham Young," *Millennial Star*, July 11, 1863, 439.

"Opened Up, in Plainness and Simplicity, the Things of God"

"I never saw any one, until I met Joseph Smith, who could tell me anything about the character, personality and dwelling-place of God, or anything satisfactory about angels, or the relationship of man to his Maker. Yet I was as diligent as any man need to be to try and find out these things.

"He took heaven, figuratively speaking, and brought it down to earth; and he took the earth, brought it up, and opened up, in plainness and simplicity, the things of God; and that is the beauty of his mission. I had a testimony, long before that, that he was a Prophet of the Lord, and that was consoling. Did not Joseph do the same to your understandings? Would he not take the Scriptures and make them so plain and simple that every person could understand?"

—Brigham Young, in *Widtsoe, Discourses* of Brigham Young, 458–459.

"I Feel Like Shouting Hallelujah"

"I feel like shouting Hallelujah, all the time, when I think that I ever knew Joseph Smith, the Prophet whom the Lord raised up and ordained, and to whom he gave keys and power to build up the Kingdom of God on earth and sustain it. These keys are committed to this people, and we have power to continue the work that Joseph commenced, until everything is prepared for the coming of the Son of Man. This is the business of the Latter-day Saints."

—Brigham Young, in Widtsoe, *Discourses of Brigham Young*, 458.

"The World My Circuit"

"When I came into this Church, I started right out as a missionary, and took a text, and began to travel on a circuit. Truth is my text, the Gospel of salvation my subject, and the world my circuit."

—Brigham Young, in Widtsoe, *Discourses of Brigham Young*, 322.

"Nothing Short of a Testimony"

"I had only traveled a short time to testify to the people, before I learned this one fact, that you might prove doctrine from the Bible till doomsday, and it would merely convince a people, but would not convert them. You might read the Bible from Genesis to Revelation, and prove every iota that you advance, and that alone would have no converting influence upon the people. Nothing short of a testimony by the power of the Holy Ghost would bring light and knowledge to them—bring them in their hearts to repentance. Nothing short of that would ever do. You have frequently heard me say that I would rather hear an Elder, either here or in the world speak only five words accompanied by the power of God, and they would do more good than to hear long sermons without the Spirit. That is true, and we know it."

—Brigham Young, in Widtsoe, *Discourses of Brigham Young*, 330.

"Brother Joseph Called Out Twelve Apostles"

"After we returned from Missouri, my brother Joseph Young and myself had been singing after preaching in a meeting; and when the meeting was dismissed, Brother Joseph Smith said, 'Come, go down to my house with me.' We went and sung to him a long time, and talked with him. He then opened the subject of the Twelve and Seventies for the first time I ever thought of it. He said, 'Brethren, I am going to call out Twelve Apostles. I think we will get together, by-and-by, and select Twelve Apostles, and select a Quorum of Seventies from those who have been up to Zion. . . .' In 1835 the last of January or in February . . . we held our meetings from day to day, and Brother Joseph called out Twelve Apostles [on 14 February.]"

—Brigham Young, in Widtsoe, *Discourses of Brigham Young*, 141–142.

"It Truly Seemed a Miracle"

"It truly seemed a miracle to look upon the contrast between our landing and departing from Liverpool [in 1841]. We landed in the spring of 1840, as strangers in a strange land and penniless, but through the mercy of God we have gained many friends, established Churches in almost every noted town and city in the kingdom of Great Britain, baptized between seven and eight thousand, printed 5,000 Books of Mormon, 3,000 Hymn Books, 2,500 volumes of the Millennial Star, and 50,000 tracts, and emigrated to Zion 1,000 souls . . . and have left sown in the hearts of many thousands the seeds of eternal truth, which will bring forth fruit to the honor and glory of God, and yet we have lacked nothing to eat, drink or wear; in all these things I acknowledge the hand of God."

—Brigham Young, in Watson, *Manuscript History*, 96–97.

"THE PROPHET PROPHESIED THAT I SHOULD LIVE"

On November 26, 1842, Brigham Young wrote,

"I was suddenly attacked with a slight fit of apoplexy. Next morning I felt quite comfortable; but in the evening at the same hour that I had the fit the day before, I was attacked with the most violent fever I ever experienced. The Prophet Joseph and Elder Willard Richards visited and administered unto me; the Prophet prophesied that I should live and recover from my sickness. He sat by me for six hours, and directed my attendants what to do for me. In about thirty hours from the time of my being attacked by the fever, the skin began to peel from my body, and I was skinned all over. I desired to be baptized in the river, but it was not until the 14th day that Brother Joseph would give his consent for me to be showered with cold water, when my fever began to break, and it left me on the 18th day, I laid upon my back, and was not turned upon my side for eighteen days. . . .

When the fever left me on the 18th day, I was bolstered up in my chair, but was so near gone that I could not close my eyes, which were set in my head. . . . While this was going on I was perfectly conscious of all that was passing around me; my spirit was as vivid as it ever was in my life, but I had no feeling in my body."

—Brigham Young, in *Millennial Star*, Mar. 12, 1864, 167.

"THE KEYS OF THE KINGDOM"

"[I]f you want Sidney Rigdon or William Law to lead you, or anybody else, you are welcome to them; but I tell you, in the name of the Lord that no man can put another between the Twelve and the

Prophet Joseph. Why? Because Joseph was their file leader, and he has committed into their hands the keys of the kingdom in this last dispensation, for all the world."

—Brigham Young, in *History of the Church*, 6:235.

"I Addressed Letters to All Governors of States and Territories"

"In the year 1845 I addressed letters to all the Governors of states and territories in the Union, asking them for an asylum, within their borders, for the Latter-day Saints. We were refused such privilege, either by silent contempt or flat out denial in every instance. They all agreed that we could not come within the limits of their territory or state."

—Brigham Young, in Widtsoe, *Discourses of Brigham Young*, 474.

"We Had Faith that We Could Raise Grain"

"When we met Mr. Bridger [proprietor of Fort Bridger, Wyoming] on the Big Sandy River [June 28, 1847], said he, 'Mr. Young, I would give a thousand dollars if I knew an ear of corn could be ripened in [the Rockies].' Said I, 'Wait eighteen months and I will show you many of them.' Did I say this from knowledge? No, it was my faith; but we had not the least encouragement—from natural reasoning and all that we could learn of this country—of its sterility, its cold and frost, to believe that we could ever raise anything. . . . We had faith that we could raise grain; was there any harm in this? Not at all. If we had not had faith, what would have become of us? We would have gone down in unbelief, have closed up every resource for our sustenance and should never have raised anything."

—Brigham Young, in Widtsoe, *Discourses of Brigham Young*, 481.

"Many Have Been Healed under My Administration"

"I am here to testify to hundreds of instances of men, women, and children being healed by the power of God, through the laying on of hands, and many I have seen raised from the gates of death, and brought back from the verge of eternity; and some whose spirits had actually left their bodies, returned again. I testify that I have seen the sick healed by the laying on of hands, according to the promise of the Savior.

"When I lay hands on the sick, I expect the healing power and influence of God to pass through me to the patient, and the disease to give way. I do not say that I heal everybody I lay hands on; but many have been healed under my administration. . . .

"I am sent for continually, though I only go occasionally, because it is a privilege of every father, who is an Elder in Israel, to have faith to heal his family, just as much so as it is my privilege to have faith to heal my family; and if he does not do it he is not living up to his privilege. It is just as reasonable for him to ask me to cut his wood and maintain his family, for if he had faith himself he would save me the trouble of leaving other duties to attend to his request."

—Brigham Young, in Widtsoe, *Discourses of Brigham Young*, 162–163.

"None of His Children Have Been Sealed to Him"

"My father died before the endowments were given. None of his children have been sealed to him. If you recollect, . . . we were very much hurried in the little time we spent [in Nauvoo] after the temple was built. The mob was there ready to destroy us; . . . but we finished the temple according to the commandment that was given to Joseph, and then took our departure. Our time, therefore, was short, and we had no time to attend to this. My father's children, consequently, have not been sealed to him. Perhaps all of his sons may go into eternity, into the spirit world, before this can be attended to; but this will make no difference; the heirs of the family will attend to this if it is not for a hundred years."

—Brigham Young, in Widtsoe, *Discourses of Brigham Young*, 401.

"I Hope to Advance in the True Knowledge of God"

"As I advance in years I hope to advance in the true knowledge of God and godliness. I hope to increase in the power of the Almighty and in influence to establish peace and righteousness upon the earth, and to bring . . . all who will hearken to the principles of righteousness, to a true sense of the knowledge of God and godliness, of themselves and the relation they sustain to heaven and heavenly beings. . . . I pray that this may be the case not only with myself but with all the Saints, that we may grow in grace and in the knowledge of the truth and be made perfect before Him."

—Brigham Young, in *Deseret News Weekly*, June 10, 1857.

"Feeling a Child-like Timidity"

"I need the wisdom of God and his Spirit to be in my heart to enable me to speak to the edification of the people. Although I have been a public speaker for thirty-seven years, it is seldom that I rise before a congregation without feeling a child-like timidity; if I live to the age of Methuselah I do not know that I shall outgrow it. There are reasons for this which I understand. When I look upon the faces of intelligent beings I look upon the image of the God I serve. There are none but what have a certain portion of divinity within them; and though we are clothed with bodies which are in the image of our God, yet this mortality shrinks before that portion of divinity which we inherit from our Father. This is the cause of my timidity."

—Brigham Young, in Widtsoe, *Discourses of Brigham Young*, 168.

"My Life Is Before the World"

"Our work, our every-day labor, our whole lives are within the scope of our religion. This is what we believe and what we try to practice. Yet the Lord permits a great many things that he never commands. . . . The Lord never commanded me to dance, yet I have danced: you all know it, for my life is before the world. Yet while the Lord has never commanded me to do it, he has permitted it. I do not know that he ever commanded the boys to go and play at ball, yet he permits it. I am not aware that he ever commanded us to build a theater, but he has permitted it, and I can give the reason why. Recreation and diversion are as necessary to our well-being as the more serious pursuits of life."

—Brigham Young, in Widtsoe, *Discourses of Brigham Young*, 238.

"I GIVE GOD THE GLORY AND THE PRAISE"

"My testimony is positive. . . . I know that the sun shines, I know that I exist and have a being, and I testify that there is a God, and that Jesus Christ lives, and that he is the Savior of the world. Have you been to heaven and learned to the contrary? I know that Joseph Smith was a Prophet of God, and that he had many revelations. Who can disprove this testimony? Any one may dispute it, but there is no one in the world who can disprove it. I have had many revelations; I have seen and heard for myself, and know these things are true, and nobody on earth can disprove them. The eye, the ear, the hand, all the senses may be deceived, but the Spirit of God cannot be deceived; and when inspired with that Spirit, the whole man is filled with knowledge, he can see with a spiritual eye, and know that which is beyond the power of man to controvert. What I know concerning God, concerning the earth, concerning government, I have received from the heavens, not alone through my natural ability, and I give God the glory and the praise."

—Brigham Young, in Widtsoe, *Discourses of Brigham Young*, 433.

"'MORMONISM' HAS DONE EVERYTHING FOR ME"

"'Mormonism' has done everything for me that ever has been done for me on the earth; it has made me happy . . . it has filled me with good feelings, with joy and rejoicing. Whereas, before I possessed the spirit of the Gospel I was troubled with that which I hear others complain of, that is, with, at times, feeling cast down, gloomy, and despondent; with everything wearing to me, at times, a dreary aspect.

"But since I have embraced the Gospel not for one-half minute, to the best of my recollection, has anything worn to me a gloomy aspect."

—Brigham Young, in Widtsoe, *Discourses of Brigham Young*, 452–453.

"I Leave to Futurity the Judgment of My Labors"

In April 1873, Brigham Young wrote to the editor of the *New York Herald*:

"The result of my labors for the last twenty-six years, briefly summed up are—The peopling of this Territory by the Latter-day Saints of about one hundred thousand souls; the founding of over two hundred cities, towns, and villages inhabited by our people, which extend to Idaho in the north, Wyoming in the east, Nevada in the west; and Arizona in the south, and the establishment of schools, factories, mills and other institutions calculated to benefit and improve our community.

"All my transactions and labors have been carried on in accordance with my calling as a servant of God. I know no difference between spiritual and temporal labors. God has seen fit to bless me with means, and as a faithful steward I use them to benefit my fellow men—to promote their happiness in this world. . . .

"My whole life is devoted to the Almighty's service, and while I regret that my mission is not better understood by the world, the time will come when I will be understood, and I leave to futurity the judgment of my labors and their result as they shall become manifest."

—"Brigham Young's reply to the *New York Herald*," *Millennial Star*, May 6, 1873, 286–287.

John Taylor

Born: November 1, 1808, Milnthorpe, England
Died: July 25, 1887, Kaysville, Utah
President of the Church: October 10, 1880, to July 25, 1887

JOHN TAYLOR

JOHN TAYLOR, SON OF JAMES and Agnes Taylor, was born on November 1, 1808, in Milnthorpe, England. As a boy, John saw in vision an angel holding a trump to his mouth and sounding a message to the nations. Although he wouldn't understand the meaning of this vision until later in life, John began to search for greater truth. In 1824, he united with the Methodists and became a Methodist exhorter. His unusual perceptions of Methodism led to his dismissal.

It was Parley P. Pratt who introduced John to Mormonism. John compared Parley's teachings to the scriptures: "I made a regular business of it for three weeks, and followed Brother Parley from place to place." Of his confidence in Mormonism, he said, "I have never doubted any principle of Mormonism since."[19]

John Taylor's testimony of the work was evident in his ordinations to the office of elder, high priest, and Apostle. Of his apostolic calling, John said, "I felt my own weakness and littleness; but I felt determined, the Lord being my helper, to endeavor to magnify it."[20]

John shared the gospel in England and Ireland, baptizing hundreds of converts. After his return to the States, he was elected to the Nauvoo City Council and named a regent of the University of Nauvoo. He was the editor of the *Times and Seasons*, the *Wasp*, and the *Nauvoo Neighbor*.

John was with Joseph Smith and his brother Hyrum on June 27, 1844, at Carthage Jail. In that loathsome jail, he sang "A Poor Wayfaring Man of Grief" before being wounded by four bullets. Although a victim of religious bigotry and brutality, John's faithful obedience endured. He said, "I expected when I came into this

Church that I should be persecuted and proscribed. I expected that the people would be persecuted, but I believed that God had spoken, that the eternal principles of truth had been revealed, and that God had a work to accomplish which was in opposition to the ideas, values, and notions of men, and I did not know but it would cost me my life before I got through."[21]

John followed the leadership of Brigham Young from Nauvoo to the Salt Lake Valley. From 1857 to 1876, he served in the Utah Territorial Legislature as speaker of the House of Representatives. From 1868 to 1870 he was a probate judge in Utah County. John's civic service ended, however, when he became the third President of The Church of Jesus Christ of Latter-day Saints.

In his administration, John encouraged temple building and regular priesthood meetings and conferences in the stakes of Zion. In 1880, he held a jubilee year to commemorate the fiftieth anniversary of the organization of the Church. During the jubilee, John forgave half of the debt owed to the Perpetual Emigration Fund and half of the delinquent tithing of the poor.

When the U.S. government tried to curtail the religious practice of plural marriage, John decried "those who would use its power to abuse the rights of others."[22] On February 1, 1885, John gave his last public sermon: "You will see trouble, trouble, trouble enough in these United States. . . . I tell you in the name of God, woe to them that fight against Zion, for God will fight against them!"[23]

John went into self-imposed exile to escape ruthless persecution by unrelenting enemies of the Church. While in exile, John wrote, "We are engaged in a great work, and laying the foundation thereof—a work that has been spoken of by all the holy prophets since the world was."[24]

John died at age seventy-eight. On his coffin was inscribed "Holiness to the Lord. Rest in Peace."

THE LIFE STORY OF JOHN TAYLOR
IN HIS OWN WORDS

"CALL UPON THE LORD IN YOUR SECRET PLACES"

"I am reminded of my boyhood. At that early period of my life I learned to approach God. Many a time I have gone into the fields, and, concealing myself behind some bush, would bow before the Lord and call upon him to guide and direct me. And he heard my prayer. At times I would get other boys to accompany me. It would not hurt you, boys and girls, to call upon the Lord in your secret places, as I did. That was the spirit which I had when a little boy. And God has led me from one thing to another. . . . My spirit was drawn out after God then; and I feel the same yet."

—John Taylor, *The Gospel Kingdom*, ed. G. Homer Durham, 46.

"I WANTED NO FABLES"

"[In May 1836] Parley P. Pratt called on me with a letter of introduction from a merchant of my acquaintance. I had peculiar feelings on seeing him. I had heard a great many stories of a similar kind to those that you have heard, and I must say that I thought my friend had imposed upon me a little in sending a man of this persuasion to me. I, however, received him courteously as I was bound to. I told him, however, plainly, my feelings, and that in our researches I wanted no fables; I wished him to confine himself to the scriptures. We talked for three hours or upwards, and he bound me as close to the scriptures as desired, proving everything he said therefrom. I afterwards wrote down eight sermons that he preached, in order that I might compare them with the word of God. I found nothing contrary. I then examined the Book of Mormon, and the prophecies concerning that; that was also correct. I then read the book of 'Doctrine and Covenants;' found nothing unscriptural there. He called upon us to repent and be baptized for the remission of sins, and, we should receive the Holy Ghost. But what is that? we inquired; the same, he answered, as it was in the Apostles' days, or nothing. A number of others and myself were baptized [May 9, 1836]."

—John Taylor, in "Three Nights' Public Discussion . . ," in *Series of Pamphlets*, by Orson Pratt . . . [1851], 17–18.

"If the Work Was True Six Months Ago, It Is True Today"

When Elder Parley P. Pratt approached John Taylor and shared doubts about the prophetic calling of Joseph Smith, John Taylor replied: "'I am surprised to hear you speak so, Brother Parley. Before you left Canada you bore a strong testimony to Joseph Smith being a Prophet of God, and to the truth of the work he has inaugurated; and you said you knew these things by revelation, and the gift of the Holy Ghost. You gave to me a strict charge to the effect that though you or an angel from heaven was to declare anything else I was not to believe it. Now Brother Parley, it is not man that I am following, but the Lord. The principles you taught me led me to Him, and I now have the same testimony that you then rejoiced in. If the work was true six months ago, it is true today; if Joseph Smith was then a prophet, he is now a prophet.'" To Elder Pratt's credit, he soon repented of his feelings and continued to be a valiant servant of the Lord.

—John Taylor, in Roberts, *Life of John Taylor*, 39–40.

"Follow the Leadings of That Spirit"

"I well remember a remark that Joseph Smith made to me. . . . Said he, 'Elder Taylor, you have been baptized, you have had hands laid upon your head for the reception of the Holy Ghost, and you have been ordained to the holy priesthood. Now if you will continue to follow the leadings of that spirit, it will always lead you right. Sometimes it might be contrary to your judgment; never mind that, follow its dictates; and if you be true to its whisperings it will in time become in you a principle of revelation so that you will know all things.'"

—John Taylor, in *Deseret News Semi-Weekly*, Jan. 15, 1878.

"I Felt My Own Weakness and Littleness"

"The work [of an Apostle] seemed great, the duties arduous and responsible. I felt my own weakness and littleness; but I felt determined, the Lord being my helper, to endeavor to magnify it. When I first entered upon Mormonism, I did it with my eyes open. I counted the cost. I looked upon it as a life-long labor, and considered that I was not only enlisted for time, but for eternity also, and did not wish to shrink now, although I felt my incompetency."

—John Taylor, in Roberts, *Life of John Taylor*, 48.

"He Has Answered My Prayers"

"There is not a man upon the earth that has put his trust in God, I do not care what part of the world he has been in, but what can say that he delivered him. I know that has been the case with me, emphatically so. I have been satisfied, when in foreign lands and in strange countries, where I had no access but to the Almighty, that he was on my side, and I know that he has answered my prayers."

—John Taylor, *The Gospel Kingdom*, ed. G. Homer Durham, 45.

"I Am a Servant of God"

"Some, in speaking of war and troubles, will say, are you not afraid? No, I am a servant of God, and this is enough, for Father is at the helm. It is for me to be as clay in the hands of the potter, to be pliable and walk in the light of the countenance of the Spirit of the Lord, and then no matter what comes. Let the lightnings flash and the earthquakes bellow, God is at the helm, and I feel like saying but little, for the Lord God Omnipotent reigneth and will continue his work until he has put all enemies under his feet, and his kingdom extends from the rivers to the ends of the earth."

—John Taylor, in *Deseret News Weekly*, Dec. 24, 1862, 202.

"You Purpose to Tar and Feather Me"

"Gentlemen, I now stand among men whose fathers fought for and obtained one of the greatest blessings ever conferred upon the human family—the right to think, to speak, to write; the right to say who shall govern them, and the right to worship God according to the dictates of their own consciences—all of them sacred, human rights, and now guaranteed by the American Constitution. I see around me the sons of those noble sires, who, rather than bow to the behests of a tyrant, pledged their lives, fortunes and sacred honors to burst those fetters, enjoy freedom themselves, bequeath it to their posterity, or die in the attempt. . . .

"But, by the by, I have been informed that you purpose to tar and feather me, for my religious opinions. Is this the boon you have inherited from your fathers? Is this the blessing they purchased with their dearest hearts' blood—this your liberty? If so, you now have a victim, and we will have an offering to the goddess of liberty. . . .

"Gentlemen come on with your tar and feathers, your victim is ready; and ye shades of the venerable patriots, gaze upon the deeds of your degenerate sons! Come on, gentlemen! Come on, I say, I am ready!"

—John Taylor, in Roberts, *Life of John Taylor*, 53–55.

"The Lord Has Been True and Faithful"

"I, myself, have traveled hundreds of thousands of miles preaching the gospel; and without purse or scrip, trusting in the Lord. Did he ever forsake me? Never, no never. I always was provided for, for which I feel to praise God my Heavenly Father. I was engaged in his work, and he told me that he would sustain me in it. He has been true to his trust; and if I have not been true to mine, I hope he will forgive me and help me to do better. But the Lord has been true and faithful, and I have never needed anything to eat or drink or wear, and was never prevented for want of means of traveling where I pleased."

—John Taylor, *The Gospel Kingdom*, ed. G. Homer Durham, 234.

"The Spirit of God Rested upon Us"

"I will tell you a circumstance that took place with me upwards of forty years ago. I was living in Canada at the time, and was a traveling Elder. I presided over a number of the churches in that district of country. A difficulty existed in a branch of the church, and steps were taken to have the matter brought before me for settlement. I thought very seriously about it, and thought it a very insignificant affair. . . . Before going to the trial I bowed before the Lord, and sought wisdom from him to conduct the affair aright, for I had the welfare of the people at heart. When we had assembled I opened the meeting with prayer, and then called upon a number of those present to pray; they did so, and the Spirit of God rested upon us. I could perceive that a good feeling existed in the hearts of those who had come to present their grievances, and I told them to bring forward their case. But they said they had not anything to bring forward. The feelings and spirit they had been in possession of had left them, the Spirit of God had obliterated these feelings out of their hearts, and they knew it was right for them to forgive one another."

—John Taylor, "The Order and Duties of the Priesthood," in *Journal of Discourses*, 21:366–367.

"You Are Welcome to Anything I Have"

"Elder [Parley P.] Pratt: 'Brother Taylor, I hear you have plenty of money?'

"Elder [John] Taylor: 'Yes, Brother Pratt, that's true.'

"Elder Pratt: 'Well, I am about to publish my 'Voice of Warning' and 'Millennial Poems,' I am very much in need of money, and if you could furnish me two or three hundred dollars I should be very much obliged.'

"Elder Taylor: 'Well, Brother Parley, you are welcome to anything I have, if it will be of service to you.'

"Elder Pratt: 'I never saw the time when means would be more acceptable.'

"Elder Taylor: 'Then you are welcome to all I have.'

"And putting his hand into his pocket Elder Taylor gave him his copper cent. A laugh followed.

"'But I thought you gave it out that you had plenty of money,' said Parley.

"'Yes, and so I have,' replied Elder Taylor. 'I am well clothed, you furnish me plenty to eat and drink and good lodging; with all these things and a penny over, as I owe nothing, is not that plenty?'"

—John Taylor, in Roberts, *Life of John Taylor*, 73.

"Streams of Fire as Thick as My Arm"

"Streams of fire as thick as my arm passed by me as these men fired [into the bedroom of Carthage Jail] . . . it looked like certain death. I remember feeling as though my time had come, but I do not know when, in any critical position, I was more calm, unruffled, energetic, and acted with more promptness and decision."

—John Taylor, *The Gospel Kingdom*, ed. G. Homer Durham, 360.

"This Is My Testimony"

"I testify that I was acquainted with Joseph Smith for years. I have traveled with him; I have been with him in private and in public; I have associated with him in councils of all kinds; I have listened hundreds of times to his public teachings, and his advice to his friends and associates of a more private nature. I have been at his house and seen his deportment in his family. I have seen him arraigned before the tribunals of his country, and seen him honorably acquitted, and delivered from the pernicious breath of slander, and the machinations and falsehoods of wicked and corrupt men. I was with him living, and with him when he died, when he was murdered in Carthage jail by a ruthless mob . . . with their faces painted, and headed by a Methodist minister, named Williams—I was there, and was myself wounded; I, at that time, received four balls in my body. I have seen him, then, under these various circumstances, and I testify before God, angels and men, that he was a good, honorable, virtuous man—that his doctrines were good, scriptural and wholesome—that his precepts were such as became a man of God—that his private and public character was unimpeachable—and that he lived and died as a man of God and a gentleman. This is my testimony."

—John Taylor, *The Gospel Kingdom*, ed. G. Homer Durham, 355.

"His Practice Was Devilish"

"The doctor, on seeing a ball lodged in my left hand, took a pen-knife from his pocket and made an incision in it for the purpose of extracting the ball therefrom, and having obtained a pair of carpenter's compasses, made use of them to draw or pry out the ball, alternately using the penknife and compasses. After sawing for some time with a dull penknife, and prying and pulling with the compasses, he ultimately succeeded in extracting the ball, which weighed about half an ounce. Some time afterwards he remarked to a friend of mine that 'I had nerves like the devil,' to stand what I did in its extraction. I really thought I had need of nerves to stand such surgical butchery, and that, whatever my nerves may be, his practice was devilish."

—John Taylor, in *History of the Church*, 7:107.

"I Feel to Rejoice"

"I rejoice in afflictions, for they are necessary to humble and prove us, that we may comprehend ourselves, become acquainted with our weakness and infirmities; and I rejoice when I triumph over them, because God answers my prayers; therefore I feel to rejoice all the day long."

—John Taylor, *The Gospel Kingdom*, ed. G. Homer Durham, 234.

"The Lord Favoured Us in Our Extremities"

"I was appointed to go to France some years ago, in company with some of the Twelve, who were appointed to go to other places. The First Presidency asked us if we would go. Yes, was the reply; we can go anywhere, for if we cannot do little things like these, I don't know what else we can do. Some people talk about doing great things; but it is not a great thing to travel a little, or to preach a little. I hear some of our Elders saying, sometimes, that they are going to do great things—to be rulers in the kingdom of God, Kings and Priests to the Most High, and are again to exalt thousands of others to thrones, principalities, and powers, in the eternal worlds; but we cannot get them out of their nests to travel a few miles here. If they cannot do this, how will they ever learn to go from world to world?

"We went, and were blessed in our journeying. We had a pretty hard time in crossing the plains, and I should not recommend people to go so late in the season as we did. We should have lost all our horses, but the hand of God was over us for our good. He delivered us out of all our dangers, and took us through safely. When we got to the Missouri River, the ice was running very strong, so that it was impossible to ferry; but in one night the river froze over, and we passed over as on a bridge, in perfect safety; but as soon as the last team was over, the ice again removed. Thus the Lord favoured us in our extremities."

—John Taylor, "Elder John Taylor's Mission to Europe in 1849–1852," in *Journal of Discourses*, 1:19–20.

"When Gathering the Fruit"

Moses W. Taylor wrote of his father, John Taylor:

"When gathering the fruit in the fall father [John Taylor] would come and inspect the baskets and selecting the largest and best fruit would say: 'Take the tithing out of this and be sure and pay it in full.'"

—Moses W. Taylor, "Stories and Counsel of Prest. Taylor," *Young Woman's Journal*, May 1905, 218.

"That Old Windbag Was Your Father"

Ezra Oakley Taylor wrote of his father, John Taylor:

"As I was growing up, it was the custom to hold Sunday afternoon meetings in the Tabernacle. All of us were expected to be there, and at a later time be able to report as to who gave the sermon, what it was about, who gave the prayers, and what hymns were sung. This particular Sunday, some of us decided to skip just this once and to get one of our friends to give us the necessary information. Then came the [family] council and sure enough Father asked me about the sermon, and who gave it. All prepared, my friend said he couldn't remember very well, I repeated his words, 'Oh, it was some old windbag, and I can't remember his name, but it was surely uninteresting.' With a twinkle in his eye, Father said, 'That old windbag was your father' and continued with the council meeting."

—Julia Neville Taylor, "An Interview with Ezra Oakley Taylor, Son of President John Taylor," Microfilm 2, in *Teachings of Presidents of the Church: John Taylor*, xix.

"It Was Always in the Spirit of Counsel"

Moses W. Taylor wrote of his father, John Taylor:

"[Father] had a strong desire to keep his children under the family influence and provided play grounds for us. Even when he was past seventy years of age he would join us in our games. He provided a large sand pile for the little ones and if I have ever had any better time in my life than I did digging in the sand, I have failed to recognize it. . . .

"I have never heard him enter into any argument with any of his family; I have never heard him and my mother contend or disagree in the presence of the children. When talking about our duties in the church, it was always in the spirit of counsel and he would frequently say, 'It would please me if you are a faithful Latter-day Saint.' He was held in such high esteem by his children that to please him seemed to be their greatest desire."

—Moses W. Taylor, "Stories and Counsel of Prest. Taylor," *Young Woman's Journal*, May 1905, 218, 219.

"I Take Pleasure in Meeting with the Saints"

"I take pleasure in meeting with the Saints. I like to break bread with them in commemoration of the broken body of our Lord and Savior Jesus Christ, and also to partake of the cup in remembrance of his shed blood. And then to reflect upon the associations connected therewith. Our relationship to God through our Lord Jesus Christ; our relationship to each other as members of the body of Christ, and our hopes concerning the future; the second appearing of our Lord Jesus Christ, when, we are given to understand, he will gird himself and wait upon us, and we shall eat bread and drink wine with him in his Father's kingdom. I like to reflect upon all these and a thousand other things connected with the salvation, happiness and exaltation of the Saints of God in this world, and in the world to come."

—John Taylor, in *Deseret News Weekly*, Jan. 15, 1873, 760.

"We Were Standing on Holy Ground"

"When I visited that holy [St. George] Temple, accompanied by my brethren who were with me, we experienced a sacred thrill of joy and a solemn, reverential sensation. As we entered its sacred portals, we felt that we were standing on holy ground, and experienced, with one of old, 'Surely this is the house of God, and the gate of heaven.' [See Genesis 28:17.] That is not simply a metaphorical expression, but a reality, for it is in that House, and it will be in the House to be built on this ground, that the most sacred ordinances of God are to be performed, which are associated with the interest and happiness of the human family, living and dead. I felt to rejoice in my heart that we had been thus far successful in the building of one temple to the name of our Father and God."

—John Taylor, in *Deseret News, Semi-Weekly*, June 19, 1877, 1.

Wilford Woodruff

Born: March 1, 1807, Farmington, Connecticut
Died: September 2, 1898, San Francisco, California
President of the Church: April 7, 1889, to September 2, 1898

WILFORD WOODRUFF

WILFORD WOODRUFF, SON OF APHEK Woodruff and Beulah Thompson, was born March 1, 1807, in Farmington, Connecticut. In his youth Wilford "pleaded with the Lord many hours in the forest, among the rocks, and in the fields, and in the mill—often at midnight for light and truth and for His Spirit to guide me in the way of salvation." At age twenty-three, as he listened to Zera Pulsipher preach of the restored gospel, "the spirit bore witness of its truth." On December 31, 1833, Wilford was baptized by Elder Pulsipher: "The snow was about three feet deep, the day was cold, and the water was mixed with ice and snow, yet I did not feel the cold."[25]

Wilford's early experiences in the Church included marching with Zion's Camp to Missouri, serving missions to the southern and eastern states, and being ordained an Apostle on April 26, 1839, at Far West, Missouri.

When poor health threatened to prevent his fulfilling a mission to England, Joseph Smith remarked, "Well, Brother Woodruff, you have started upon your mission."

"Yes," Wilford said, "but I feel and look more like a subject for the dissecting room than a missionary."

Joseph replied, "What did you say that for? Get up, and go along; all will be right with you." On that mission to England, Wilford brought more than "eighteen hundred souls" to the waters of baptism.[26]

While serving a mission with Brigham Young to the eastern states in 1844, Wilford learned of the martyrdom of Joseph Smith and his brother Hyrum. Wilford wrote, "Brother Young took the bed and I the armchair, and then we veiled our faces and gave vent to our grief. Until now I had not shed a tear since the death of the Prophet. My soul had been nerved up like steel."[27]

Wilford kept a daily journal for sixty-three years and a history of the leading men in the Church. In referring to his writings, Wilford penned, "I seem to be a marked victim of the adversary. I can find but one reason for this: the devil knew if I got into the Church of Jesus Christ of Latter-day Saints, I would write the history of that Church and leave on record the works and teachings of the prophets, of the apostles and elders."[28]

In 1877 at the close of the dedicatory services of the St. George Temple, Wilford was appointed to preside over that temple. In 1879 persecution against plural marriage caused him to go into exile: "For the first time in my life I have had to flee from my enemies for the gospel's sake. . . . They are trying to arrest me for obeying the law of God in reference to Plural Marriage."[29]

At the death of President John Taylor in 1887, Wilford became the President of the Church. "It is a position I have never looked for," he wrote. "I pray God . . . to give me grace equal to my day."[30] His administration was fraught with government persecution. Persecution subsided, in part, on October 6, 1890, when Wilford presented a manifesto ending plural marriage: "I want to say to all Israel that the step which I have taken in issuing this Manifesto has not been done without earnest prayer before the Lord."[31]

When Wilford neared the end of his life, he summarized his journals and concluded that from 1834 to 1895 he had traveled 172,269 miles, held 7,555 meetings, attended 75 semiannual general conferences of the Church, attended 344 quarterly conferences, preached 3,526 discourses, established 77 preaching places in missions, organized 51 branches, received 18,977 letters, written 11,519 letters, assisted in confirming 8,952 Saints, labored 603 days in the Endowment House, and traveled through England, Scotland, Wales, six islands of the sea, twenty-three states, and five U.S. territories in the cause of righteousness.[32]

Wilford died on September 2, 1898, in San Francisco, California. His remains were conveyed by rail from San Francisco to Salt Lake City, where his funeral was held in the tabernacle.

THE LIFE STORY OF WILFORD WOODRUFF IN HIS OWN WORDS

"I CAME NEAR BEING KILLED BY A SURLY BULL"

"When six years of age, I came near being killed by a surly bull. My father and I were feeding pumpkins to the cattle, [and] a surly bull drove my cow away from the one she was eating. I took the pumpkin he had left, upon which he pitched at me. My father told me to throw down the pumpkin and run. I ran down a steep hill, and took the pumpkin with me, being determined that the cow should have her rights. The bull pursued. As he was about to overtake me, I stepped into a post hole and fell; the bull leaped over me, after the pumpkin, and tore it to pieces with his horns, and would have served me in the same way, had I not fallen."

—"History of Wilford Woodruff (From His Own Pen): Chapter of Accidents," *Millennial Star*, June 10, 1865, 359–360.

"GENTLENESS AND MERCY ARE BETTER EVERY WAY"

"When I was a boy and went to school, the schoolmaster used to come with a bundle of sticks about eight feet long, and one of the first things we expected was to get a whipping. For anything that was not pleasing to him we would get a terrible thrashing. What whipping I got then did not do me any good. . . . Kindness, gentleness and mercy are better every way."

—Wilford Woodruff, *Deseret News Weekly*, June 22, 1889, 823.

"The Protection and Mercy of God Has Been over Me"

"I have broken both legs—one in two places—both arms, my breast bone and three ribs, and had both ankles dislocated. I have been drowned, frozen, scalded and bit by a mad dog—have been in two water wheels under full head of water—have passed through several severe fits of sickness, and encountered poison in its worst forms—have landed in a pile of railroad ruins—have barely been missed by the passing bullets, and have passed through a score of other hair-breadth escapes.

"It has appeared miraculous to me, that with all the injuries and broken bones which I have had, I have not a lame limb, but have been enabled to endure the hardest labor, exposures and journeys—have often walked forty, fifty, and one occasion, sixty miles in a day. The protection and mercy of God has been over me, and my life thus far has been preserved; for which blessings I feel to render the gratitude of my heart to my Heavenly Father, praying that the remainder of my days may be spent in His service and in the building up of His kingdom."

—"History of Wilford Woodruff (From His Own Pen): Chapter of Accidents," *Millennial Star*, June 24, 1865, 392.

"I Would Have Gone a Thousand Miles to Have Seen a Prophet"

"In my early manhood I prayed day and night that I might live to see a prophet. I would have gone a thousand miles to have seen a prophet, or a man that could teach me the things that I read of in the Bible. I could not join any church, because I could not find any church at that time that advocated these principles. I spent many a midnight hour, by the river side, in the mountains, and in my mill . . . calling upon God that I might live to see a prophet or some man that would teach me of the things of the kingdom of God as I read them."

—"Discourse by President Wilford Woodruff," *Millennial Star*, Nov. 21, 1895, 741.

"No Longer Needed"

"Before I ever heard of 'Mormonism,' when reading the Scriptures, I often wondered why it was that we had no prophets, no apostles, no gifts of graces, no healings by the power of God, no visions, no angels, no revelations, no voice of God. I often wondered why these things were not continued among the children of men, why they were not enjoyed by the different churches and denominations of the day, and in my conversation with theologians and divines, I often referred to these things, but they all told me that such supernatural manifestations were unnecessary in our day and age of the world, that such power was only necessary in a day of darkness, among an ignorant generation of people; they needed Prophets to lead them; but we who live in the blaze of Gospel light need no such thing; we need no revelation, only that which is in the Bible; we need no visitation of angels now, those things were given to establish the doctrine of Christ, and when it was once established they were no longer needed."

—Wilford Woodruff, "The Church and Kingdom of God, etc.," in *Journal of Discourses*, 2:195–196.

"I First Met Joseph Smith"

"Before I saw Joseph I said I did not care how old he was, or how young he was; I did not care how he looked—whether his hair was long or short; the man that advanced that revelation was a prophet of God. I knew it for myself. I first met Joseph Smith in the streets of Kirtland. He had on an old hat, and a pistol in his hand. Said he, 'Brother Woodruff, I've been out shooting at a mark, and I wanted to see if I could hit anything'; and, says he, 'Have you any objection to it?' 'Not at all,' says I; 'there is no law against a man shooting at a mark, that I know of.'

"He invited me to his house. He had a wolf skin, which he wanted me to help him to tan; he wanted it to sit on while driving his wagon team. Now, many might have said, 'You are a pretty Prophet;

shooting a pistol and tanning a wolf skin.' Well, we tanned it, and used it while making a journey of a thousand miles. This was my first acquaintance with the Prophet Joseph. And from that day until the present, with all the apostasies that we have had, and with all the difficulties and afflictions we have been called to pass through, I never saw a moment when I had any doubt with regard to this work. I have had no trial about this. While the people were apostatizing on the right hand and on the left, and while apostles were urging me to turn against the Prophet Joseph, it was no temptation to me to doubt this work or to doubt that Joseph Smith was a Prophet of God."

—"Discourse by President Woodruff," *Millennial Star*, Oct. 5, 1891, 627–628.

"I Have Had the Ministrations of Angels"

"I have never prayed for the visitation of an angel, but I have had the ministrations of angels several times in my life.

"One visitation I received in Kentucky, at the house of A.[braham] O. Smoot's mother, while on my first mission. . . . I went into a little room where there was a sofa to pray alone. I felt full of joy and rejoicing at the promises God had made to me through the Prophet. While I was upon my knees praying, my room was filled with light. I looked and a messenger stood by my side. I arose and this personage told me he had come to instruct me. He presented before me a panorama. He told me he wanted me to see with my eyes and understand with my mind what was coming to pass in the earth before the coming of the Son of Man."

—Wilford Woodruff, *Deseret News Weekly*, Nov. 7, 1896, 641–642.

"By the Help of God"

"I have waded swamps and swum rivers, and have asked my bread from door to door; and have devoted nearly fifty years to this work. And why? Was there gold enough in California to have hired me to do it? No, verily; and what I have done and what my brethren have done, we have done because we were commanded of God. And this is the position we occupy to-day. We have preached and labored at home and abroad, and we intend to continue our labors, by the help of God, as long as we can have liberty to do it, and until the Gentiles prove themselves unworthy of eternal life, and until the judgments of God overtake the world, which are at the door."

—Wilford Woodruff, "Liberty of Conscience, etc.," in *Journal of Discourses*, 23:130.

"Has Not Received a College Diploma"

"I was once preaching to a large assembly in Collinsville, Connecticut; when I got through, a young clergyman came forward, and asked me if I had received any diploma from college. I answered him, 'No.'

"'Do you know,' said he, 'that a man who has not received a college diploma has no right to preach?'

"'No, sir,' I said, 'I do not know it.'

"'Well, sir,' he said, 'that is the case.'

"I then asked him to inform me how it was that Jesus preached, without receiving a college diploma?"

—Wilford Woodruff, "Simplicity of the Gospel, etc.," in *Journal of Discourses*, 18:219.

"We Had the Privilege of Beholding the Face of the Prophet"

"When the members of Zion's Camp were called, many of us had never beheld each other's faces; we were strangers to each other and many had never seen the prophet. We had been scattered abroad, like corn sifted in a sieve, throughout the nation. We were young men, and were called upon in that early day to go up and redeem Zion, and what we had to do we had to do by faith. We assembled together from the various states at Kirtland and went up to redeem Zion, in fulfilment of the commandment of God unto us. God accepted our works as He did the works of Abraham. We accomplished a great deal, though apostates and unbelievers many times asked the question, 'What have you done?' We gained an experience that we never could have gained in any other way. We had privilege of beholding the face of the prophet, and we had the privilege of travelling a thousand miles with him, and seeing the workings of the Spirit of God with him, and the revelations of Jesus Christ unto him and the fulfilment of those revelations."

—Wilford Woodruff, "The Holy Ghost—Laboring in Faith, etc.," in *Journal of Discourses*, 13:158.

"I Have Been Inspired and Moved Upon to Keep a Journal"

"I have been inspired and moved upon to keep a journal and write the affairs of this Church as far as I can. I did not understand why my feelings were exercised so much in the early age of this Church, but I understand it now. I seldom ever heard Brother Joseph or the Twelve preach or teach any principle but what I felt as uneasy as a fish out of water until I had written it. Then I felt right. I could write a sermon of Joseph's a week after it was delivered almost word for word, and after it was written, it was taken from me or from my mind. This was a gift from God unto me."

—Journal of Wilford Woodruff, Mar. 17, 1857.

"Get Up and Move That Carriage"

"I drove my carriage one evening into the yard of Brother Williams. Brother Orson Hyde drove a wagon by the side of mine. I had my wife and children in the carriage. After I turned out my team and had my supper, I went to bed in the carriage. I had not been there but a few minutes when the Spirit said to me, 'Get up and move that carriage.' I told my wife I had to get up and move the carriage. She said, 'What for?' I said, 'I don't know.' That is all she asked me on such occasions; when I told her I did not know, that was enough. I got up and moved my carriage. . . . I then looked around me and went to bed. The same Spirit said, 'Go and move your animals from that oak tree.' . . . I went and moved my horses and put them in a little hickory grove. I again went to bed.

"In thirty minutes a whirlwind came up and broke that oak tree off within two feet from the ground. It swept over three or four fences and fell square in that dooryard, near Brother Orson Hyde's wagon, and right where mine had stood. What would have been the consequences if I had not listened to that Spirit? . . . That was the still, small voice to me—no earthquake, no thunder, no lightning; but the still, small voice of the Spirit of God."

—Wilford Woodruff, in *Deseret News Weekly*, Sept. 5, 1891.

"Round Up Your Shoulders and Bear It"

"When we went upon our first foreign mission Joseph said to us, 'No matter what may come upon you, round up your shoulders and bear it, and always sustain and defend the interests of the Church and Kingdom of God.'

"When we took our departure his demeanor in parting was something that I had never noticed or experienced before. After crossing the Mississippi River I crawled to the side of a house and lay down upon a side of sole leather, while suffering from the chills and fever. While resting there the Prophet Joseph came along and saw me. He gave me some parting advice in answer to some remarks made, and then told me to get up and go on, and all would be well with me. That is the way I parted with him upon that occasion. From that day to this I have noticed the steady growth and increase of this people."

—Wilford Woodruff, "The City of Enoch," in *Journal of Discourses*, 24:53.

"The Spirit of the Lord Said to Me, 'Go South'"

"I was in Staffordshire in the year 1840. I was in the town of Stanley and held a meeting in the City Hall. I had a week's appointments out in that town. Before I rose to speak to the people, the Spirit of the Lord said to me, 'this is the last meeting you will hold with this people for many days.' I told the congregation when I arose what the Spirit of the Lord had manifested to me. They were as much surprised as I was. I did not know what the Lord wanted, but I saw the purpose of God afterwards. The Spirit of the Lord said to me, 'Go south.' I traveled eighty miles; went into the south of England. As soon as I arrived, I met John Benbow. It was clearly made manifest to me why I had been called thither. I had left a good field, where I was baptizing every night in the week. When I got to this place, I found a people—some 600 of them—who had broken off from the Wesleyan Methodists and formed themselves into a sect called the United Brethren. I found that they were praying for light and truth and that they had gone about as far as they could go. I saw that the Lord had sent me to them. I went to work amongst them and ultimately baptized their superintendent, forty preachers and some 600 members; I baptized every member of that denomination, but one. Altogether some 1800 were baptized in that field of labor. I suppose some of those then baptized may be in this congregation to-day. I name these things to show how we have to be governed and led by the revelations of God day by day. Without this we can do nothing."

—Wilford Woodruff, "A Double Birthday—The Authority of the Priesthood, etc.," in *Journal of Discourses*, 21:315.

"Joseph Smith Visited Me a Great Deal after His Death"

"Joseph Smith visited me a great deal after his death, and taught me many important principles. The last time he visited me was while I was in a storm at sea. I was going on my last mission to preside in England. . . . The Prophet laid before me a great many things. Among other things he told me to get the Spirit of God; that all of us needed it. He also told me what the Twelve apostles would be called to go through on the earth before the coming of the Son of Man, and what the reward of their labors would be. . . .

"The last time I saw him was in heaven. In the night vision I saw him at the door of the temple in heaven. He came and spoke to me. He said he could not stop to talk with me because he was in a hurry. The next man I met was Father Smith; he could not talk with me because he was in a hurry. I met a half a dozen brethren who had held high positions on earth and none of them could stop to talk with me because they were in a hurry. I was much astonished. By and by I saw the Prophet again, and I got the privilege to ask him a question. 'Now,' said I, 'I want to know why you are in a hurry. I have been in a hurry all through my life; but I expected my hurry would be over when I got into the kingdom of heaven, if I ever did.' Joseph said: 'I will tell you, Brother Woodruff. Every dispensation that has had the Priesthood on the earth and has gone into the celestial kingdom, has had a certain amount of work to do to prepare to go to the earth with the Savior when He goes to reign on the earth. Each dispensation has had ample time to do this work. We have not. We are the last dispensation, and so much work has to be done, and we need to be in a hurry in order to accomplish it.'"

—Wilford Woodruff, in *Deseret News Weekly*, Nov. 7, 1896.

"Don't You nor Your Company Go Aboard That Steamer"

"When I got back to Winter Quarters from the pioneer journey, President Young said to me, 'Brother Woodruff, I want you to take your wife and children and go to Boston, and stay there until you can gather every Saint of God in New England and Canada and send them up to Zion.' I did as he told me. It took me two years to gather everybody, and I brought up the rear with a company. When I got into Pittsburgh with this company it was dusk, and I saw a steamer just preparing to go out. I walked right up to the captain and asked him if he was ready to go out. He said he was. 'How many passengers have you?' 'Two hundred and fifty.' 'Can you take another hundred?' 'I can.' 'Then,' said I, 'I would like to go aboard with you.' The words were hardly out of my mouth when the Holy Ghost said to me. 'Don't you nor your company go aboard that steamer.' That was enough; I had learned the voice of the Spirit. I turned and told the captain that I had made up my mind not to go at present. . . .It was a dark night, and before the steamer had gone far she took fire, and all on board was lost. We should probably have shared the same fate, had it not been for that monitor within me."

—Wilford Woodruff, in *Deseret News Weekly*, Nov. 7, 1896.

"BUILT OF CUT GRANITE STONE"

"When in the western country, many years ago, before we came to the Rocky Mountains, I had a dream. I dreamed of being in these mountains, and of seeing a large fine looking temple erected in one of these valleys which was built of cut granite stone, I saw that temple dedicated, and I attended the dedicatory services, and I saw a good many men that are living to-day in the midst of this people. . . . When the foundation of that temple was laid I thought of my dream and a great many times since. And whenever President Young held a council of the brethren of the Twelve and talked of building the temple of adobe or brick, which was done I would say to myself, 'No, you will never do it'; because I had seen it in my dream built of some other material. I mention these things to show you that things are manifested to the Latter-day Saints sometimes which we do not know anything about, only as they are given by the Spirit of God."

—Wilford Woodruff, "Revelation, etc." in *Journal of Discourses*, 21:299–300.

"THE SPIRITS OF THE DEAD GATHERED AROUND ME"

"I will here say that two weeks before I left St. George, the spirits of the dead gathered around me, wanting to know why we did not redeem them. Said they, 'You have had the use of the Endowment House for a number of years, and yet nothing has ever been done for us. We laid the foundation of the government you now enjoy, and we never apostatized from it, but we remained true to it and were faithful to God.'

"These were the signers of the Declaration of Independence, and they waited on me for two days and two nights. I thought it very singular, that notwithstanding so much work had been done, and yet nothing had been done for them. The thought never entered my heart, from the fact, I suppose, that heretofore our minds were reaching after our more immediate friends and relatives.

"I straightway went into the baptismal font and called upon Brother McAllister to baptize me for the signers of the Declaration of Independence, and fifty other eminent men, making one hundred in all, including John Wesley, Columbus, and others. I then baptized him for every President of the United States, except three; and when their cause is just, somebody will do the work for them."

—Wilford Woodruff, "Not Ashamed of the Gospel, etc.," in *Journal of Discourses*, 19:229.

"My Family Dwell with Me in Glory"

"I have thought many a time that if I labored until I was as old as Methuselah and by that means could have my family dwell with me in glory in the eternal worlds, it would pay me for all the pain and suffering I could endure in this world. . . .

". . . I have had the blessing and privilege of redeeming in the Temple of our God some four thousand of my father's and my mother's kindred. I speak of this because it is one of our blessings, the fullness and glory of which we will never know until the vail is opened."

—Wilford Woodruff, in *Deseret News Weekly*, August 17, 1889; Wilford Woodruff, in *Deseret News Weekly*, Feb. 24, 1894.

"Thou Hast Certainly Chosen the Weak Things of This World"

Following the death of President John Taylor on July 25, 1887, Wilford Woodruff recorded,

"This places me in a very peculiar situation, a position I have never looked for during my life. But in the providence of God it is laid upon me, and I pray God my Heavenly Father to give me grace equal to my day. It is a high and responsible position for any man to occupy and a position that needs great wisdom. I never expected to outlive President Taylor. . . . But it has come to pass. . . . I can only say, Marvelous are thy ways, O Lord God Almighty, for thou hast certainly chosen the weak things of this world to perform thy work on the earth. May thy servant Wilford be prepared for whatever awaits him on earth and have power to perform whatever is required at his hands by the God of Heaven. I ask this blessing of my Heavenly Father in the name of Jesus Christ, the Son of the Living God."

—Journal of Wilford Woodruff, July 25, 1887.

"I Want to Live as Long as I Can Do Good"

"I want to live as long as I can do good; but not an hour longer than I can live in fellowship with the Holy Spirit, with my Father in heaven, my Savior, and with the faithful Latter-day Saints. To live any longer than this, would be torment and misery to me. When my work is done I am ready to go; but I want to do what is required of me."

—Wilford Woodruff, "On the Death of Elder Ezra T. Benson," in *Journal of Discourses,* 13:327.

"I Have Known That This Was the Work of God"

"My whole life almost has been spent in this Church; and from the time I came into the Church I went on missions and have never ceased altogether from that day to this. I have always rejoiced in this, and do to-day. When I die and lay down my body, I do not want anybody to rise up and say that I have neglected my duty in trying to give him salvation as far as I could. I have always rejoiced in preaching the Gospel; I have rejoiced in administering the ordinances of life and salvation at home and abroad, because I have known that this was the work of God, and I know it is to-day."

—"Discourse by President Wilford Woodruff," *Millennial Star,* May 14, 1896, 310.

"I Am True and Faithful unto Death"

"At my death I wish the historian of the Church to publish a brief account of my life, labors, and travels as an Elder and an Apostle in the Church of Jesus Christ of Latter-day Saints. I wish my body washed clean and clothed in clean white linen, according to the order of the Holy Priesthood, and put into a plain, decent coffin, made of native wood, with plenty of room. I do not wish any black made use of about my coffin, or about the vehicle that conveys my body to the grave. I do not wish my family or friends to wear any badge of mourning for me at my funeral or afterwards, for, if I am true and faithful unto death, there will be no necessity for anyone to mourn for me. I have no directions to give concerning the services of my funeral, any further than it would be pleasing to me for as many of the Presidency and Twelve Apostles who may be present to speak as may be thought wisdom. Their speech will be to the living.

"If the laws and customs of the spirit world will permit, I should wish to attend my funeral myself, but I shall be governed by the counsel I receive in the spirit world.

"I wish a plain marble slab put at the head of my grave, stating my name and age, and that I died in the faith of the Gospel of Christ and in the fellowship of the Saints."

—Wilford Woodruff, in Cowley, *Wilford Woodruff*, 622.

Lorenzo Snow

Born: April 3, 1814, Mantua, Ohio
Died: October 10, 1901, Salt Lake City, Utah
President of the Church: September 13, 1898, to October 10, 1901

LORENZO SNOW

Lorenzo Snow, son of Oliver Snow and Rosetta Leonora Pettibone, was born April 3, 1814, in Mantua, Ohio. After meeting the Prophet Joseph Smith, Lorenzo said, "Joseph Smith is a most remarkable man. I want to get better acquainted with him. Perhaps, after all, there is something more to Joseph Smith and to Mormonism than I have ever dreamed."[33]

Lorenzo was baptized in June 1836 in Ohio's Chagrin River. A few days later, while in the act of calling upon the Lord, he heard the sound of "'rustling of silk robes.' Immediately the Holy Ghost descended upon him, enveloping his entire person and permeating his body from the crown of his head to the soles of his feet. He was as completely immersed in the spirit of the Holy Ghost as he had been immersed in the water."[34]

In his patriarchal blessing Lorenzo was promised, "Thou hast a great work to perform in thy day and generation. God has called thee to the ministry. Thou must preach the gospel of thy Savior to the inhabitants of the earth."[35] Following that counsel, he preached the gospel in Ohio, Missouri, Kentucky, Illinois, England, Italy, and the islands of the sea. Of his preaching, Lorenzo wrote, "The Lord was with me, and I was greatly blessed in performing my arduous labors."[36]

Lorenzo presided over the temporary LDS encampment of Mount Pisgah, Iowa Territory, before leading a pioneer company to the Salt Lake Valley. For decades, he served in the Utah State Legislature and presided over the Saints living in Brigham City, Utah. In 1889 he was sustained as President of the Quorum of the Twelve

Apostles. Four years later, he was called to be the first president of the Salt Lake Temple. In that temple, Lorenzo received a divine manifestation of the Savior and was instructed by Him to reorganize the First Presidency following the death of Wilford Woodruff.[37]

Lorenzo accepted the Lord's call as President of the Church "with the same sense of diffidence that had characterized his demeanor throughout life. 'If I had had the power to escape it honorably . . . I would never have been found in my present position.'"[38] Abraham Owen Woodruff said, "President Snow . . . now carries a heavy load—the indebtedness of the Church, for which he was not responsible. This grave responsibility has killed one Prophet. It is my sincere belief that my father [Wilford Woodruff] would now be living if it were not for the great responsibility which rested upon him. President Snow is in his 86th year."[39]

In May 1899 Lorenzo received a revelation to recommit the Saints to live the law of tithing. Lorenzo promised the Latter-day Saints that by "paying . . . a full and honest tithing—not only would the Church be relieved of its great indebtedness, but through the blessings of the Lord this would also be the means of freeing the Latter-day Saints from their individual obligations."[40]

Of his life's labors, Lorenzo said, "I never desired but one thing, one office in this Church, and that was to be an Elder, and that I received under the direction of Joseph Smith, the Prophet, I have gone along from one thing to another, with much fear, knowing my inability. I devoted myself wholly to discharging my duties and the Lord has helped me through, and he will continue to help me."[41]

Lorenzo Snow died on October 10, 1901, of pneumonia.

The Life Story of Lorenzo Snow in His Own Words

"This Was the Turning Point in My Life"

Lorenzo Snow wrote of his journey with Elder David W. Patten in 1835:

"Our conversation fell upon religion and philosophy, and being young and having enjoyed some scholastic advantages, I was at first disposed to treat his opinions lightly, especially so as they were not always clothed in grammatical language; but as he proceeded in his earnest and humble way to open up before my mind the plan of salvation, I seemed unable to resist the knowledge that he was a man of God and that his testimony was true.

"I felt pricked in my heart. This he evidently perceived, for almost the last thing he said to me after bearing his testimony, was that I should go to the Lord before retiring at night and ask him for myself. This I did with the result that from the day I met this great Apostle, all my aspirations have been enlarged and heightened immeasurably. This was the turning point in my life."

—Lorenzo Snow, in Wilson, *Life of David W. Patten*, v.

"A Perfect Knowledge That God Lives"

"One day while engaged in my studies, some two or three weeks after I was baptized, I began to reflect upon the fact that I had not obtained a knowledge of the truth of the work. . . .

"I laid aside my books, left the house and wandered around through the fields under the oppressive influence of a gloomy, disconsolate spirit, while an indescribable cloud of darkness seemed to envelop me. I had been accustomed, at the close of the day, to retire for secret prayer to a grove, a short distance from my lodgings, but at this time I felt no inclination to do so.

"The spirit of prayer had departed, and the heavens seemed like brass over my head. At length, realizing that the usual time had come for secret prayer, I concluded I would not forego my evening service, and, as a matter of formality, knelt as I was in the habit of doing, and in my accustomed retired place, but not feeling as I was wont to feel.

"I had no sooner opened my lips in an effort to pray, than I heard a sound, just above my head, like the rustling of silken robes, and immediately the Spirit of God descended upon me, completely enveloping my whole person, filling me from the crown of my head to the soles of my feet, and O, the joy and happiness I felt! No language can describe the instantaneous transition from a dense cloud of mental and spiritual darkness into a refulgence of light and knowledge, as it was at that time imparted to my understanding. I then received a perfect knowledge that God lives, that Jesus Christ is the Son of God, and of the restoration of the Holy Priesthood, and the fulness of the gospel.

"It was a complete baptism—a tangible immersion in the heavenly principle or element, the Holy Ghost; and even more real and physical in its effects upon every part of my system than the immersion by water; dispelling forever, so long as reason and memory last, all possibility of doubt or fear in relation to the fact handed down to us historically, that the 'Babe of Bethlehem' is truly the Son of God; also the fact that He is now being revealed to the children of men, and communicating knowledge, the same as in the apostolic times. I was perfectly satisfied."

—Lorenzo Snow, *Juvenile Instructor*, Jan. 15, 1887, 22–23.

"Well Acquainted with Joseph Smith the Prophet"

"Perhaps there are very few men now living who were so well acquainted with Joseph Smith the Prophet as I was. I was with him oftentimes. I visited with him in his family, sat at his table, associated with him under various circumstances, and had private interviews with him for counsel. I know that Joseph Smith was a Prophet of God; I know that he was an honorable man, a moral man, and that he had the respect of those who were acquainted with him. The Lord has shown me most clearly and completely that he was a Prophet of God, and that he held the Holy Priesthood."

—Lorenzo Snow, "Testimony that Joseph was a Prophet of God and an honorable and moral man," in Conference Report, Oct. 7, 1900, 61.

"You Will Be Great"

"I remember an incident which occurred in Kirtland when I received my first patriarchal blessing from Father Smith. A better man never existed, nor was there a man better-loved than he. I was introduced by my sister Eliza R., though at that time I was not a Latter-Saint and had no idea of becoming one. . . . He said, 'You will be great, and as great as you want to be, as great as God Himself, and you will not wish to be greater.' I could not understand this, but years after in Nauvoo while talking upon a principle of the gospel, the Spirit of God rested powerfully upon me and showed me more clearly than I can now see your faces a certain principle and its glory, and it came to me summarized in this brief sentence: 'As man is now, God once was; as God is now man may be.' The Spirit of God was on me in a marvelous manner all that day, and I stored that great truth away in my mind. I felt that I had learnt something that I ought not to communicate to others."

—Lorenzo Snow, in *Deseret Evening News*, June 15, 1901.

"The First Time I Was Called upon to Bear My Testimony"

"I remember the first time I was called upon to bear my testimony. . . . It was something I very much dreaded, yet at the same time I felt that it was my duty to get up, but I waited, and waited. One bore testimony, another gave his testimony, then another, and they were nearly through, but I still dreaded to get up. I had never spoken before an audience. . . . I [finally] concluded it was about time for me to get up. I did so. Well, how long do you suppose I talked? I judge about half a minute—it couldn't possibly have been more than a minute. That was my first effort; and the second, I think, was about the same. I was bashful, . . . but I made up my mind, solidly and firmly, that whenever I was called upon to perform a duty of this nature or of any other, I would do it no matter what might be the result. That is a part of the foundation of my success as an Elder in Israel."

—Lorenzo Snow, in Eliza R. Snow Smith, *Biography and Family Record of Lorenzo Snow* [1884], 16.

"I Had Never Intended to Be a Preacher"

"I had never intended to be a preacher, and it was nothing but a perfect knowledge that it was my duty to do so, that I was willing to go forth upon this business—a knowledge that my salvation depended upon my going forth and proclaiming these glad tidings to the world, and I went, and could testify to every man and woman in any nation or community wherever I traveled, that I was authorized to preach the Gospel and administer in its ordinances, which pertain to a knowledge of eternal life, a knowledge of time and eternity, and thus establish the divine authenticity of my mission."

—Lorenzo Snow, "Discourse," *Millennial Star*, Apr. 18, 1887, 242–243.

"The Holy Ghost Rested Mightily upon Me"

"It was a very difficult thing for me to get up there and preach to my kindred and the neighbors who were called in. I remember that I prayed nearly all day preceding the night I was to speak. I went out by myself and asked the Lord to give me something to say. My aunt told me afterwards that she almost trembled when she saw me getting up to speak, but I opened my mouth, and what I said I never did know, but my aunt said I spoke fine for about three-quarters of an hour. . . . I believed and felt an assurance that a Spirit of inspiration would prompt and give me utterance. I had sought by prayer and fasting—I had humbled myself before the Lord, calling on Him in mighty prayer to impart the power and inspiration of the holy Priesthood; and when I stood before that congregation, although I knew not one word I could say, as soon as I opened my mouth to speak, the Holy Ghost rested mightily upon me, filling my mind with light and communicating ideas and proper language by which to impart them."

—Lorenzo Snow, in Smith, *Biography and Family Record of Lorenzo Snow*, 16.

"I Was a Humble Elder of the Church of Christ"

"I was once traveling in a strange country on a mission, and had been refused entertainment many times, and my chances for sleeping in a hay-stack were very good. Presently I came to a hotel. We usually avoided such places, but my affairs were desperate, and I approached the proprietor and told him that I was without means, preaching the gospel, and asked him to give me entertainment. He replied that he was running his hotel to make money, and that I was very welcome to a room in his house and meals at his table upon payment of the regular prices for such commodities. I started to go away, but, upon a little reflection, returned to the man, and again told him that I was a humble elder of the Church of Christ, preaching the gospel, warning the people and calling upon them to repent and turn unto the Lord. I quoted to him the words of the Savior, recorded in Matt. 25, 31–46, where He tells of the coming of the Son of Man in His glory, when He shall divide the sheep from the goats and shall bless those on His right hand because they ministered unto Him, but shall cast out those on His left hand, because they ministered not unto Him;

and when those on His left hand shall ask when they saw the Son of Man in want and ministered not unto Him, He shall say unto them, 'Inasmuch as ye did it not to one of the least of these, ye did it not to me.' After having quoted these things, and borne testimony that I was a humble disciple of Jesus Christ, I started to leave him, but he called after me, saying, 'Where are you going? Come in here and eat, and stay as long as you desire.' I returned and was well entertained, and no word was ever said to me about paying for the same."

—Lorenzo Snow, in Thomas Hull, "Instructions to Missionaries," *Improvement Era*, Dec. 1899, 128.

"A PRECIOUS GIFT TO ME"

"On another occasion, one evening, I was preaching in a large room of a private house, and afterwards learned that a portion of my audience had gathered for the purpose of mobbing me. They had arranged with a party that lay concealed at a little distance, and within call, to join them immediately on my leaving the house to return to my lodgings, and all proceed together to execute their schemes of vengeance. It was a very cold night, and after the close of the services I stood with my back to the chimney fire, with a number of others—some of whom belonged to the mob party. One of the latter persons amid the jostling of the crowd, accidentally brought his hand in contact with one of the pockets in the skirt of my coat, which struck him with sudden alarm on his feeling, what he supposed to be, a large pistol. He immediately communicated the discovery to his affrighted coadjutors, all of whom directly withdrew, and, to their fellows outside, imparted the astounding news that the 'Mormon' Elder was armed with deadly weapons. That was sufficient—the would-be outlaws abandoned their evil designs for fear of signal punishment; but the supposed pistol which caused their alarm and my protection, was my pocket Bible, a precious gift to me from the dearly beloved Patriarch, Father Joseph Smith."

—Lorenzo Snow, in Smith, *Biography and Family Record of Lorenzo Snow*, 37–38.

"A Little Amusement in Hunting Turkeys"

"In Adam-ondi-Ahman, while gradually recovering from the effects of a malignant fever which had detained me a fortnight in Far West, under the constant and skilful nursing of my sister Eliza, for some time I was unable to either do, or read much. One day, to while away the slowly passing hours, I took my gun with the intention of indulging in a little amusement in hunting turkeys, with which that section of the country abounded. From boyhood I had been particularly, and I may say strangely attached to a gun. Hunting in the forests of Ohio was a pastime that to me possessed the most fascinating attractions. It never occurred to my mind that it was wrong—that indulging in 'what was sport to me was death to them;' that in shooting turkeys, squirrels, etc., I was taking life that I could not give; therefore I indulged in the murderous sport without the least compunction of conscience.

"But at this time a chance came over me. While moving slowly forward in pursuit of something to kill, my mind was arrested with the reflection on the nature of my pursuit—that of amusing myself by giving pain and death to harmless, innocent creatures that perhaps had as much right to life and enjoyment as myself. I realized that such indulgence was without any justification, and feeling condemned, I laid my gun on my shoulder, returned home, and from that time to this have felt no inclination for that murderous amusement."

—Lorenzo Snow, in Smith, *Biography and Family Record of Lorenzo Snow*, 27–28.

"I Laid My Hands upon His Head"

Aboard the ship Swanton in 1843, Lorenzo Snow wrote: "The captain's steward, a young German, met with an accident which threatened his life. Being a very moral, sober and steady young man, having been with the captain [on] several voyages, he had succeeded greatly in winning the affections of the captain, officers and crew; the Saints also had become much attached to him. Hence the prospect of his death . . . created a great sensation of sorrow and grief throughout the whole ship.

"He would bleed at his mouth, attended with severe cramping and fits. At last, after having tried various remedies to no purpose, all hopes of his life were given up. The sailors, before retiring to their beds, were requested by the captain to go into the cabin one by one to bid him farewell; which accordingly was done without the least expectation of seeing him alive the next morning. Many eyes were wet with tears as they returned from the cabin.

"Sister Martin [a Latter-day Saint] while sitting alone by his bedside expressed to him her wish that I might be called on and administer to him and perhaps he might yet be restored. To this he gave a cheerful consent. I was asleep in my berth when the message came, it being about twelve o'clock of the night. I arose immediately and proceeded to the cabin. . . .

"As I passed along I met the captain at the cabin door, who appeared to have been weeping. 'I am glad you have come, Mr. Snow,' he said, 'though it is of no use, for it must soon be over with the steward.' I stepped into his room and sat down by his bed. His breathing was very short and seemed as one dying. He could not speak loud, but signified his wish [that] I should administer to him. . . .

"I laid my hands upon his head, and had no sooner got through the administration than he arose up into a sitting posture, [slapped] his hands together, shouting praises to the Lord for being healed; very soon after, he arose from his bed [and] went out of the cabin and walked the deck. . . . The steward was baptized when we reached New Orleans; and on parting with him made me a present of a Bible, which I now keep."

—Lorenzo Snow, Journal and Letterbook, 1836–1845, 72–83, cited in *Teachings of Presidents of the Church: Lorenzo Snow*, 13–16.

"To Spare the Life of the Child"

In 1850, while serving a mission among the Waldenses in the Piedmont region of Italy, Lorenzo Snow wrote:

"Sept. 6th.—This morning my attention was directed to Joseph Guy, a boy three years of age, the youngest child of our host. Many friends had been to see the child, as to all human appearance, his end was nigh at hand. I went to see him in the afternoon: death was making havoc of his body; his former healthy frame was now reduced to a skeleton, and it was only by close observation we could discern he was alive. . . .

"Sept. 7th.—This morning, I proposed . . . that we should fast, and retire to the mountains, and pray. As we departed, we called and saw the child; his eyeballs turned upwards: his eyelids fell and closed: his face and ears were thin, and wore the pale marble hue, indicative of approaching dissolution. The cold perspiration of death covered his body, and the principle of life was nearly exhausted. Madame Guy and other females were sobbing, while Monsieur Guy hung his head. . . .

"After a little rest upon the mountains, aside from any likelihood of interruption, we there called upon the Lord in solemn prayer, to spare the life of the child."

Lorenzo Snow came down from the mountains and gave the child a blessing:

"From that hour he began to amend; and with a heart filled with gratitude to our heavenly Father, I am happy to say, that in a few days he left his bed, and joined his little companions."

—Lorenzo Snow, "Organization of the Church in Italy," *Millennial Star*, Dec. 15, 1850, 371.

"Only Do What Duty Demanded"

"In performing the mission of soliciting means [for the Perpetual Emigrating Fund] from the Saints who, after having been robbed and plundered, had performed a journey of more than one thousand miles, and just located in an unwatered, desolate recess of the great 'American Desert,' I found myself inducted into an uphill business. With very few exceptions, the people had very little, or nothing they could possibly spare. . . . The efforts and willingness, everywhere manifested, to eke out a portion of the little—the feeling of liberality and greatness of soul, which everywhere I met in the midst of poverty, the warm-hearted greetings I received even where comparative indigence held court, filled my heart with exceeding great joy. One man insisted that I should take his only cow, saying that the Lord had delivered him, and blessed him in leaving the old country and coming to a land of peace; and in giving his only cow, he felt that he would only do what duty demanded, and what he would expect from others, were the situation reversed."

—Lorenzo Snow, in Smith, *Biography and Family Record of Lorenzo Snow*, 108.

"You Have Magnified Your Priesthood"

"When President Young was aroused to call upon the people to repent and reform . . . , he talked very strongly as to what ought to be done with some people—that their Priesthood ought to be taken from them, because of their failure to magnify it as they should have done. The brethren who lived in those days will remember how vigorously he spoke in this direction. Well, it touched Brother Franklin's heart, and it touched mine also; and we talked the matter over to ourselves. We concluded we would go to President Young and offer him our Priesthood. If he felt in the name of the Lord that we had not magnified our Priesthood, we would resign it. We went to him, saw him alone, and told him this. I guess there were tears in his eyes when he said, 'Brother Lorenzo, Brother Franklin, you have magnified your Priesthood satisfactorily to the Lord. God bless you.'"

—Lorenzo Snow, in *Deseret News Semi-Weekly*, Dec. 19, 1899, 5, cited in *Teachings of Presidents of the Church: Lorenzo Snow*, 117, 119.

"Asked the Lord to Spare His Life"

In 1864 Lorenzo Snow boarded a small boat to go ashore on the island of Maoi. The boat capsized, and he was tossed into the ocean. William Cluff, a missionary, related:

"The first I saw of Brother Snow was his hair floating upon the water around one end of the capsized boat. As soon as we got him into our boat, we told the boatmen to pull for shore with all possible speed. His body was stiff, and life apparently extinct.

"Brother A. L. Smith and I were sitting side by side. We laid Brother Snow across our laps, and, on the way to shore, we quietly administered to him and asked the Lord to spare his life, that he might return to his family and home.

"On reaching the shore, we carried him a little way to some large barrels that were lying on the sandy beach. We laid him face downwards on one of them, and rolled him back and forth until we succeeded in getting the water he had swallowed out of him. . . .

"We did not only what was customary in such cases . . . but also what the Spirit seemed to whisper to us.

"After working over him for some time, without any indications of returning life, the by-standers said that nothing more could be done for him. But we did not feel like giving him up, and still prayed and worked over him, with an assurance that the Lord would hear and answer our prayers.

"Finally we were impressed to place our mouth over his and make an effort to inflate his lungs, alternately blowing in and drawing out the air, imitating, as far as possible, the natural process of breathing. This we persevered in until we succeeded in inflating his lungs. After a little, we perceived very faint indications of returning life. A slight wink of the eye, which, until then, had been open and death-like, and a very faint rattle in the throat, were the first symptoms of returning vitality. These grew more and more distinct, until consciousness was fully restored. . . . We did not only what was customary in such cases . . . but also what the Spirit seemed to whisper to us."

—Lorenzo Snow, in William Cluff, *Biography and Family Record of Lorenzo Snow*, 278–279.

"He Called Me Back"

In March 1891, while speaking at a conference in Brigham City, Lorenzo Snow learned of the death of Ella Jensen, the daughter of Jacob Jensen. He left the conference with Rudger Clawson, president of the Box Elder Stake, to go to the Jensen home. Jacob Jensen recounted what happened after they arrived at his home:

"After standing at Ella's bedside for a minute or two, President Snow asked if we had any consecrated oil in the house. I was greatly surprised, but told him yes and got it for him. . . .

"During the administration I was particularly impressed with some of the words which he used and can well remember them now. He said: 'Dear Ella, I command you, in the name of the Lord, Jesus Christ, to come back and live, your mission is not ended. You shall yet live to perform a great mission.'

"He said she should yet live to rear a large family and be a comfort to her parents and friends. I well remember these words. . . .

"After President Snow had finished the blessing, he turned to my wife and me and said: 'Now do not mourn or grieve any more. It will be all right. Brother Clawson and I are busy and must go, we cannot stay, but you just be patient and wait, and do not mourn, because it will be all right.' . . .

"Ella remained in this condition for more than an hour after President Snow administered to her, or more than three hours in all after she died. We were sitting there watching by the bedside, her mother and myself, when all at once she opened her eyes. She looked about the room, saw us sitting there, but still looked for someone else, and the first thing she said was: 'Where is he? Where is he?' We asked, 'Who? Where is who?' 'Why, Brother Snow,' she replied. 'He called me back.'"

—Jacob Jensen, in LeRoi C. Snow, "Raised from the Dead," *Improvement Era*, Sept. 1929, 884–886.

"This Is the Testimony of Your Grandfather"

Alice Pond wrote of a conversation she had with her grandfather Lorenzo Snow in the Salt Lake Temple:

"In the large corridor leading into the celestial room, I was walking several steps ahead of grand-pa when he stopped me and said: 'Wait a moment, Allie, I want to tell you something. It was right here that the Lord Jesus Christ appeared to me at the time of the death of President Woodruff. He instructed me to go right ahead and reorganize the First Presidency of the Church at once and not wait as had been done after the death of the previous presidents, and that I was to succeed President Woodruff.'

"Then grand-pa came a step nearer and held out his left hand and said: 'He stood right here, about three feet above the floor. It looked as though He stood on a plate of solid gold.'

"Grand-pa told me what a glorious personage the Savior is and described His hands, feet, countenance and beautiful white robes, all of which were of such a glory of whiteness and brightness that he could hardly gaze upon Him.

"Then [grand-pa] came another step nearer and put his right hand on my head and said: 'Now, grand-daughter, I want you to remember that this is the testimony of your grand-father, that he told you with his own lips that he actually saw the Savior, here in the Temple, and talked with Him face to face.'"

—Alice Pond, in LeRoi C. Snow, "An Experience of My Father's," *Improvement Era*, Sept. 1933, 677.

"I Have No Disposition to Shirk Any Responsibility"

"I can assure you, brethren and sisters, that I had no ambition to assume the responsibility which now rests upon me. If I could have escaped it honorably I should never have been found in my present position. I have never asked for it, nor have I ever asked the assistance of any of my brethren that I might attain to this position, but the Lord revealed to me and to my brethren that this was His will, and I have no disposition to shirk any responsibility nor to decline to occupy any position that the Lord requires me to fill. I have tried to serve Him, to overcome the weaknesses of the flesh and to bring myself with every power and faculty of my nature into complete subservience to His will, so that I might eventually reach the highest glory which it is possible for man to attain."

—Lorenzo Snow, in *Deseret News Weekly*, Oct. 8, 1898.

"The Lord Has Done It"

At the Brigham Young Academy on March 31, 1899, Lorenzo Snow said:

"I feel that whatever I have accomplished that it is not Lorenzo Snow, and the scenes that have brought me to this position as President of the Church—it is not Lorenzo Snow, but the Lord has done it. When Jesus was upon the earth He made this remarkable expression; I have thought of it and it is before me constantly in all of my labors: 'I can of myself do nothing; as I hear I judge, and my judgment is just.' Now, why did He say that His judgment was just? He says, because 'I seek not my own will but the will of my Father who sent me.' That is the principle, my brethren and sisters, that I have endeavored to act upon ever since it was revealed to me that my Father in heaven, and your Father in heaven, exists. I have endeavored to do His will. . . .

"It is the Lord that you honor when you honor me and my counselors and the Quorum of the Twelve. We have discovered that a long time since, every one of us, that of ourselves we could do nothing. Only as far as we followed that principle which Jesus followed when He was in the world has success followed our efforts; and it will be so with you."

—Lorenzo Snow, "Anniversary Exercises," *Deseret Evening News*, Apr. 7, 1899, 9–10, in *Teachings of Presidents of the Church: Lorenzo Snow*, 148.

"One Case Where a Refusal Was Given"

"It is a strange thing that among the thousands of letters which I have received from those who have been called to go upon missions—mostly young men—I do not think of but one case where a refusal was given. Why is this? It is because the spirit of love and of immortality, the Spirit of the Almighty, is upon these young elders, and they have received manifestations which inspire them to do that which otherwise no inducement could prompt them to do."

—Lorenzo Snow, "Opening Address," in Conference Report, Apr. 5, 1901, 3.

"I Stood on Holy Ground"

Mr. Prentis of South Carolina wrote of Lorenzo Snow: "I had expected to find intellectuality, benevolence, dignity, composure, and strength depicted upon the face of the President of The Church of Jesus Christ of Latter-day Saints; but when I was introduced [*sic*] to President Lorenzo Snow, for a second I was startled to see the holiest face but one I had ever been privileged to look upon. His face was a power of peace, his presence a benediction of peace. In the tranquil depths of his eyes were not only the 'home of silent prayer' but the abode of spiritual strength. As he talked of the more sure word of prophecy and the certainty of the hope which was his, and the abiding faith which had conquered the trials and difficulties of a tragic life, I watched the play of emotions and studied with fascinated attention, the subtle shades of expression which spoke so plainly the workings of his soul; and the strangest feeling stole over me, that I stood on holy ground."

—Mr. Prentis, in "Life and Character Sketch of Lorenzo Snow," *Improvement Era*, June 1899, 569–570.

"You Visit with Him Long, You Love Him"

Reverend W. D. Cornell wrote of Lorenzo Snow: "I was taken into his august presence by his courteous and experienced secretary, and found myself shaking hands with one of the most congenial and lovable men I ever met—a man who has the peculiar ability to dispossess one at once of all uneasiness in his presence—a master in the art of conversation, with a rare genius, enabling him to make you feel a restful welcome in his society.

"President Snow is a cultured man, in mind and soul and body. His language is choice, diplomatic, friendly, scholarly. His mannerisms show the studied grace of schools. The tenor of his spirit is as gentle as a child. You are introduced to him. You are pleased with him. You converse with him, you like him. You visit with him long, you love him."

—Reverend W. D. Cornell, in "Mormonism in Salt Lake," *Millennial Star*, Sept. 14, 1899, 579.

Joseph F. Smith

Born: November 13, 1838, Far West, Missouri
Died: November 19, 1918, Salt Lake City, Utah
President of the Church: October 17, 1901, to November 19, 1918

JOSEPH F. SMITH

JOSEPH FIELDING SMITH, SON OF Hyrum Smith and Mary Fielding, was born November 13, 1838, at Far West, Missouri. When Joseph was two months old, a mob ransacked his family home: "When the mob entered the room where I was, the bed on the floor was thrown on to the other completely smothering me up."[42] Miraculously, he survived the ordeal. He was taken by his mother from Missouri across the Mississippi River to safety in Illinois. Unfortunately, Illinois also proved difficult for him and his family. His father, Hyrum Smith, was assassinated in Carthage Jail in June 1844.

Joseph and his family fled from further persecution in Illinois to Iowa and then to the Salt Lake Valley. At age fifteen, Joseph was called to labor as a missionary in the Hawaiian Islands. On the first of what would become five missions, Joseph penned, "I well know that I am young and inexperienced at present, therefore I wish to be humble, prayerful before the Lord, that I may be worthy of the blessings and love of God to protect me at all times."[43]

On July 1, 1866, Brigham Young said, "Hold on, shall I do as I feel [led]? I always feel well to do as the Spirit constrains me. It is my mind to ordain Brother Joseph F. Smith to the Apostleship, and to be one of my counselors."[44] At age twenty-seven, Joseph began his service in the Quorum of the Twelve Apostles and the First Presidency of the Church. He served as a counselor to Brigham Young, John Taylor, Wilford Woodruff, and Lorenzo Snow.

From 1901 to 1918 Joseph served as President of The Church of Jesus Christ of Latter-day Saints. During his administration, two declarations were issued by the First Presidency—"The Origin of Man," presenting the doctrine of the Church on the origin of the human race, and "The Role of the Father and the Son," outlining the nature of the Godhead. In 1903 Joseph appeared before a U.S. Senate investigation committee in Washington, D.C. Though he received "scandalous treatment from the public press on account of [his] testimony before the Committee," his testimony clarified the abuse and false accusations hurled against LDS Church leaders.[45]

On October 3, 1918, Joseph had a vision of the Savior's visit to the spirits of the dead. This vision, known as the "Redemption of the Dead," is contained in Doctrine and Covenants 138. A few weeks after the vision, Joseph died of pleurisy. Bishop Charles W. Nibley said of him, "As a preacher of righteousness, who could compare with him? He was the greatest that I ever heard—strong, powerful, clear, appealing."[46]

The Life Story of Joseph F. Smith in His Own Words

"As a Child I Knew the Prophet Joseph Smith"

"As a child I knew the Prophet Joseph Smith. As a child I have listened to him preach the gospel that God had committed to his charge and care. As a child I was familiar in his home, in his household, as I was familiar under my own father's roof. I have retained the witness of the Spirit that I was imbued with, as a child, and that I received from my sainted mother, the firm belief that Joseph Smith was a prophet of God; that he was inspired as no other man in his generation, or for centuries before, had been inspired; that he had been chosen of God to lay the foundations of God's Kingdom."

—Joseph F. Smith, *Gospel Doctrine*, 493.

"Childlike He Put It in His Pocket"

Joseph Fielding Smith wrote of his father, Joseph F. Smith:
"On one occasion, Joseph F. . . . who was then about five years of age, found in his father's desk a sum of several dollars. . . . Childlike he put it in his pocket and went out to play, happy in hearing the dollars jingle in his pocket. To his great consternation one of the neighbors took him to his mother in great excitement because the boy had stolen the money from its secreted place. Never, said he, would he forget the fright that was given him when he was told that he was a thief. What he did was a

perfectly innocent act that any normal child might have done. However the impression remained with him all his days."

—Joseph Fielding Smith, in Gibbons, *Joseph F. Smith*, 9.

"He Kissed Me Goodbye"

At age sixty-eight, President Joseph F. Smith visited Nauvoo with other LDS leaders from Salt Lake City. Stopping on one particular street in Nauvoo, he said:

"This is the exact spot where I stood when the brethren came riding up on their way to Carthage. Without getting off his horse father learned over in his saddle and picked me up off the ground. He kissed me goodbye and put me down again and I saw him ride away."

When standing in the Mansion House in Nauvoo, he added:

"In this room the bodies of the martyrs lay in their coffins, after they had been brought from Carthage and dressed for burial. I remember my mother lifting me up to look upon the faces of my father and the Prophet, for the last time."

—Joseph F. Smith, in Nibley, *Presidents of the Church*, 183–184.

"Her Faith and Example Will Ever Be Bright in My Memory"

"I can remember my mother in the days of Nauvoo. I remember seeing her and her helpless children hustled into a flat boat with such things as she could carry out of the house at the commencement of the bombardment of the city of Nauvoo by the mob. I remember the hardships of the Church there and on the way to Winter Quarters, on the Missouri river, and how she prayed for her children and family on her wearisome journey. . . . I can remember all the trials incident to our endeavors to move out with the Camp of Israel, coming to these valleys of the mountains without teams sufficient to draw our wagons; and being without the means to get those teams necessary, she yoked up her cows and calves, and tied two wagons together, and we started to come to Utah in this crude and helpless condition, and my mother said—'The Lord will open the way;' but how He would open the way no one knew. . . .

"Do you not think that these things make an impression upon the mind? Do you think I can forget the example of my mother? No; her faith and example will ever be bright in my memory."

—Joseph F. Smith, in *Deseret News Semi-Weekly*, Jan. 5, 1892, 3.

"I Saw My Mother Kneeling Down in Prayer"

In the fall of 1847, Joseph F. Smith was "soaked to the skin, fatigued, disheartened and almost exhausted" after searching for lost oxen:

"In this pitiable plight I was the first to return to our wagons, and as I approached I saw my mother kneeling down in prayer. I halted for a moment and then drew gently near enough to hear her pleading with the Lord not to suffer us to be left in this helpless condition, but to lead us to recover our lost team, that we might continue our travels in safety. When she arose from her knees I was standing nearby. The first expression I caught upon her precious face was a lovely smile, which discouraged as I was, gave me renewed hope and an assurance I had not felt before. . . .

"[She said,] 'I will just take a walk out and see if I can find the cattle.'"

Her finding of the lost oxen led Joseph F. Smith to say,

"It was one of the first practical and positive demonstrations of the efficacy of prayer I had ever witnessed. It made an indelible impression upon my mind, and has been a source of comfort, assurance and guidance to me throughout all of my life."

—Joseph F. Smith, *Life of Joseph F. Smith*, 132–134.

"Would You Deny Me a Blessing?"

"I recollect most vividly a circumstance that occurred in the days of my childhood. My mother was a widow, with a large family to provide for. One spring when we opened our potato pits, she had her boys get a load of the best potatoes and she took them to the tithing office; potatoes were scarce that season. I was a little boy at the time, and drove the team. When we drove up to the steps of the tithing office, ready to unload the potatoes, one of the clerks came out and said to my mother, 'Widow Smith, it's a shame that you should have to pay tithing.' . . . He chided my mother for paying her tithing, called her anything but wise or prudent; and said there were others who were strong and able to work that were supported from the tithing office. My mother turned upon him and said: '. . . Would you deny me a blessing? If I did not pay my tithing, I should expect the Lord to withhold his blessings from me. I pay my tithing, not only because it is a law of God, but because I expect a blessing by doing it.'"

—Joseph F. Smith, *Gospel Doctrine*, 228–229.

"I Felt a Newness of Life"

Of his baptism on May 21, 1852, in City Creek near Temple Square in Salt Lake City, Joseph F. Smith wrote:

"I felt in my soul that if I had sinned—and surely I was not without sin—that it had been forgiven me; that I was indeed cleansed from sin; my heart was touched, and I felt that I would not injure the smallest insect beneath my feet. I felt as if I wanted to do good everywhere to everybody and to everything. I felt a newness of life, a newness of desire to do that which was right. There was not one particle of desire for evil left in my soul. I was but a little boy, it is true, when I was baptized; but this was the influence that came upon me, and I know that it was from God, and was and ever has been a living witness to me of my acceptance of the Lord."

—Joseph F. Smith, *Gospel Doctrine*, 96.

"Don't Whip Her with That"

"My little sister Martha was called up to be punished. I saw the school teacher bring out the leather strap, and he told the child to hold out her hand. I just spoke up loudly and said, 'Don't whip her with that,' and at that he came at me and was going to whip me; but instead of whipping me, I licked him, good and plenty."

—Joseph F. Smith, in Gibbons, *Joseph F. Smith*, 26–27.

"To Keep My Word, My Promises, My Integrity"

"Without anything to start with in the world, except the example of my mother, I struggled along with hard knocks in early life. . . . And so I have passed along more than sixty years with no one to care for me or take one thought of me except the servants of the Lord; some of them having been my kinsmen, and they were always kind to me and to mine. I was fortunate to be left among them, but I have had to watch my step, my 'P's' and 'Q's', so to say, for fear I would do something that would diminish my standing and involve my honor and my word. If there is anything on earth I have tried to do as much as anything else, it is to keep my word, my promises, my integrity, to do what it was my duty to do."

—Joseph F. Smith, in Gibbons, *Joseph F. Smith*, 327–328.

"Showed Me the Truth"

"When I as a boy started out in the ministry, I would frequently go out and ask the Lord to show me some marvelous thing, in order that I might receive a testimony. But the Lord withheld marvels from me, and showed me the truth, line upon line, precept upon precept, here a little and there a little, until he made me to know the truth from the crown of my head to the soles of my feet, and until doubt and fear had been absolutely purged from me. He did not have to send an angel from the heavens to do this, nor did he have to speak with the trump of an archangel. By the whisperings of the still small voice of the Spirit of the living God, he gave to me the testimony I possess."

—Joseph F. Smith, *Gospel Doctrine*, 7.

"I Am Clean"

Of his mission to the Sandwich Islands, Joseph F. Smith recalled:

"I dreamed that I was on a journey, and I was impressed that I ought to hurry—hurry with all my might, for fear I might be too late. I rushed on my way as fast as I possibly could, and I was only conscious of having just a little bundle, a handkerchief with a small bundle wrapped in it. I did not realize just what it was, when I was hurrying as fast as I could; but finally I came to a wonderful mansion, if it could be called a mansion. It seemed too large, too great to have been made by hand, but I thought I knew that was my destination. As I passed towards it, as fast as I could, I saw a notice, 'Bath.' I turned aside quickly and went into the bath and washed myself clean. I opened up this little bundle that I had, and there was a pair of white, clean garments, a thing I had not seen for a long time. . . . I put them on. Then I rushed to what appeared to be a great opening, or door. I knocked and the door opened, and the man who stood there was the Prophet Joseph Smith. He looked at me a little reprovingly, and the first words he said: 'Joseph, you are late.' Yet I took confidence and said:

"'Yes, but I am clean—I am clean!'

". . . That vision, that manifestation and witness that I enjoyed at that time has made me who I am, if I am anything that is good, or clean, or upright before the Lord, if there is anything good in me. That has helped me out in every trial and through every difficulty."

—Joseph F. Smith, *Gospel Doctrine*, 542–543.

"This Experience Taught Me a Good Lesson"

"I never but once was the cause of a disturbance. That was in Sheffield, [England]. . . . We had a large audience. . . . I said that 'the authority of the Apostles of today was the same as that held by the Apostles of Christ's day, and that the word of the modern Apostles was as good as the word of ancient Apostles.' Somebody in the audience cried out 'blasphemy!' This was too much for my boyish temper to bear; the proposition I had made seemed so clear, so plain and so indisputable to my mind, I could not brook a shout of 'blasphemy,' and I let loose on my opponent, upon apostate Christianity, hireling ministers, and upon those who opposed the truth in general, in my best licks, and by the time I got through, I had stirred up the emissaries of his Satanic Majesty until they were red-hot, and the parrot and monkey show began in good shape! Bro. Gibson tried to quell the riot, but the excited mob would not listen to him—would not hear any more, and made for our stand! We slipped through the crowd, and made for home. But some of the leaders were aching to get hold of me, and hung round for hours to get a chance. Well, this experience taught me a good lesson. Thereafter I moderated my fervor."

—Joseph F. Smith, in Holzapfel and Shupe, *Joseph F. Smith*, 97.

"They Were Men of God"

"I have served from my youth up along with such men as Brigham Young, Heber C. Kimball, Willard Richards, George A. Smith, Jedediah M. Grant, Daniel H. Wells, John Taylor, George Q. Cannon, and Wilford Woodruff and his associates, and Lorenzo Snow and his associates, the members of the twelve apostles, the seventies, and the high priests in the Church of Jesus Christ of Latter-day Saints for more than sixty years; and, that my word may be heard by every stranger within the sound of my voice, I want to testify to you that better men than these have never lived within the range of my acquaintance. I can so testify because I was familiar with these men, grew up from babyhood with them, associated with them in council, in prayer and supplication, and in travel from settlement to settlement throughout the country here, and in crossing the plains. I have heard them in private and in public, and I bear my testimony to you that they were men of God, true men, pure men, God's noblemen."

—Joseph F. Smith, *Gospel Doctrine*, 169.

"It Is Surprising to Hear the Multitude of Questions"

"It is surprising to hear the multitude of questions that are continuously sent to the Presidency of the Church, and to others of my brethren who are in leading positions, for information upon some of the most simple things that pertain to the Gospel. Hundreds of questions, communications, and letters are sent to us from time to time asking information and instruction on matters that are so plainly written in the revelations of God—contained in the Book of Mormon, the Doctrine and Covenants, the Pearl of Great Price, and the Bible—it seems that any one who can read should understand."

—Joseph F. Smith, "Unnecessary Questions," in Conference Report, Apr. 1915, 138.

"I Went as I Was Called"

"I was called on a mission after I had served four years on a homestead [in October 1873] and it was only necessary for me to remain one year more to prove up and get my title to the land; but President [Brigham] Young said he wanted me to go to Europe on a mission, to take charge of the mission there. I did not say to him, 'Brother Brigham, I cannot go; I have got a homestead on my hands, and if I go I will forfeit it.' I said to Brother Brigham, 'All right, President Young; whenever you want me to go I will go; I am on hand to obey the call of my file leader.' And I went. I lost the homestead, and yet I never complained about it; I never charged Brother Brigham with having robbed me because of this. I felt that I was engaged in a bigger work than securing 160 acres of land. I was sent to declare the message of salvation to the nations of the earth. I was called by the authority of God on the earth, and I did not stop to consider myself and my little personal rights and privileges; I went as I was called, and God sustained and blessed me in it."

—Joseph F. Smith, in *Deseret News Semi-Weekly*, Apr. 28, 1896, 1.

"Shall I Do as I Feel Led?"

On July 1, 1866, Wilford Woodruff recorded:

"I met at the Prayer Circle with President Young John Taylor W. Woodruff G. A. Smith G. Q. Cannon & Joseph F Smith. John Taylor Prayed & . . . President Young arose from his knees. . . . Of a sudden he stoped & Exclaimed hold on, 'Shall I do as I feel led? I always [feel] well to do as the Spirit Constrains me. It is my mind to Ordain Brother Joseph F. Smith to the Apostleship, and to be one of my Councillors.'

"He then Called upon Each one of us for an Expression of our Feelings and we Individually responded that it met our Harty approval. . . . After which Brother Joseph F. Smith knelt . . . we laid our hands upon him."

—Wilford Woodruff Diary, July 1, 1866, in Holzapfel and Shupe, *Joseph F. Smith*, 38.

"I Know that My Redeemer Lives"

On April 29, 1901, at the death of his nineteen-year-old daughter, Alice, Joseph F. Smith wrote:

"Our hearts are still bowed down in the earth where the remains of our Sweet girl and those of her little Brothers and Sister repose in dust. . . . But we will do the best we can, by the help of the Lord, and from our hearts we feel that our Sleeping treasures are all in His holy keeping and will soon awake from the dust to immortality and eternal life. But for the precious assurance and glorious hope in the Gospel of Christ, life would not only not be worth the living, but it would be an infamous and damning farce! But, 'O, what joy this sentence gives, I know that my Redeemer lives!' Thank God."

—Joseph F. Smith to Joseph R. Smith, May 14, 1901, Church History Library; in *Teachings of Presidents of the Church: Joseph F. Smith*, 86.

"My Days Grow Better and Better"

On his thirty-sixth birthday in 1874, Joseph F. Smith wrote: "The day was cold, bleak and dreary, a fit and proper anniversary of the dark and trying day of my birth; When my father [Hyrum] and his brother [Joseph] were confined in a dungeon for the gospel's sake and the saints were being driven from their homes in Missouri by a merciless mob. The bright sunshine of my soul has never thoroughly dispelled the darkening shadows cast upon it by the lowering gloom of that evening period.

"Yet the merciful hand of God and his kindliest providences have ever been extended visibly toward me, even from my childhood, and my days grow better and better thru humility and the pursuit of wisdom and happiness in the kingdom of God; The objects of my life becoming more apparent as time advances and experience grows. Those objects being the proclamation of the gospel, or the establishment of the kingdom of God on the earth; The salvation of souls, and most important of which to me—that of myself and family."

—Joseph F. Smith diary, Nov. 13, 1874, in Gibbons, *Joseph F. Smith*, 98.

"MAMA, MAMA, MY DEAR OLD MAMA"

Bishop Charles W. Nibley wrote:

"As we landed at the wharf in Honolulu, the native Saints were out in great numbers with their wreaths of leis, beautiful flowers of every variety and hue. . . . In the midst of it all I noticed a poor, old, blind woman, tottering under the weight of about ninety years, being led in. She had a few choice bananas in her hand. It was her all—her offering. She was calling, 'Iosepa, Iosepa.' Instantly, when [Joseph F. Smith] saw her, he ran to her and clasped her in his arms, hugged her, and kissed her over and over again, patting her on the head saying, 'Mama, Mama, my dear old Mama.' And with tears streaming down his cheeks he turned to me and said, 'Charlie, she nursed me when I was a boy, sick and without anyone to care for me. She took me in and was a mother to me.'"

—Charles W. Nibley, "Reminiscences," cited in Smith, *Gospel Doctrine*, 519–520.

"A Little Child Was Sitting by Its Mother"

"I witnessed a little circumstance in our meeting this afternoon in the aisle; a little child was sitting by its mother on a seat. Somebody came along and took the little child off its seat, and occupied the seat himself, leaving the child to stand. I want to say to you, my brethren and sisters, that that act sent a pang to my heart. I would not, for anything . . . grieve the heart of a little child in the house of God, lest an impression should be left upon its mind that would make the house of worship a distasteful place, and it would prefer not to come within its walls, than to come and be offended."

—Joseph F. Smith, *Gospel Doctrine*, 283.

"Promise I Made to God"

"In looking over the experience of my life, I cannot now discern, and do not remember a circumstance, since the beginning of my experience in the world, where I have felt, for a moment, to slacken or relax in the pledge and promise that I made to God and to the Latter-day Saints, in my youth. . . . As an elder in Israel I tried to be true to that calling; I tried to my utmost to honor and magnify that calling, and I strove, with all the intelligence and fervor of my soul, to be true to it. I have no knowledge nor recollection of any act of mine, or any circumstance in my life where I proved untrue or unfaithful to these callings in the Priesthood of the Son of God. Later in my life, when I was called to act as an apostle, and was ordained an apostle, and set apart to be one of the Twelve, I strove to honor that calling, to be true to it, and to my brethren, to the household of faith, and to the covenants and obligations involved in receiving this holy Priesthood which is after the order of the Son of God. I am not aware that I ever violated one of my obligations or pledges in these callings to which I have been called. I have sought to be true and faithful to all these things."

—Joseph F. Smith, *Gospel Doctrine*, 504.

"I Have Not Lived Alone These Five Months"

On October 4, 1918, Joseph F. Smith told a general conference audience:

"I will not, I dare not, attempt to enter upon many things that are resting upon my mind this morning, and I shall postpone until some future time, the Lord being willing, my attempt to tell you some of the things that are in my mind, and that dwell in my heart. I have not lived alone these five months. I have dwelt in the spirit of prayer, of supplication, of faith and of determination; and I have had my communication with the Spirit of the Lord continuously."

—Joseph F. Smith, "Continuous Communication with the Spirit of the Lord," in Conference Report, Oct. 1918, 2.

"To Enjoy More Fully Every Gift and Blessing"

"I am looking forward to the time when I shall have passed away from this stage of existence, there I shall be permitted to enjoy more fully every gift and blessing that have contributed to my happiness in this world; everything. I do not believe that there is one thing that was designed or intended to give me joy or make me happy, that I shall be denied here after, provided I continue faithful; otherwise my joy cannot be full. . . . I refer to the happiness experienced in seeking to do the will of God on earth as it is done in heaven. We expect to have our wives and husbands in eternity. We expect our children will acknowledge us as their fathers and mothers in eternity. I expect this; I look for nothing else. Without it, I could not be happy."

—Joseph F. Smith, *Gospel Doctrine*, 65.

Heber J. Grant

Born: November 22, 1856, Salt Lake City, Utah
Died: May 14, 1945, Salt Lake City, Utah
President of the Church: November 23, 1918, to May 14, 1945

HEBER J. GRANT

HEBER JEDEDIAH GRANT, SON OF Jedediah Grant and Rachel Ivins, was born November 22, 1856, in Salt Lake City. Nine days after Heber's birth, his father died. His mother Rachel was left to care for him and to teach him of his destiny: "Behave yourself, Heber, and you will someday be an apostle."[47]

In his youth Heber adopted a motto from Ralph Waldo Emerson: "That which we persist in doing becomes easier for us to do: not that the nature of the thing itself is changed, but that our power to do is increased."[48] With this motto as his guide, Heber succeeded in becoming an acclaimed penman, baseball pitcher, banker, and businessman.

In 1882, President John Taylor called Heber to fill a vacancy in the Quorum of the Twelve Apostles. Heber viewed the calling "beyond anything I was worthy of, and . . . the thought came to me, 'You know . . . that John Taylor is a prophet of God, and to decline this office . . . is equivalent to repudiating the prophet.'"

Heber said to President Taylor, "I will accept the office and do my best."[49] Yet for months he struggled to overcome feelings of personal failure and turned to the Lord in prayer. While praying, he saw in vision a council in heaven: "In this council the Savior was present, my father was there, and the Prophet Joseph Smith was there. The Prophet Joseph Smith and my father mentioned me and requested that I be called to that position [apostleship]. . . . It was given to me that I had done nothing to entitle me to that exalted position, except that I had lived a clean, sweet life. It was because of their faithful labors that I was called. . . .

It was also given to me that . . . from that day it depended upon me and upon me alone as to whether I made a success of my life or a failure."[50]

From 1918 to 1945 Heber served as President of The Church of Jesus Christ of Latter-day Saints. As President, Heber strongly opposed the repeal of Prohibition and the Eighteenth Amendment to the United States Constitution. Despite his plea for Latter-day Saints to not repeal Prohibition, Utah became the thirty-sixth state to vote for the repeal. When Heber received word of the vote, he said, "I have never felt so humiliated in my life over anything as that the state of Utah voted for the repeal of Prohibition."[51] From that point on Heber was adamant in proclaiming the need for Latter-day Saints to live the Word of Wisdom. Heber said, "There is seldom a conference when someone does not take it upon himself to tell us: 'Please do not speak on the Word of Wisdom. We hear it so much, we are sick and tired of it.'"[52]

Heber also spoke on the need for members to live within their means and avoid debt. He believed debt and speculation were the major causes of the Great Depression. Under his guidance and direction, the Church implemented the welfare program. When the United States became embroiled in World War II, his was the voice of comfort that buoyed up Latter-day Saints.

Heber died on May 14, 1945, in Salt Lake City. At his funeral, his counselor David O. McKay characterized him as persistent in his loyalty to friends and to God.[53]

The Life Story of Heber J. Grant in His Own Words

"Some Day You Will Be an Apostle"

"My mother always told me, 'Behave yourself, Heber, and some day you will be an apostle. If you do not behave yourself, you will not be, because we have a revelation recorded in the Doctrine and Covenants which specifically states there is a law irrevocably decreed in heaven before the foundations of the world upon which all blessings are predicated, and when we obtain any blessing from God, it is by obedience to that law upon which its predicated.' [Doctrine and Covenants 130:20.] I said, 'Mother, I do not want to be an Apostle. I do not want to be a bishop. I do not want to be anything but a businessman. Just get it out of your head.'"

—Heber J. Grant, in Hinckley, *Faith of Our Pioneer Fathers*, 69–71.

"One Can Learn to Sing"

"I have, all the days of my life, enjoyed singing very much. When I was a little boy ten years of age I joined a singing class, and the professor told me that I could never learn to sing. Some years ago [a man] told me that I could sing, but he said he would like to be forty miles away while I was doing it. . . .

"I make these remarks because I feel that we ought to encourage our young people to learn to sing. From the standpoint of a singer, I have lost thirty-three years of my life. . . . I did not learn until forty-three years of age, and I have spent four or five months trying to learn to sing the hymns, 'God moves in a mysterious way,' and 'O My Father.' I have learned one because of the sentiments and my love for the author, and the other because the late President Wilford Woodruff loved it better than any other hymn in the hymn book." Heber then sang the hymn 'O My Father,' before saying, "I have but one object tonight in speaking and singing, and that is to encourage the young men and young ladies not to waste thirty or forty years of their lives before undertaking to sing. . . . By continued effort one can learn to sing that has no knowledge of music whatever, as was the case with me."

—Heber J. Grant, "My Soul Delighteth in the Song of the Heart," in Conference Report, Apr. 1900, 61–62.

"I Spent Hours and Hours Throwing the Ball"

"As I was an only child, my mother reared me very carefully. Indeed, I grew up more or less under the principles of a hothouse plant, a growth which is long and lengthy but not substantial. I learned to sweep and to wash and wipe dishes but did little stone throwing and little indulgence in works which are interesting to boys, which develop their physical frames. Therefore, when I joined the baseball club, the boys of my own age and a little older played in the first nine, those younger than I played in the second, and those still younger, in the third, and I played with them. One of the reasons for this was that I could not throw the ball from one base to another, and another reason was that I lacked the strength to run or bat the ball. When I picked up the ball, the boys would generally shout, 'Throw it here, sissy!' So much fun was engendered on my account by my youthful companions that I solemnly vowed that I would play baseball in the nine that would win the championship in the territory of Utah. My mother was keeping boarders for a living at the time, and I shined their boots until I saved a dollar, which I invested in a baseball, and spent hours and hours throwing the ball at Bishop Edwin D. Woolley's barn, which caused him to refer to me as the laziest boy in the Thirteenth Ward. Often my arm would ache so that

I could scarcely go to sleep at night, but I kept on practicing and finally succeeded in getting into the second nine of our club. Subsequently, I joined a better club and eventually played in the nine that won the championship in California, Colorado, and Wyoming, and thus made good my promise to myself and retired from the baseball arena."

— Heber J. Grant, in Hinckley, *Heber J. Grant*, 37–38.

"The Greatest Scribbler on Earth"

"When a youth, attending school, a man was pointed out to me who kept books in Wells, Fargo and Co's. Bank, in Salt Lake City, and it was said that he received a salary of one hundred and fifty dollars a month. Well do I remember figuring that he was earning six dollars a day, Sundays omitted, which seemed to me an enormous amount. . . . I dreamed of being a book-keeper, and of working for Wells, Fargo & Co., and immediately joined the book-keeping class in the Deseret University, in the hope some day of earning what I thought at that time to be an immense salary. . . .

"Well do I remember the amusement I furnished my fellow-students. One remarked when looking at my books, 'What is it; hen tracks?' Another said, 'Has lightning struck an ink bottle?' These remarks and others, while not made to hurt my feelings but in good-natured fun, nevertheless cut deep, and aroused within me a spirit of determination. I resolved to live to set copies for all who attended the university, and to be the teacher of penmanship and book-keeping in that institution. Having a purpose and also 'the will to labor,' and agreeing with Lord Lytton that, 'In the bright lexicon of youth there's no such word as fail,' I commenced to employ my spare time in practicing penmanship, continuing year after a year until I was referred to as 'the greatest scribbler on earth.'

"The result was that some years later, I secured a position as book-keeper and policy clerk in an insurance office. Although at fifteen, I wrote a very nice hand, and it was all that was needed to satisfactorily fill the position which I then held, yet I was not fully satisfied but continued to dream, and 'scribble,' when not otherwise occupied. I worked in the front part of A. W. White & Co's. bank, and, when not busy, volunteered to assist with the bank work, and to do anything and everything I could to employ my time, never thinking whether I was to be paid for it or not, but having only a desire to work and learn. Mr. Morf, the book-keeper in the bank, wrote well, and took pains to assist me in my efforts to become proficient as a penman. I learned to write so well that I often earned more before and after office hours by writing cards, invitations, etc., and making maps, than the amount of my regular salary. Some years later, a diploma at the Territorial Fair was awarded me for the finest penmanship in Utah."

—Heber J. Grant, "The Nobility of Labor," *Improvement Era*, Dec. 1899, 82–83.

"The Marvelous Testimony which That Man Bore"

"There stand out in my life many incidents in my youth, of wonderful inspiration and power through men preaching the gospel in the spirit of testimony and prayer. I call to mind one such incident when I was a young man, probably seventeen or eighteen years of age. I heard the late Bishop Millen Atwood preach a sermon in the Thirteenth Ward. I was studying grammar at the time, and he made some grammatical errors in his talk.

"I wrote down his first sentence, smiled to myself, and said: 'I am going to get here tonight, during the thirty minutes that Brother Atwood speaks, enough material to last me for the entire winter in my night school grammar class.' We had to take to the class for each lesson two sentences, or four sentences a week, that were not grammatically correct, together with our corrections.

"I contemplated making my corrections and listening to Bishop Atwood's sermon at the same time. But I did not write anything more after that first sentence—not a word; and when Millen Atwood stopped preaching, tears were rolling down my cheeks, tears of gratitude and thanksgiving that welled up in my eyes because of the marvelous testimony which that man bore of the divine mission of Joseph Smith, the prophet of God, and of the wonderful inspiration that attended the prophet in all his labors. . . .

"During all the years that have passed since then, I have never been shocked or annoyed by grammatical errors or mispronounced words on the part of those preaching the gospel."

— Heber J. Grant, in *Gospel Standards*, comp. G. Homer Durham, 294–295.

"Away from My Widowed Mother"

When Heber J. Grant was offered an appointment to study at the United States Naval Academy, he said:

"For the first time in my life I did not sleep well; I lay awake nearly all night long, rejoicing that the ambition of my life was to be fulfilled. I fell asleep just a little before daylight; my mother had to wake me.

"I said: 'Mother, what a marvelous thing it is that I am to have an education as fine as that of any young man in all Utah. I could hardly sleep; I was awake until almost daylight this morning.'

"I looked into her face; I saw that she had been weeping.

"I have heard of people, who, when drowning, had their entire life pass before them in almost a few seconds. I saw myself as an admiral in my mind's eye. I saw myself traveling all over the world in a ship, away from my widowed mother. I laughed and put my arms around her, and kissed her and said:

"'Mother, I do not want a naval education. I am going be a business man and shall enter an office right away and take care of you, and have you quit keeping boarders for a living.'

"She broke down and wept and said that she had not closed her eyes but had prayed all night that I would give up my life's ambition so that she would not be left alone."

— Heber J. Grant, in *Gospel Standards*, comp. G. Homer Durham, 349.

"I Wanted to Be Married for Time and Eternity"

"I shall always be grateful, to the day of my death, that I did not listen to some of my friends when, as a young man not quite twenty-one years of age, I took the trouble to travel all the way from Utah County to St. George to be married in the St. George Temple. That was before the railroad went south of Utah County, and we had to travel the rest of the way by team. It was a long and difficult trip in those times, over unimproved and uncertain roads, and the journey each way required several days.

"Many advised me not to make the effort—not to go all the way down to St. George to be married. They reasoned that I could have the president of the stake or my bishop marry me, and then when the Salt Lake Temple was completed, I could go there with my wife and children and be sealed to her and have our children sealed to us for eternity.

"Why did I not listen to them? Because I wanted to be married for time and eternity—because I wanted to start life right. Later I had cause to rejoice greatly because of my determination to be married in the temple at that time rather than to have waited until some later and seemingly more convenient time."

—Heber J. Grant, "Beginning Life Together," *Improvement Era*, Apr. 1936, 198–199.

"That Is Jeddy Grant's Boy"

"I know nothing of course of the advice and counsel of a father because mine died when I was a baby, but I have learned of his reputation from others. People assure me that Jedediah M. Grant was one of the noblemen of this Church.

"I remember at one time asking Captain William H. Hooper to sign some bonds for me, when I was a youngster of twenty just starting in business.

"He said: 'I never do such a thing; never do such a thing.'

"I had no more than returned to my office when a young messenger came from the bank and told me the captain wanted to see me.

"I said, 'I don't want to see him.'

"'Well, he sent me to bring you to the bank.'

"I went back, and he said: 'Boy, boy, give me those bonds.' I did so, and he signed them. Then he said: 'When you went out I turned to Mr. Hills and said, 'Lew, who is that boy? He has been [greeting] me on the streets for years. I don't know who he is. I never sign a bond for somebody I don't know. Who is he?' He said, 'Why that is Jeddy Grant's boy, Heber J. Grant.' 'Jeddy Grant's boy? Bring him back. I would sign that bond if I knew I had to pay it.'"

—Heber J. Grant, "His Father," in Conference Report, Oct. 1934, 4.

"I Shed Tears of Humiliation"

"I went to Grantsville, the largest ward in the Tooele Stake of Zion, and I approached the Lord with much the same attitude as Oliver Cowdery when he told the Lord, 'I want to translate,' and the Lord told him he could translate. But, failing, he was later told, he did not study it out, and he did not pray about it, and he did not do his share [see Doctrine and Covenants 9:7–8]. . . . I got up and talked for five minutes, and I sweat as freely, I believe, as if I had been dipped in a creek, and I ran out of ideas completely. I made as complete a 'fizzle,' so to speak, of my talk, as a mortal could make. . . .

"I walked several miles away from that meetinghouse, out into the fields, among the hay and straw stacks, and when I got far enough away, so that I was sure nobody saw me, I knelt down behind one of those stacks and I shed tears of humiliation. I asked God to forgive me for not remembering that men can not preach the gospel of the Lord Jesus Christ with power, with force, and with inspiration only as they are blessed with power which comes from God; and I told him there, as a boy, that if he would forgive me for my egotism, if he would forgive me for imagining that without his Spirit any man can proclaim the truth and find willing hearts to receive it, to the day of my death I would endeavor to remember from whence the inspiration comes, when we are proclaiming the gospel of the Lord Jesus Christ, the plan of life and salvation again revealed to earth."

—Heber J. Grant, "Significant Counsel to the Young People of the Church," *Improvement Era*, Aug. 1921, 871–872.

"Boys, Count Me In"

"When I was a young man of twenty-four, presiding over the Tooele stake of Zion, passing a base-ball game one day, I heard the boys profane. I did not correct them, but I called to one of the players and said: 'Next time you have a baseball game, boys, count me in. I used to play in the nine that won the championship in our territory.' The boys did count me in, and I often played with them. The fact that the president of the stake came and played with them was the reason, I think, that no oaths were used in all the games that I played. I never saw finer deportment in my life than those boys exhibited upon the ball field."

—Heber J. Grant, "The Place of the Young Men's Mutual Improvement Associations in the Church," *Improvement Era*, Aug. 1912, 877.

"Give That Man Twenty Dollars"

"I remember once while sitting in the State Bank I saw an aged brother passing, by the name of John Furster. He was one of the first men baptized in Scandinavia. As he passed the bank window, the Spirit whispered to me, 'Give that man twenty dollars.' I went up to the teller, handed him my I.O.U. for $20, walked down the street and overtook Mr. Furster in front of the Z.C.M.I. store. I shook hands with him and left the twenty dollars in his hand. Some years later I learned that that morning Brother Furster had been praying for sufficient means to enable him to go to Logan and do a little work in the temple there. At the time, the Salt Lake Temple was not completed. The twenty dollars was just the amount he needed, and years later he thanked me with tears running down his cheeks, for having given him this money."

—Letter from Heber J. Grant to N. L. Nelson, Apr. 1, 1914, cited in *Teachings of Presidents of the Church: Heber J. Grant*, 142.

"I Know what You Were Going to Say"

"On the 6th of October, 1882, I met brother George Teasdale at the south gate of the temple. His face lit up, and he said: 'Brother Grant, you and I'—very enthusiastically—and then he commenced coughing and choking, and went on into [the] meeting and did not finish his sentence. It came to me as plainly, as though he had said the words: '. . . Are going to be chosen this afternoon to fill the vacancies in the Quorum of the Twelve Apostles.'

"I went to the meeting, and my head swelled, and I thought to myself, 'Well, I am going to be one of the apostles,' and I was willing to vote for myself, but the conference adjourned without anyone being chosen.

"Ten days later I received a telegram saying, 'You must be in Salt Lake tomorrow without fail.' I was then president of [the] Tooele Stake. The telegram came from my partner, Nephi W. Clayton. When I got to the depot, I said: 'Nephi, why on earth are you calling me back here? I had an appointment out in [the] Tooele Stake.'

"'Never mind,' he said, 'it was not I who sent for you; it was Brother Lyman. He told me to send the telegram and sign my name to it. He told me to come and meet you and take you to the President's office. That is all I know.'

"So I went to the President's office, and there sat Brother Teasdale, and all of the ten apostles, and the Presidency of the Church, and also Seymour B. Young and the members of the Seven Presidents of the Seventies. And the revelation was read calling Brother Teasdale and myself to the apostleship, and Brother Seymour B. Young to be one of the Seven Presidents of the Seventies.

"Brother Teasdale was blessed by President John Taylor, and George Q. Cannon blessed me.

"After the meeting I said to Brother Teasdale, 'I know what you were going to say to me on the sixth of October when you happened to choke half to death and then went into the meeting.'

"He said, 'Oh, no, you don't.'

"'Yes, I do,' and I repeated it: 'You and I are going to be called to the apostleship.'

"He said, 'Well, that is what I was going to say, and then it occurred to me that I had no right to tell it, that I had received a manifestation from the Lord.' He said, 'Heber, I have suffered the tortures of the damned for ten days, thinking I could not tell the difference between a manifestation from the Lord and one from the devil, that the devil had deceived me.'

"I said, 'I have not suffered like that, but I never prayed so hard in my life for anything as I did that the Lord would forgive me for the egotism of thinking that I was fit to be an apostle, and that I was ready to go into that meeting ten days ago and vote for myself to be an apostle.'"

—Heber J. Grant, "My Call to the Apostleship," in Conference Report, Oct. 3, 1942, 24–25.

"THE POWER OF THE LIVING GOD IS HERE ON THE EARTH"

"I shall never forget the occasion when a friend appealed to me, upon learning that the doctor had announced that his daughter, stricken with diphtheria, would die before morning. He asked me to pray for that daughter, and after leaving his office I prayed with all the earnestness of my soul that God would heal that girl. While praying, the inspiration came to me: 'The power of the living God is here on the earth. The Priesthood is here. Hurry! Hurry! . . . Go and rebuke the power of the destroyer, and the girl shall live.'

"The doctor waiting upon that girl, said she could not live till morning; but when morning came he explained that he could not comprehend it, and that he believed the girl was going to get well. He could not refrain from expressing his surprise at the change in the girl's condition over night. The power of the living God rebuked the destroyer."

—Heber J. Grant, "An Illustration of the Destroyer Rebuked," in Conference Report, Apr. 1925, 9–10.

"The Will of the Lord Shall Be Done"

"About an hour before my wife died, I called my children into her room and told them that their mother was dying and for them to bid her good-bye. One of the little girls, about twelve years of age, said to me: 'Papa, I do not want my mamma to die. I have been with you in the hospital in San Francisco for six months; time and time again when mamma was in distress you administered to her and she has been relieved of her pain and quietly gone to sleep. I want you to lay hands upon my mamma and heal her.'

"I told my little girl that we all had to die sometime, and that I felt assured in my heart that her mother's time had arrived. She and the rest of the children left the room.

"I then knelt down by the bed of my wife (who by this time had lost consciousness). . . . I told the Lord that I lacked the strength to have my wife die and to have it affect the faith of my little children in the ordinances of the gospel of Jesus Christ; and I supplicated the Lord with all the strength that I possessed, that He would give to that little girl of mine a knowledge that it was His mind and His will that her mamma should die.

"Within an hour my wife passed away, and I called the children back into the room. My little boy about five and a half or six years of age was weeping bitterly, and the little girl twelve years of age took him in her arms and said: 'Do not weep, do not cry, Heber; since we went out of this room the voice of the Lord from heaven has said to me, 'In the death of your mamma the will of the Lord shall be done.'"

— Heber J. Grant, in *Gospel Standards*, comp. G. Homer Durham, 360–361.

"Would You Like to Wash Out My Mouth?"

Frances Grant Bennett said of her father, Heber J. Grant:

"An incident occurred which made so profound an impression on me that I have remembered it all my life. I used some language father didn't approve of, and he told me he would have to wash such words out of my mouth. He scrubbed out my mouth thoroughly with soap and said, 'Now your mouth is clean. I don't ever want you to make it dirty with such words again.'

"Several days later at the breakfast table, father was telling a story, and in quoting someone else he used a profane expression. I was quick to pick it up.

"'Papa,' I said, 'you washed my mouth out for saying words like that.'

"'So I did,' he answered. 'And I shouldn't say them any more than you should. Would you like to wash out my mouth?'

"'I certainly would.' I got the laundry soap and did a thorough job of it."

—Bennett, *Glimpses of a Mormon Family*, 15–16.

"Father Was There Waiting"

Lucy Grant Cannon said of her father, Heber J Grant:
"A few days before Christmas as I was preparing some little gifts for a needy family, father walked in and I showed him the things, telling him about the family as I had gathered the story from the mother. I mentioned that I must get my temple clothes ready; I was lending them to the woman to use the next morning. The next day when she came to return my clothing she told me when she went into the temple gate father was there waiting. He had never seen her before, only, knowing her by my description, he stopped her and handed her an envelope as he wished the family a happy Christmas. The envelope contained twenty dollars."

—Lucy Grant Cannon, "A Father Who Is Loved and Honored," *Improvement Era*, Nov. 1936, 682.

George Albert Smith

Born: April 4, 1870, Salt Lake City, Utah
Died: April 4, 1951, Salt Lake City, Utah
President of the Church: May 21, 1945, to April 4, 1951

GEORGE ALBERT SMITH

GEORGE ALBERT SMITH, SON OF John Henry Smith and Sarah Farr, was born April 4, 1870, in Salt Lake City. George descended from a long line of faithful leaders—his father and grandfather served in leading quorums of the Church.

At age ten, George fell in love with his future wife, Lucy Emily Woodruff. He "expected to marry her" although she showed much disdain for his boyish pranks. On May 25, 1892, George and Lucy were married in the Manti Temple. Soon after their marriage, George accepted a mission call to the southern states, where intense prejudice threatened to destroy the work of God. After completing an honorable mission, George returned to his family in Salt Lake City. To support his family, he worked as a salesman for ZCMI department store and as a receiver for the United States Land Office.

In 1903 George was called to the Quorum of the Twelve Apostles. He served in the same quorum with his father, John Henry Smith. While serving as an Apostle of the Lord Jesus Christ, George wrote a personal creed: "I would be a friend to the friendless and find joy in ministering to the needs of the poor. I would visit the sick and afflicted and inspire in them a desire for faith to be healed. I would teach the truth to the understanding and blessing of all mankind. I would seek out the erring one and try to win him back to the righteous and happy life. . . . I would not become an enemy to any living soul."[54] Using the creed as his guide, George became known for his kindness to children and his concern for the handicapped, sick, and poor.

In 1909 George became very ill. Although there was never a definitive diagnosis of his health problem, many attributed his illness to a serious case of la grippe, a type of influenza.[55] The illness left him with emotional and physical problems. A three-year bout of depression, discomfort, and discouragement followed. A turning point in his health was a dream in which he saw his grandfather, George A. Smith, and told him of his continuing faithfulness to the Smith name.[56] Although health issues and public speaking remained a struggle, George put his trust in God and pressed forward to fulfill his apostolic responsibilities.

In 1945, George Albert Smith was sustained as President of The Church of Jesus Christ of Latter-day Saints. During his administration, he encouraged Latter-day Saints to be kind. One of his public acts of kindness was sending supplies to war-torn Europe. On his birthday, April 4, 1951, George died at age eighty-one.

The Life Story of George Albert Smith in His Own Words

"It Was Such a Simple Prayer"

"I was trained at the knee of a Latter-day Saint mother [Sarah Farr Smith]. One of the first things I remember was when she took me by the hand and led me upstairs. In the room there were two beds, the bed in which my parents slept, and a little trundle bed over on the other side. I can remember it as if it were yesterday. When we got upstairs, she sat down by my little trundle bed. She had me kneel in front of her. She folded my hands and took them in hers, and taught me my first prayer. I will never forget it. I do not want to forget it. It is one of the loveliest memories that I have in life, an angelic mother sitting down by my bedside and teaching me to pray.

"It was such a simple prayer, but . . . that prayer opened for me the windows of heaven. That prayer extended to me the hand of my Father in heaven, for she had explained to me what it all meant as far as a little child could understand. From that day until now, while I have covered approximately a million miles in the world among our Father's other children, every day and every night, wherever I have been, when I have gone to my bed or arisen from it, I have felt I was close to my Heavenly Father. He is not far away."

—George Albert Smith, "Mother's Teachings," in Conference Report, Oct. 1946, 150–151.

"I WAS PLAYING OUTSIDE WITH THE OTHER CHILDREN"

During his childhood, George Albert Smith was afflicted with typhoid fever. The doctor told his mother that George should stay in bed for three weeks, eat no solid food, and drink some coffee.

George later recalled: "When [the doctor] went away, I told mother that I didn't want any coffee. I had been taught that the Word of Wisdom, given by the Lord to Joseph Smith, advised us not to use coffee.

"Mother had brought three children into the world and two had died. She was unusually anxious about me."

Young George asked for a priesthood blessing: "When the doctor came the next morning I was playing outside with the other children. He was surprised. He examined me and discovered that my fever was gone and that I seemed to be well.

"I was grateful to the Lord for my recovery. I was sure that he had healed me."

—George Albert Smith, "Boyhood Experiences," *Juvenile Instructor*, Feb. 1943, 73.

"I REMEMBER WITH DEEP APPRECIATION HIS KINDNESS"

"Although a small child when Brigham Young passed away, I knew him; I have sat upon his knee and I remember with deep appreciation his kindness to my mother and to me when Father was in England as a missionary. I have been well acquainted with the other Presidents and believe that they were all men of God. It is inconceivable that our Heavenly Father would choose any other kind to preside over his church.

"I have known the members of the Quorum of the Twelve since I was a small boy, and since I became of age I have been intimate with all of them. They have been a remarkable group of men."

—George Albert Smith, "Humble but Great Men," in Conference Report, Apr. 1931, 31.

"Ordained Me a Deacon"

"I remember, as if it were yesterday, when John Tingey placed his hands on my head and ordained me a deacon. I had the matter so presented to me and the importance of it, that I felt it was a great honor. The result was, it was a blessing to me, and then after awhile other ordinations came to me. But in each case the foundation was laid in my mind that here was an opportunity for another blessing."

—George Albert Smith, "Responsibilities of a Bishop," in Conference Report, Oct. 1948, 181.

"It Made an Impression on My Mind"

"When I was about fourteen years of age, I read the fortieth chapter of Alma in the Book of Mormon in our Sunday School class. It made an impression on my mind that has been helpful when death has taken loved ones away. . . . It is one place in the scriptures that tells us where our spirits go when they leave this body, and I have wanted to go to that place called paradise ever since."

—George Albert Smith, "Early Life," in Conference Report, Apr. 1949, 83–84.

"Accountable for Your Thoughts"

"It was fortunate that part of my instruction [at the Brigham Young Academy] came under Dr. Karl G. Maeser, that outstanding educator who was the first builder of our great Church schools. . . . I cannot remember much of what was said during the year that I was there, but there is one thing that I will probably never forget. I have repeated it many times. . . . Dr. Maeser one day stood up and said:

"'Not only will you be held accountable for the things that you do, but you will be held responsible for the very thoughts that you think.'

"Being a boy, not in the habit of controlling my thoughts very much, it was quite a puzzle to me what I was to do, and it worried me. In fact, it stuck to me just like a burr. About a week or ten days after that it suddenly came to me what he meant. I could see the philosophy of it then. All at once there came to me this interpretation of what he had said: Why of course, you will be held accountable for your thoughts because when your life is complete in mortality, it will be the sum of your thoughts. That one suggestion has been a great blessing to me all my life, and it has enabled me upon many occasions to avoid thinking improperly because I realize that I will be, when my life's labor is complete, the product of my thoughts."

—George Albert Smith, "Pres. Smith's Leadership Address," *Deseret News*, Feb. 16, 1946.

"THOU SHALT BECOME A MIGHTY APOSTLE"

On January 16, 1884, Zebedee Coltrin came to the Smith home and inquired after George Albert Smith. Brother Coltrin indicated that he was a patriarch and "had not been able to sleep or be at peace with himself for the past few days because of the feeling that he should come and give George a blessing."

Patriarch Coltin pronounced the following blessing upon George Albert Smith:

"[T]hou wast called and chosen of the Lord from before the foundation of the earth was laid to come forth in this dispensation to assist in building up the Zion of God upon the earth, and thou shalt be enabled to bring many to a knowledge of the truth, for thy voice shall be as the voice of a trumpet in declaring the words of the Lord to the nobles of the earth, and many shall believe in thy words and embrace the gospel of the Son of God.

". . . [And] thou shalt become a mighty Apostle in the Church and kingdom of God upon the earth for none of thy father's family shall have more power with God than thou shalt have, for none shall exceed thee, for thy reward shall be great in the heavens, for the blessing of thy father and of thy grandfather shall rest upon thee and thou shalt become a man of mighty faith before the Lord, even like unto that of the brother of Jared, and thou shalt remain upon the earth until thou art satisfied with life, and shall be numbered with the Lord's anointed and shall become a king and a priest unto the Most High."

—Doyle L. Green, "Tributes Paid President George Albert Smith," *Improvement Era*, June 1951, 404–405.

"WE STAYED AND ENJOYED THE INSPIRATION OF THE ALMIGHTY"

"I remember as a young man and missionary in the Southern States, the first conference I attended. It was out in the woods on a farm in Mississippi. We didn't have comfortable seats to sit on. The brethren had been permitted to cut down a few trees and lay the trunks of those trees across the stumps which were left. We balanced ourselves on those or else sat on the ground. Our meeting started right after breakfast time, and we didn't even think it was necessary to have anything more to eat until evening. We stayed and enjoyed the inspiration of the Almighty, and we certainly were blessed, notwithstanding the inconveniences and discomforts which surrounded us. At that time there was considerable hostility manifested in Mississippi and other states in the South, but we just felt as if we had walked into the presence of our Heavenly Father, and all fear and anxiety left. That was my first experience in the mission field attending a conference."

—George Albert Smith, "Incidents from Missionary Life," in Conference Report, Oct. 1945, 115.

"GRATEFUL TO MY HEAVENLY FATHER FOR PROTECTING ME"

"Elder Stout and I were traveling along a high precipice. Our little walk was narrow; on one side was the wall of the mountain, on the other side, the deep, deep river. We had no light and there were no stars and no moon to guide us. . . .

". . . Elder Stout was ahead of me and as I walked along I felt the hard surface of the trail under my feet. In doing so I left the wall of the mountain, which had acted as a guide and a steadying force. After I had taken a few steps away from the mountain wall itself, I felt impressed to stop immediately, that something was wrong. I called to Elder Stout and he answered me. The direction from which his voice came indicated I was on the wrong trail, so I backed up until I reached the wall of the mountain and again proceeded forward. . . .

"We arrived safely at our destination about eleven o'clock at night. I soon discovered I had lost my comb and brush, and the next morning we returned to the scene of my accident. I recovered my property, and while there my curiosity was stimulated and aroused to see what had happened the night before when I had lost my way in the dark. As missionaries we wore hob-nails in the bottom of our shoes to make them last longer, so that I could easily follow our tracks in the soft dirt. I retraced my steps to the point where my tracks left the mountainside and discovered that in the darkness I had wandered to the edge of a deep precipice. Just one more step and I would have fallen over into the river and been drowned. I felt very ill when I realized how close I had come to death. I also was very grateful to my Heavenly Father for protecting me. I have always felt that if we are doing the Lord's work and ask him for his help and protection, he will guide and take care of us."

—George Albert Smith, "How My Life Was Preserved," George Albert Smith Family Papers, box 121, scrapbook 1, 43–44, in *Teachings of George Albert Smith*, 194–195.

"I WAS SURE . . . THE LORD WOULD PROTECT ME"

"About midnight we [George and President J. Golden Kimball] were awakened with a terrible shouting and yelling from the outside. Foul language greeted our ears as we sat up in bed to acquaint ourselves with the circumstances. It was a bright moonlit night and we could see many people on the outside. President Kimball jumped up and started to dress. The men pounded on the door and used filthy language ordering the Mormons to come out, that they were going to shoot them. President Kimball asked me if I wasn't going to get up and dress and I told him no, I was going to stay in bed, that I was sure the Lord would take care of us. In just a few seconds the room was filled with shots. Apparently the mob had divided itself into four groups and were shooting into the corners of the house. Splinters were flying over our heads in every direction. There were a few moments of quiet, then another volley of shots was fired and more splinters flew. I felt absolutely no terror. I was very calm as I lay there, experiencing one of the most horrible events of my life, but I was sure . . . that the Lord would protect me, and he did.

"Apparently the mob became discouraged and left. The next morning when we opened the door, there was a huge bundle of heavy hickory sticks such as the mob used to beat the missionaries in the South."

—George Albert Smith, "How My Life Was Preserved," George Albert Smith Family Papers, box 121, scrapbook 1, 43–44, in *Teachings of the Presidents of the Church: George Albert Smith*, xvii–xviii.

"WE PASSED A LITTLE INDIAN SETTLEMENT"

"I boarded the train and started home, and we passed a little Indian settlement at the side of the track. I saw evidence that there were quite a number of Indians there, so I reached over and touched the man who was sitting in the seat in front of me, and I said, 'Do you know what Indians these are?'

"He said, 'They are the Catawbas.'. . .

"I asked, 'Do you know where they come from?'

"He said, 'Do you mean the Catawbas?'

"I replied, 'Any Indians.'

"He said, 'Nobody knows where the Indians came from.'

"'Oh,' I said, 'yes, they do.' I was talking then to a man about forty-five or fifty years old, and I was twenty-one.

"He questioned, 'Well, where did they come from?'

"I answered, 'They came from Jerusalem six hundred years before the birth of Christ.'

"'Where did you get that information?' he asked.

"I told him, 'From the history of the Indians.'

"'Why,' he said, 'I didn't know there was any history of the Indians.'

"I said, 'Yes, there is a history of the Indians. It tells all about them.'

"Then he looked at me as much as to say: My, you are trying to put one over on me.

"But he said, 'Where is this history?'

"'Would you like to see one?' I asked. And he said that he certainly would. I reached down under the seat in my little log-cabin grip and took out a Book of Mormon and handed it to him. . . ."

Many years later George saw this man again:

"[The man] said, 'I want to tell you something. I read that book, and I was so impressed with it that I made up my mind I would like to take a trip down into Central America and South America, and I took that book with me in my bag when I went down there. As a result of reading it, I knew more about those people than they knew about themselves.'"

—George Albert Smith, "The Pathway of Righteousness," *Improvement Era*, April 1950, 362, 410.

"I Recognized Him as My Grandfather"

"A number of years ago I was seriously ill. In fact, I think everyone gave me up but my wife. With my family I went to St. George, Utah, to see if it would improve my health.

"One day . . . I lost consciousness of my surroundings and thought I had passed to the Other Side. I found myself standing with my back to a large and beautiful lake, facing a great forest of trees. There was no one in sight, and there was no boat upon the lake or any other visible means to indicate how I might have arrived there. I realized, or seemed to realize, that I had finished my work in mortality and had gone home. . . .

"I began to explore, and soon I found a trail through the woods which seemed to have been used very little, and which was almost obscured by grass. I followed this trail, and after I had walked for some time and had traveled a considerable distance through the forest, I saw a man coming towards me. I became aware that he was a very large man, and I hurried my steps to reach him, because I recognized him as my grandfather [George A. Smith]. In mortality he weighed over three hundred pounds, so you may know he was a large man. I remember how happy I was to see him coming. I had been given his name and had always been proud of it. When Grandfather came within a few feet of me, he stopped. His stopping was an invitation for me to stop. Then . . . he looked at me very earnestly and said: 'I would like to know what you have done with my name.'

"Everything I had ever done passed before me as though it were a flying picture on a screen—everything I had done. Quickly this vivid retrospect came down to the very time I was standing there. My whole life had passed before me. I smiled and looked at my grandfather and said:

"'I have never done anything with your name of which you need be ashamed.'

"He stepped forward and took me in his arms, and as he did so, I became conscious again of my earthly surroundings. My pillow was as wet as though water had been pouring on it—wet with tears of gratitude that I could answer unashamed."

—George Albert Smith, "Your Good Name," *Improvement Era*, March 1947, 139.

"I Rejoice to Testify"

"I have been in the valley of the shadow of death in recent years, so near the other side that I am sure that [if not] for the special blessing of our heavenly Father I could not have remained here. But, never for one moment did that testimony that my heavenly Father has blessed me with become dimmed. The nearer I went to the other side, the greater was my assurance that the gospel is true. Now that my life has been spared I rejoice to testify that I know the gospel is true, and with all my soul I thank my heavenly Father that he has revealed it to me."

—George Albert Smith, "The Promise of Eternal Life Conditional," in Conference Report, Oct. 1921, 42.

"My Brother, You Have Been Misinformed"

"I recall an experience I once had. I was riding on a train in England. My companion in the compartment was a Presbyterian minister, and when he gave me the opportunity to do so, I told him I was a member of the Church of Jesus Christ of Latter-day Saints. With amazement he said, 'Aren't you ashamed of yourself to belong to such a group?'

"I smiled at him and said, 'My brother, I would be ashamed of myself not to belong to that group, knowing what I know.' Then that gave me the opportunity I desired to talk to him and explain to him some of the things we believe."

—George Albert Smith, "Freely Have Ye Received: Freely Give," *Ensign*, June 1972, 33–34.

"The Cover Was Elegantly Embossed with Gold"

"In Chicago a number of years ago, during the Century of Progress Exposition, I went into our Church booth one day and inquired of the missionaries as to who had charge of the great cultural and scientific fair.

"They told me the man's name was Dawes, and I asked, 'Is he the brother of Charles G. Dawes, who was vice president of the United States and also ambassador to Great Britain?'

"And they answered, 'Yes.'

"'Well,' I said, 'I am delighted to know that. I happen to know him.'

"... I went to the telephone and called his office. His secretary ... told Mr. Dawes that George Albert Smith of Salt Lake City was there and wanted to meet him, and he told her to have me come over. So, instead of running me behind a hundred people to wait my turn, she took me to a side door, and there stood before me a tall man whom I had never seen before in my life. . . .

"'Well,' I said, 'I have come to tell you that this is a wonderful fair, and to express to you my appreciation for what you have done in organizing and seeing it through. It is marvelous what has been accomplished. . . . Now, I understand that you are a busy man, and that is all I wanted to come and say, and to congratulate and thank you.'

"'That is very considerate,' he said. 'Come in.' . . .

"So I went in, out of ideas and out of breath, almost. He insisted on my sitting down, and the next thing I said was: 'By the way, Mr. Dawes, where do your people come from?'

"'Do you mean in America?' he asked.

"'I mean anywhere.'

"He said, 'Are you interested in genealogy?'

"'I certainly am,' I answered. 'We have one of the finest genealogical libraries in Salt Lake City.'

"He said, 'Excuse me just a moment,' and walked out of his office and came back with a carton about the size of an old family Bible. He took his knife, opened the carton, and took out a package wrapped in white tissue paper. He took the tissue paper off and put on the table one of the most beautifully bound books I have ever seen. It was well printed and profusely illustrated, and the cover was elegantly embossed with gold.

"As I looked it over, I said, 'Mr. Dawes, that is a beautiful piece of work.'

"'It ought to be. It cost me twenty-five thousand dollars.'

"'Well,' I said, 'it is worth it.'

"He said, 'Is it worth anything to you?'

"I said, 'It would be if I had it.'

"He said, 'All right, you may have it!'—twenty-five thousand dollars worth of genealogy placed in my hand by a man whom I had met only five minutes before! Well, I was amazed. Our visit continued but a short while longer. I told him how delighted I was to have it and that I would place it in the genealogical library in Salt Lake City.

"Before I left the room, he said, 'Mr. Smith, this is my mother's genealogy, the Gates' genealogy. We are also preparing my father's genealogy—the Dawes' family. It will be one just like this. When it is finished, I would like to send you a copy of that also.'

"Fifty thousand dollars of genealogy!—and just because I tried to be polite to someone. I do not think that was an accident."

—George Albert Smith, "On Searching for Family Records," *Improvement Era*, Aug. 1946, 491, 540.

"I Talked to Him about the Gospel"

George Albert Smith had a conversation with a man on a train who was raised in a Latter-day Saint family but was no longer participating in the Church:

"I talked to him about the gospel of Jesus Christ. . . . And he said as we discussed the principles of the gospel, 'These things interest me.' We visited quite a long time, and when we finished, that good man, I believe he was a good man, said to me, 'I would give all that I possess to have the assurance that you have. . . .'

"I said, 'My brother, you don't have to give all that you possess to have that assurance. All you have to do is to search the scriptures prayerfully. Go where they may be explained to you. Seek the truth, and the beauty of the truth will appeal to you, and . . . you can know as I know that God lives, that Jesus is the Christ, that Joseph Smith is a prophet of the Living God.'"

—George Albert Smith, "Assurance of Eternal Life," in Conference Report, Oct. 1948, 165–166.

"I Have Borne Witness of the Divinity of This Work"

At the April 1925 general conference of the Church, George Albert Smith said:

"In the past two months I have traveled more than eleven thousand miles in this wonderful land of America, from the eastern seaboard to the western seaboard. I have borne witness of the divinity of this work, I have found great and good men outside the pale of this, or of any church, who are apparently anxious to know what the end will be as a result of the condition that this world finds itself in. It has been my privilege to explain to some of these men my faith in the divine mission of Jesus Christ; my knowledge that our Heavenly Father loves his children, as he always has done; the assurance that has burned into my soul, for which I am grateful, that I know that the work of our Heavenly Father is upon the earth, that the gospel of Jesus Christ will solve the problem and be a panacea for the ills that afflict mankind."

—George Albert Smith, "The Gospel a Panacea for the Ills of Mankind," in Conference Report, Apr. 1925, 68.

"Our Souls Were Subdued"

At the October 1934 general conference of the Church, George Albert Smith said:

"Here, sixty-nine years ago, this building [the Salt Lake Tabernacle] was opened, and from that time until now many marvelous instructions have been given to the Latter-day Saints. I have been in this house when the Spirit of God has been poured out upon us and there were few eyes not moistened by tears. Our souls were subdued. We felt to repent of our sins."

—George Albert Smith, "In This Building," in Conference Report, Oct. 1934, 51.

"Why, Brother Smith, It Enabled Me to Understand the Bible"

"I remember a good many years ago when I was down in California, I met a man who was a great geologist, whose name was Robert Hill. While being employed in research in Mexico and Central America by the Smithsonian Institute or National Museum, a Book of Mormon fell into his hands, and he read it. He was working under the direction of the department at Washington, where they collect curiosities from the various sections of the country. . . .

"When he read the Book of Mormon he asked for a leave of absence. He came to Salt Lake City and inquired for somebody who would indicate to him the source of the Book of Mormon, for he said, 'This book explains some things that the scientists are unable to harmonize.' Dr. James E. Talmage took him in hand and informed him as to the source of the Book of Mormon, how it had been revealed, how the people had come here under the direction of our Heavenly

Father and built up this country. Before Robert Hill left, he said, 'This is what I have been looking for,' and he was baptized and became a member of the Church of Jesus Christ of Latter-day Saints. He returned to Mexico, and I saw him later in Los Angeles. When I asked him what effect the Book of Mormon had on his life, he said, 'Why, Brother Smith, it enabled me to understand the Bible as I have never understood it before.'"

—George Albert Smith, "Conversion through Book of Mormon," in Conference Report, Oct. 1948, 6–7.

"MY FRIENDS, YOU LOOK SO HOT AND TIRED"

Martha Stewart Hatch said of her grandfather, George Albert Smith:

"Once on a hot summer day there was some problem happening under the street near Grandfather's home in Salt Lake City, and some workers from the city had come to fix it. It was hot outdoors, the sun shone fiercely, and the job at hand was a pick-and-shovel kind that made the sweat pour off the men's faces and backs as they dug into the roadway. The workers were not careful with their language. . . .

"Someone went out and asked the men to stop their foul talk, and in the process pointed out that Brother Smith lived right there—couldn't they show some respect and keep quiet, please? With that the men let loose a new string of bad words. Quietly, Grandfather prepared some lemonade and placing some glasses and the pitcher on a tray he carried it out to the struggling men with, 'My friends, you look so hot and tired. Why don't you come and sit under my trees here and have a cool drink?' Their anger gone, the men responded to the kindness with meekness and appreciation. After their pleasant little break they went back to their labor and finished their work carefully and quietly."

—Madsen, *The Lord Needed a Prophet*, 130–131.

"I Wish I Knew Who It Was"

Elder Spencer W. Kimball wrote:

"It was reported to [President George Albert Smith] that someone had stolen from his buggy the buggy robe. Instead of being angry, he responded: 'I wish we knew who it was, so that we could give him the blanket also, for he must have been cold; and some food also, for he must have been hungry.'"

—Spencer W. Kimball, *Miracle of Forgiveness*, 284.

"This Coat Is Yours"

Elder Thomas S. Monson wrote:

"On a cold winter morning, the street cleaning-crew [in Salt Lake City] was removing large chunks of ice from the street gutters. The regular crew was assisted by temporary laborers who desperately needed the work. One such [man] wore only a lightweight sweater and was suffering from the cold. A slender man with a well-groomed beard stopped by the crew and asked the worker, 'You need more than that sweater on a morning like this. Where is your coat?' The man replied that he had no coat to wear. The visitor then removed his own overcoat, handed it to the man and said, 'This coat is yours. It is heavy wool and will keep you warm. I just work across the street.' The street was South Temple. The good Samaritan who walked into the Church Administration Building to his daily work and without his coat was President George Albert Smith."

—Thomas S. Monson, "My Brother's Keeper," *Ensign*, May 1990, 47.

"I Know That My Redeemer Liveth"

Elder Robert L. Simpson, a counselor in the Presiding Bishopric of the Church, said:

"President Smith passed away on his 81st birthday, April 4, 1951. During the final moments of his life, with his family close by, his son asked, "Father, is there something you'd like to say to the family—something special?"

"With a smile, he reaffirmed the testimony he had shared numerous times throughout his life: 'Yes, only this: I know that my Redeemer liveth; I know that my Redeemer liveth.'"

—Robert L. Simpson, "The Power and Responsibilities of the Priesthood," in *Speeches of the Year*, Mar. 31, 1964, 8.

David O. McKay

Born: September 8, 1873, Huntsville, Utah
Died: January 18, 1970, Salt Lake City, Utah
President of the Church: April 9, 1951, to January 18, 1970

David O. McKay

David O. McKay, son of David McKay and Jennette Evans, was born September 8, 1873, in Huntsville, Utah. David's father set the standard in his home by serving in the Utah Senate and as a bishop of the Eden and Huntsville wards. More important, he shared with David his abiding testimony of Jesus Christ. David's mother taught him to respect life, to be confident, and to maintain personal discipline. David said, "My home life from babyhood to the present time has been the greatest factor in giving me moral and spiritual standards and in shaping the course of my life."[57]

At age seven, David became the man of the house when, over the course of a single year, his father left home to fulfill a mission in the British Isles and his sister died. At age twelve, David served as president of his deacons quorum, and at age thirteen he received his patriarchal blessing. "The eye of the Lord is upon thee," the patriarch said. "The Lord has a work for thee to do." [58]

As a teenager, David enrolled in the Weber Stake Academy and studied the works of Robert Burns and William Shakespeare. He later attended the University of Utah. During his years at the university, he played on the football team, was a popular pianist, and was elected class president. In 1897 he received a teaching certificate and an offer to teach at the Weber Stake Academy.

Before accepting the offer, David fulfilled a mission to Great Britain. On that mission he learned "sincere prayer is answered sometime, somewhere."[59] After completing an honorable mission, he returned to the states. On January 2, 1901, David married Emma

Ray Riggs in the Salt Lake Temple; they became the first couple married in that temple in the twentieth century.

On April 8, 1906, David was sustained as a member of the Quorum of the Twelve Apostles. In 1918 he was appointed General Sunday School Superintendent and in 1919 Church Commissioner of Education. On November 3, 1922, David was appointed president of the European Mission. While fulfilling that assignment, he coined the phrase, "Every member a missionary."[60] In 1934 he began his service as a counselor in the First Presidency of the Church, a position he held for twenty-seven years.

On April 9, 1951, David O. McKay became the ninth President of The Church of Jesus Christ of Latter-day Saints. During his presidency, David radiated good will: "What you sincerely in your heart think of Christ will determine what you are, will largely determine what your acts will be."[61] Family was another key touchstone of his presidency. As he spoke of the importance of family, David, quoting J. E. McCulloch, advised, "No other success can compensate for failure in the home."[62]

David died in his ninety-sixth year on January 18, 1970, the same day the five hundredth stake of the Church was organized.

The Life Story of David O. McKay in His Own Words

"The Kingdom of God or Nothing"

"Just above the pulpit in the meetinghouse where as a boy I attended Sunday services, there hung for many years a large photograph of the late President John Taylor, and under it, in what I thought were gold letters, this phrase:

"'The Kingdom of God or Nothing.'

"The sentiment impressed me as a mere child years before I understood its real significance. I seemed to realize at that early date that there is no other church or organization that approaches the perfection or possesses the divinity that characterizes the church of Jesus Christ. As a child I felt this intuitively; in youth, I became thoroughly convinced of it; and today I treasure it as a firm conviction of my soul."

—David O. McKay, in Middlemiss, *Cherished Experiences*, 15.

"Don't Be Afraid. Nothing Will Hurt You"

"When a very young child in the home of my youth, I was fearful at night. I traced it back to a vivid dream when two [Native Americans] came into the yard. I ran to the house for protection, and one of them shot an arrow and hit me in the back. Only a dream, but I felt that blow, and I was very much frightened, for in the dream they entered the house and frightened Mother.

"I never got over it. Adding to that were the fears of Mother, for when Father was away, Mother would never go to bed without looking under the bed; so burglars were real to me, or wicked men who could come in and try to take advantage of Mother and the young children.

"One night I could not sleep. I was only a boy, and I fancied I heard noises around the house. Mother was away in another room. My brother Thomas by my side was sleeping soundly. I could not sleep, and I became terribly fearful, and I decided that I would do as my parents had taught me to do—pray.

"I thought I could not pray without getting out of bed and kneeling, and that was a terrible test. But I finally did bring myself to get out of bed and kneel and pray to God to protect Mother and the family. And a voice as clearly to me as mine is to you said, 'Don't be afraid. Nothing will hurt you.' Where it came from, what it was, I am not saying. You may judge. To me it was a direct answer, and there came an assurance that I should never be hurt in bed at night."

—David O. McKay, "Elder David O. McKay," in Conference Report, Apr. 1912, 52; see also David Lawrence McKay, *My Father*, 77–79.

"The Life and Influence of a Perfect Mother"

"The older I grow, the more deeply grateful I am for the life and influence of a perfect mother.

"Among my most precious soul treasures, is the memory of Mother's prayers by the bedside, of her affectionate touch as she tucked the bed clothes around my brother and me, and gave each a loving, good night kiss. We were too young and roguish, then, fully to appreciate such devotion, but not too young to know that Mother loved us.

"It was this realization of Mother's love, with a loyalty to the precepts of an exemplary father, which more than once during fiery youth, turned my steps from the precipice of temptation."

—David O. McKay, *Treasures of Life*, 41–42.

"Joseph Smith Was a Prophet of God"

"It has been easy for me to understand and believe the reality of the visions of the Prophet Joseph. It was easy for me in youth to accept his vision, the appearance of God the Father and his Son, Jesus Christ to the boy praying. I thought of nothing else. Of course that is real. It was easy for me to believe that Moroni came to him there in the room. Heavenly beings were real from my babyhood on, and as years came those impressions strengthened by reason and strengthened by the inspiration of God directly to my soul.

"I know that those visions were real, and that Joseph Smith was a prophet of God, and when we say this it means that I know that Jesus lives, that Christ is our Redeemer and that this is his Church. We are merely his representatives."

—David O. McKay, "Address," in Conference Report, Oct. 1951, 182–183.

"The Anticipated Manifestation Had Not Come"

"Somehow in my youth I got the idea that we could not get a testimony unless we had some manifestation. I read of the first vision of the Prophet Joseph Smith, and I knew that he knew what he had received was of God. I heard my father's testimony of a voice that had come to him, and somehow I received the impression that that was the source of all testimony. . . .

"I remember riding over the hills of Huntsville one afternoon, thinking of these things and concluding that there in the silence of the hills was the best place to get that testimony. I stopped my horse, threw the reins over his head, withdrew just a few steps, and knelt by the side of a tree. The air was clear and pure, the sunshine delightful; the growing verdure and flowers scented the air. . . .

"I knelt down and with all the fervor of my heart poured out my soul to God and asked him for a testimony of this gospel. I had in mind that there would be some manifestation; that I should receive some transformation that would leave me absolutely without doubt.

"I got up, mounted my horse, and as he started over the trail, I remember rather introspectively searching myself and involuntarily shaking my head, saying to myself, 'No, sir, there is no change; I am just the same boy I was before I knelt down.' The anticipated manifestation had not come. Nor was that the only occasion.

"However, it did come, but not in the way I had anticipated."

—David O. McKay, *Treasures of Life*, 228–230.

"Do Your Duty, That Is Best"

"I went to college, graduated from the University [of Utah]. While still [at the] University, [I] received the call to go on a mission. I did not like it, because I had my hope after graduation of a teaching position. William M. Stewart, head of the normal department, had offered me a school there in Salt Lake County, at what I thought was a good salary, and I would pay back my parents for what they had done. The sacrifices they had made to send me and my brother and sisters to college. Now here I am to go on a mission and have to be supported again by my father. I think he anticipated my feelings about that time, and wrote the letter accompanying the call from box B at that time, because he said, 'You decide what to do. Do not be influenced by your surroundings. We leave it to you to decide whether you will accept the call or not.'

"[Well,] I did what was perhaps presumptuous on my part at that time period. I thought I would go to the President of the Church, tell him that I have a position to teach, about William Stewart, and if I accept this position I cannot do it for two years or more, and I shall not graduate until June, and that was January, 1897. Brother George Reynolds made an opportunity [for me] to meet the President. He listened. 'Well, you finish your school . . . and graduate in June, and when you are ready to accept this call, you let us know. Goodbye.'

"By the time graduation was over I had sent to him and to my father and all—my father was a bishop—I am ready to go and to answer my call. And in August, the 7th of August 1897, I said goodbye to my folks, companions and all.

"I had not heard a voice. I had not—I still had that same desire that made me kneel on the hillside and out in the meadow across the spring creek, same thing. I still knew that we would have to live in such a way as to merit our call or guidance. It came unto my mind during that period, 'Do my duty,' and I learned this couplet. 'Do your duty, That is best. Leave unto the Lord the rest.'"

—David O. McKay, "North British Missionary Meeting," Mar. 1, 1961, in *Clare Middlemiss Notebooks*, 1955–1980, ms. 9427, unpaginated.

"Were They Right or Was I?"

"One gloomy, misty morning [as a missionary] I was distributing tracts in Stirling, Scotland. I had been away from my home in Huntsville only a few months, but I had already encountered the opposition that prejudice and bigotry were hurling against the Church. For the first time in my life, I had felt the sting of ostracism. . . .

"This ostracism was because of our religion.

"Our church was considered as unwholesome, as something to be despised. Was it? Yet, after all, was it really worth the seeming sacrifices that my companion and I and thousands of others were making for it? Most surely someone was deceived. Either I was wrong or the people were. They seemed sincere in their opposition to my Church. I was sincere in my advocacy of it. Were they right or was I?

"With these thoughts and feelings and a hundred others associated with them, I took my tracts that morning and entered a 'close,' [a series of small houses] distributing them from door to door from the ground floor to the top. When I came down a half dozen or more housewives were assembled at the entrance of the 'close.' As I passed the one staring remarked, ['You can go on home. You can't have any of our poor lassies.']

"Scarcely four months had passed since the sweetest girl in all the world had led me to hope that she would give me her hand, as well as her heart, to me upon my return from my mission; so nothing could have been farther from my mind that morning than the desire to win the favor of any other girl. So the woman that sneered was deceived.

But her taunt had in it such a vile accusation, viz., that I was there to traffic in the virtue of women, and to cover such traffic with the garb of religion!

"The most real thing to me in all the world were my own thoughts and feelings, and I knew as I knew nothing else that those women, and all who thought as they, though the number might run into millions, were deceived.

"A few days later my companion and I met a minister, who accused us of not being Christians because we believed in the Book of Mormon. Again I knew, knew beyond a shadow of a doubt, that, in company with all my associates, I accepted Christ and him crucified. The very purpose of my being in Stirling [Scotland] was to bear witness that the living Christ had again spoken to man; to testify that there is no other name given under heaven whereby mankind may be saved. . . .

"False accusations thus became a means of clarifying my mind regarding 'Mormonism' and the world as no other experience in my life had clarified it. Study, devotion to duty, and inspiration of the Lord later made clear my vision of the glorious principles of salvation, and gave me communion with my Friend and Savior, the Redeemer of the world."

—David O. McKay, "Where Knowledge Is Absolute," Jan. 11, 1923, in *Clare Middlemiss Notebooks*, 1955–1980, ms. 9427, unpaginated.

"GOD IS MINDFUL OF YOU"

"I remember, as if it were yesterday, the intensity of the inspiration of that occasion [a meeting in Scotland conducted by President James L. McMurrin, a counselor in the European Mission Presidency]. . . .

"James L. McMurrin gave what has since proved to be a prophecy. I had learned by intimate association with him that James McMurrin was pure gold. His faith in the gospel was implicit. No truer man, no man more loyal to what he thought was right ever lived. So when he turned to me and gave what I thought then was more of a caution than a promise, his words made an indelible impression upon me. Paraphrasing the words of the Savior to Peter, Brother McMurrin said: 'Let me say to you, Brother David, Satan hath desired you that he may sift you as wheat, but God is mindful of you.' . . .

"At that moment there flashed in my mind temptations that had beset my path, and I realized even better than President McMurrin, or any other man, how truly he had spoken when he said, 'Satan hath desired thee.' With the resolve then and there to keep the faith, there was born a desire to be of service to my fellowmen; and with it came a realization, a glimpse at least, of what I owed to the elder who first carried the message of the restored gospel to my grandfather and grandmother, who had accepted the message years before in the north of Scotland and in South Wales."

—David O. McKay, "Prophecy of James L. McMurrin," in Conference Report, Oct. 1968, 86.

"WHATE'ER THOU ART, ACT WELL THY PART"

In 1898 David O. McKay and his missionary companion, Elder Peter Johnson, saw an inscription written on a stone arch. David recalled:

"I said to my companion: 'That's unusual! I am going to see what the inscription is.' When I approached near enough, this message came to me, not only in stone, but as if it came from One in whose service we were engaged:

"'Whate'er Thou Art, Act Well Thy Part.'. . .

"God help us to follow that motto. It is just another expression of Christ's words: 'He that will do the will of God shall know of the doctrine, whether the work is of God, or whether I speak of myself,' [see John 7:17] and that testimony leads us all to the guidance of the Holy Spirit in life."

—David O. McKay, "Address," in Conference Report, Oct. 1956, 91.

"I HAVE ASKED YOUR DAUGHTER TO BE MINE IN MARRIAGE"

Hoping to receive the consent of Dr. Obadiah H. Riggs to marry his daughter Emma Ray Riggs, David O. McKay wrote:

"Her sweetness of disposition, her virtue, her intelligence, her unselfish nature—in short, her perfect qualities, won my love. When she told me that this affection was reciprocated, my happiness seemed complete. . . . I have asked your daughter to be mine in marriage, and now I ask you, Dr. Riggs, her father, if you will give your consent. She has given hers. . . . In return for this I can give her nothing but a true love and a heart and mind whose one desire is to make her happy."

—David O. McKay, "Letter of David O. McKay to Dr. Obadiah H. Riggs," Dec. 9, 1900, ms. 668, box 1, in David Oman McKay Papers.

"WARM THE CAN"

David Lawrence McKay wrote of his father, David O. McKay:

"My first memory of Weber is of playing with the papers in Father's wastebasket. Father's office was squeezed into the vestibule between the inner and outer doors because the Moench Building then the only building on [the Weber Academy] campus was severely overcrowded. Father was determined to do something about these conditions. . . .

"When the Church agreed to match the funds to get the required $120,000, Father felt keenly his responsibility to raise the necessary first $60,000. . . .

"President Joseph F. Smith said, 'David, how are you getting along with the building?'

"I said, 'Not very well. At first we had large contributions as you know ranging from $5,000 down to $25, etc., but now the contributions are small and slow. It reminds me of an experience when I was a boy in Huntsville. Mother had molasses in some cans in the cellar. When I inverted a can, molasses would come out in a great glob, but no matter how long I held that can inverted, I could not get out the last drop.'

"He smiled and said, 'Shall I tell you how to get out that last drop?'

"I said, 'Yes.'

"'Warm the can.'

"We followed that advice and were pleased to dedicate that building which is now west of the Moench Building."

—David Lawrence McKay, *My Father*, 37–38.

"Father Was Speechless"

David Lawrence McKay wrote of his father, David O. McKay:

"On 8 April 1906, Father was called and sustained to the Quorum of the Twelve. As he told us children the story later, he and Mother had gone to Salt Lake City at conference time, taking Llewelyn and me to visit Mother's cousin Bell White and her husband, Parley, for lunch. During the meal, a telephone call came, asking Father to come immediately to the office of Francis M. Lyman, president of the Quorum of the Twelve Apostles. . . . [Father] felt that perhaps he might be asked to become a member of the Church Board of Education. Elder George Albert Smith, then an apostle, met him at Temple Square and escorted him to the office of President Lyman.

"As Father told us the story later, Elder Lyman opened the conversation: 'So, you're David O. McKay.'

"'Yes, sir.'

"'Well, David O. McKay, the Lord wants you to be a member of the Quorum of the Twelve Apostles.'

"Father was speechless.

"'Well,' continued Elder Lyman, 'haven't you anything to say?'

"Father was finally able to respond, 'I am neither worthy nor able to receive such a call.'

"'Not worthy! Not worthy!' exclaimed Elder Lyman. 'What have you been doing?'

"Father explained, 'I have never done anything in my life of which I am ashamed.'

"'Well, then,' pursued a calmer Elder Lyman, 'don't you have faith the Lord can make you able?'

"'Yes sir,' responded Father humbly. 'I have that faith.'

"'Very well, then,' said Elder Lyman briskly. 'Don't say anything about this until your name is presented in conference this afternoon.'

"Father, somewhat dazed, returned to the Whites' apartment. On his way, he encountered his father, who asked if he had been called to the Board of Education. 'I've been asked not to say anything about this until it's announced,' Father explained, and Grandfather replied, 'Then don't say anything.'

"Father didn't. It must have been very hard for him to say nothing to Mother—and equally difficult for her not to ask. They left Llewelyn and me with our cousins and went to the afternoon session. It was in the last few minutes of the closing session that President Smith presented the names of General Authorities for sustaining, including the new apostle on the list, without commentary. When Mother heard, 'George F. Richards, Orson F. Whitney, and David O. McKay,' she burst into tears. She heard someone behind them say, 'There's the wife of one of them. See, she's crying.'"

—David Lawrence McKay, *My Father*, 38–40.

"I Cannot See a Scar on Your Face"

In March 1916, the Ogden River overflowed its banks, causing the bridge near the mouth of the canyon to become unstable. David O. McKay recounted:

"We [David and his brother Thomas E.] jumped into a little Ford car and dashed through the rain and mud. . . . I saw the pile of rocks there at the bridge, and it seemed to be intact just as it had been the day before. So jocularly I said, 'I'm going across the bridge. Can you swim?' With that I stepped on the gas and dashed across the bridge, only to hear Thomas E. say, 'Oh, look out! There's a rope!' The watchman who left at seven o'clock had stretched the derrick rope across the road, and his successor, the day watchman, had not arrived. I reached for the emergency brake but was too late. The rope smashed the window, threw back the top, and caught me just in the chin, severing my lip, knocking out my lower teeth, and breaking my upper jaw. . . .

"About nine o'clock that morning I was on the operating table. . . . They sewed my upper jaw in place and took fourteen stitches in my lower lip and lacerated cheek. One of the attendants remarked, 'Too bad; he will be disfigured for life.' Certainly I was most unrecognizable. When I was wheeled back to my room in the hospital, one of the nurses consolingly remarked, 'Well, Brother McKay, you can wear a beard,' meaning that thus I might hide my scars.

". . . Three very close friends . . . called and administered to me. In sealing the anointing, [one of them] said, 'We bless you that you shall not be disfigured and that you shall not have pain.'. . .

"Saturday evening Dr. William H. Petty called to see if the teeth that were still remaining in the upper jaw might be saved. It was he who said, 'I suppose you are in great pain.' I answered, 'No, I haven't any pain.' . . . Sunday morning President Heber J. Grant came up from Salt Lake City. . . . He entered and said, 'David, don't talk; I'm just going to give you a blessing.' . . .

"The following October . . . I sat at a table near where President Grant was sitting. I noticed that he was looking at me somewhat intently, and then he said, 'David, from where I am sitting I cannot see a scar on your face!' I answered, 'No, President Grant, there are no scars.'"

—David O. McKay "A Personal Experience of Divine Healing," transcription July 10, 1945, in Middlemiss, *Cherished Experiences*, 138–140.

"How Weighty This Responsibility Seems"

After being sustained as President of the Church, David O. McKay said in the April 1951 general conference:

"I wish it were within my power of expression to let you know what my true feelings are on this momentous occasion. I would wish that you might look into my heart and see there for yourselves just what these feelings are.

"It is just one week ago today that the realization came to me that this responsibility of leadership would probably fall upon my shoulders. I received word that President George Albert Smith had taken a turn for the worse, and that the doctors felt that the end was not far off. I hastened to his bedside, and with his weeping daughters, son, and other kinfolk, I entered his sick room. For the first time, he failed to recognize me.

"Then I had to accept the realization that the Lord had chosen not to answer our pleadings as we would have had them answered, and that he was going to take him home to himself. . . . As President Clark and I were considering problems of import pertaining to the Church, he, ever solicitous of the welfare of the Church, and of my feelings, would say, 'The responsibility will be yours to make this decision,' but each time I would refuse to face what, to him, seemed a reality.

"When that reality came, as I tell you, I was deeply moved. And I am today, and pray that I may, even though inadequately, be able to tell you how weighty this responsibility seems."

—David O. McKay, "Responsibility of Leadership," in Conference Report, Apr. 9, 1951, 157.

"I Recognized Him at Once as My Savior!"

While sailing toward what is now Western Samoa, David O. McKay wrote on May 10, 1921:

"The reflection of the afterglow of a beautiful sunset was most splendid! . . . Pondering still upon this beautiful scene, I lay in my [bed] at ten o'clock that night. . . .

"I then fell asleep, and beheld in vision something infinitely sublime. In the distance I beheld a beautiful white city. Though it was far away, yet I seemed to realize that trees with luscious fruit, shrubbery with gorgeously tinted leaves, and flowers in perfect bloom abounded everywhere. The clear sky above seemed to reflect these beautiful shades of color. I then saw a great concourse of people approaching the city. Each one wore a white flowing robe and a white headdress. Instantly my attention seemed centered upon their leader, and though I could see only the profile of his features and his body, I recognized him at once as my Savior! The tint and radiance of his countenance were glorious to behold. There was a peace about him which seemed sublime—it was divine!

"The city, I understood, was his. It was the City Eternal; and the people following him were to abide there in peace and eternal happiness.

"But who were they?

"As if the Savior read my thoughts, he answered by pointing to a semicircle that then appeared above them, and on which were written in gold the words:

"'These are They Who Have Overcome the World—Whom Have Truly Been Born Again!'"

— David O. McKay, in Middlemiss, *Cherished Experiences*, 59–60.

"That Little Boy Is Ours"

"I remember . . . when [my wife and I] said goodbye to a little boy 2½ years of age. That is now nearly thirty years ago. But when people say, 'How many children have you?' I answer unhesitatingly, 'five boys and two girls,' although there are only four boys and two girls in active life here. But that little boy is ours. I sometimes try to picture him now as a young man. He was just a two-and-one-half year-old sweet baby when we said good-bye to him, and our heartstrings were torn. . . . But I like to picture him now as grown as our boys who are here."

—David O. McKay at the funeral service of David Blair Kinnersley, Sept. 13, 1947, in *Clare Middlemiss Notebooks*, no. 4, 1955–1980, ms. 9427, unpaginated.

"My Voice Was as Resonant and Clear as It Ever Was"

"[In the spring of 1921 in New Zealand] a thousand people assembled for the afternoon service. They came with curiosity and high expectations. It was my duty to give them a message, but I was not only too hoarse to speak and be heard by that crowd, but I was also ill.

"However, with a most appealing prayer in my heart for divine help and guidance, I arose to perform my duty. My voice was tight and husky. . . .

"Then happened what had never before happened to me. I entered into my theme with all the earnestness and vehemence I could command and spoke as loud as possible. Feeling my voice getting clearer and more resonant, I soon forgot I had a voice and thought only of the truth I wanted my hearers to understand and accept. For forty minutes I continued with my address, and when I concluded, my voice was as resonant and clear as it ever was. . . .

"When I told Brother Cannon and some other brethren how earnestly I had prayed for the very blessing I had received, he said, 'I too, was praying—never prayed more fervently for a speaker in my life.'"

— David O. McKay, in Middlemiss, *Cherished Experiences*, 58–59.

"Take This Handkerchief to Your Mother with My Blessing"

"One Sunday, June 29, 1952, Sister McKay and I were in . . . the 'Mercedes Palast' Theater, the largest hall in North Berlin [Germany].

"Prior to the meeting I had received word through the presidency of the East German Mission that one of the members of the Church in that mission—a sister—had lost her husband and eldest son under Communist rule. She had been driven from her home, and was subsequently exposed to the rigors of the weather and lack of nutrition until she finally became paralyzed and had been confined to her bed for five years. She had heard of my coming to Berlin, and being unable to travel herself, she expressed the desire that her two little children—a boy and a girl about ten and twelve years of age—be sent over to meet the President of the Church. This good sister said, 'I know if I send my children to shake hands with President McKay, and then they come home and take my hand—if I can hold their little hands in mine—I know that I shall get better.'. . .

"Anticipating meeting them, I took a new handkerchief; and when that little girl and boy came along, I went to them and shook their hands, and said, 'Will you take this handkerchief to your mother with my blessing?' I later learned that after I had shaken hands with them, they would not shake hands with anyone else, for they did not want to touch anyone with their hands until they got back to their mother. . . .

"When Sister McKay returned to Salt Lake City, she wrote to the mission president's wife and asked her to find out how the mother of the two little children was getting along. In her reply, the mission president's wife wrote:

'This sister thanks the Lord every day for the blessing and the handkerchief which President McKay sent through her two children, and she has faith that she will fully recover and I believe so, too. Immediately after the children came home, her feet and toes began to get feeling in them, and this feeling slowly moved up into her legs. And now she gets out of bed alone and seats herself on a chair, and then, with her feet and the chair, works all the way around to the kitchen sink, where she has the children bring her the dishes to wash, and other things, and is very thankful that she is able to help now.'"

—David O. McKay, "Behind the Iron Curtain," June 29, 1952, transcription, in Middlemiss, *Cherished Experiences*, 142–144.

"I KNEW YOU WOULD COME"

Llewelyn R. McKay wrote of his father, David O. McKay:

"When the travelers to the South Seas were at Suva (Fiji Islands) January 8, 1955, word was received at the office that a Mrs. Sally Skips, a patient of the leper colony (two miles from the city) was anxious to see father. She had met him when she was a little girl in Samoa thirty-four years ago when father and Hugh J. Cannon were touring missions. Of course it was impossible for her to leave the colony. Although other plans had been made, and father's appointments were full, he remarked, 'This lady has as much right as anyone else to speak with me, and since she has expressed the desire to see me and cannot come to us, then we shall go to her.'

"Subsequently, a taxi was called which took father, mother, and Brother Murdock to a group of cottages on a hillside. The matron in charge of the colony sent an assistant to fetch the afflicted woman, but he soon returned with the explanation that Mrs. Skipps was too ill to leave her room.

"'Well,' said father, 'if it is permitted, we shall go to her cottage.'

"Just off a corridor in a small ward waited a middle-aged Samoan woman sitting on her bed, and as she greeted her visitors, tears streamed down her face. . . . 'I knew you would come, if it were at all possible,' she said in good English.

"After receiving a blessing from father, she gratefully waved farewell."

—Llewelyn R. McKay, in "South Sea Islands Members Pay Devotions to Leader," *Church News*, Jan. 29, 1955; Llewelyn R. McKay, *Home Memories*, 152–153.

"The President of the Church Keeps His Appointments"

L. Glen Snarr of the *Deseret News* wrote of David O. McKay:

"In Salt Lake City one Thursday, a Sunday School class had been granted the great favor of an appointment with the President. Unfortunately he was called to the hospital where his brother Thomas E. lay critically ill. The children were naturally disappointed. A member of the Council of the Twelve greeted the class and talked with them.

"Many busy men would have considered the matter closed, but the next Sunday morning found President McKay driving eight miles to a small chapel south of the city. Entering the building he inquired where this particular class met. Imagine the thrill experienced in that little classroom when the door opened and the President walked in. After explaining why he was not in his office, he shook hands with the teacher and with each of the children and left his blessing.

"'I want you children to know,' he said, 'that the President of the Church keeps his appointments if at all possible.'"

—Glenn Snarr, in "Memories of a Prophet" *Improvement Era*, Feb. 19, 1970, 72.

"What a Prophet of God Must Really Look Like"

Arch L. Madsen, president of Bonneville International and of KSL, wrote of David O. McKay:

"I remember being in New York when President McKay returned from Europe. Arrangements had been made for pictures to be taken, but the regular photographer was unable to go, so in desperation the United Press picked their crime photographer—a man accustomed to the toughest type of work in New York. He went to the airport, stayed there two hours, and returned later from the darkroom with a tremendous sheaf of pictures. He was supposed to take only two. His boss immediately chided him. 'What in the world are you wasting time and all those photographic supplies for?'

"The photographer replied very curtly, saying he would gladly pay for the extra materials, and they could even dock him for the extra time he took. It was obvious that he was very touchy about it. Several hours later the vice-president called him to his office, wanting to learn what happened. The crime photographer said, 'When I was a little boy, my mother used to read to me out of the Old Testament, and all my life I have wondered what a prophet of God must really look like. Well, today I found one.'"

—Arch L. Madsen, in "Memories of a Prophet," *Improvement Era*, Feb. 1970, 72.

"MORMON PROPHET GETS CITATION"

"He would often steal away to Huntsville to ride his horse. . . . One morning in the summer he went up to ride about 5:30 . . . and he was in a hurry. He had a very important meeting at the Church office building at 8:30 or 9:00. He was speeding down Harrison Blvd. in Ogden to go up the canyon [when] 'he saw a red light flashing behind him.'

"He stopped the car and a traffic officer came up and said, 'Oh I'm sorry; I didn't realize it was you.' David said, 'Young man, if I was going one mile over the speed limit, you give me a ticket. You do your duty.'

"So he got his ticket all right. The next day when he got to the Church Office Building, there were about fifteen newspaper articles on his desk. The *Ogden Examiner* had printed a front-page article, 'Mormon Prophet gets citation.' I guess if he was like most people he would have called up the editor and told him 'a thing or two.' . . .

"He called him and said, 'I have been reading the article about me in your paper. I wanted to thank you. You have been able to straighten up a lot of people around here who think that I am slowing up.'"

—Robert L. Simpson, interview in St. George, Utah, by Mary Jane Woodger, Oct. 1997; transcript, McKay Research Project, in author's possession.

"We've Just Seen a Miracle"

David Lawrence McKay wrote of his father, David O. McKay:

"At October conference, I read [my father's] Saturday night priesthood address, and my brother Bob read his opening and closing conference addresses. We began to worry that he might ask one of us to read the dedicatory prayer for the [Oakland, California] temple dedication, scheduled for 17 November [1964].

"'Has he asked you, Bob?' I queried one day in late October.

"'No,' my brother answered. 'Has he asked you?'

"'No.'

"There seemed to be no more to say. President Hugh B. Brown, then Father's first counselor, asked a week or so later, 'Lawrence, has your father said anything about who is going to dedicate the Oakland Temple?'

"'No,' I reported, 'he hasn't, President Brown.'

"November arrived, and still no one was appointed. . . .

"[At the dedication] Father was helped over to the rickety temporary pulpit, which he grasped as he stood. Then he began to talk. . . . He spoke for 30 minutes and then still standing offered the dedicatory prayer for another 30 minutes. His articulation [became] as clear as it was ten years ago. When he finished, his counselors helped him to his seat. Your mother, with tears on her cheeks, turned to me and said, 'Lawrence, we've just seen a miracle.'"

—David Lawrence McKay, *My Father*, 262–264.

Joseph Fielding Smith

Born: July 19, 1876, Salt Lake City, Utah
Died: July 2, 1972, Salt Lake City, Utah
President of the Church: January 23, 1970, to July 2, 1972

JOSEPH FIELDING SMITH

JOSEPH FIELDING SMITH, SON OF Joseph F. Smith and Julina Lambson, was born July 19, 1876, in Salt Lake City. As a child, Joseph loved to read the scriptures. "From my earliest recollection," he said, "from the time I could first read, I have received more pleasure and greater satisfaction out of the study of the scriptures . . . than from anything else in all the world."[63]

In 1899 Joseph accepted a mission call to serve in Great Britain. Missionary service proved difficult for him; not only was he naturally reserved and quiet, but he didn't baptize anyone. After returning to his family in Salt Lake City, Joseph accepted a position with the Church Historian's Office. He enjoyed the employment so much that he found occasions to be associated with that office for the next seventy years.

In 1910 Joseph was called to the Quorum of the Twelve Apostles. For the next sixty-two years, he was known as the Apostle who clarified important doctrines and published gospel scholarship. His public addresses and more than twenty-five scholarly books focused on the importance of maintaining doctrinal purity. His capacity to write about the principles and doctrines of the gospel became the hallmark of his ministry. His public addresses left no doubt where he stood on gospel principles. As a result, his public persona was that of a serious and somber man.

"When [Joseph] is gone people will say, he is a good man, sincere, orthodox, etc.," said his wife, Ethel. "They will speak of him as the public knows him, but the man they have in mind is very different from the man I know. The man I know is a kind, loving, husband and father whose greatest ambition in life is to make his family happy, entirely forgetful of self in his efforts to do this. . . .

"The man I know is most gentle, and if he feels that he has been unjust to anyone the distance is never too far for him to go and, with loving words or kind deeds, erase the hurt. . . . He enjoys a good story and is quick to see the humor of a situation, to laugh, and to be laughed at, always willing to join in any wholesome activity. The man I know is unselfish, uncomplaining, considerate, thoughtful, sympathetic. . . . That is the man I know."[64]

Joseph Fielding Smith became the tenth President of The Church of Jesus Christ of Latter-day Saints. At age ninety-six, he was the oldest man to ever hold that position. During his two-and-a-half-year administration, Joseph consolidated Church magazines into three publications—*Ensign*, *New Era*, and *Friend*. He designated Monday night for family home evening and authorized the formation of LDS Social Services. In a testimony given in 1972, Joseph prayed for the membership of the Church: "O God our Heavenly and Eternal Father, look down in love and in mercy upon this thy church and upon the members of the church who keep thy commandments. Let thy Spirit dwell in our hearts forever; and when the trials and woes of this life are over, may we return to thy presence, with our loved ones, and dwell in thy house forever."[65]

Joseph died on July 2, 1972, in Salt Lake City.

The Life Story of Joseph Fielding Smith In His Own Words

"From My Earliest Recollection"

"From my earliest recollection, from the time I first could read, I have received more pleasure and greater satisfaction out of the study of the scriptures, and reading of the Lord Jesus Christ, and of the Prophet Joseph Smith, and the work that has been accomplished for the salvation of men, than from anything else in all the world."

—Joseph Fielding Smith, "Born of Goodly Parents," in Conference Report, Apr. 1930, 91.

"Among My Fondest Memories"

Of his father, Joseph Fielding Smith wrote:

"My father was the most tender-hearted man I ever knew. . . . Among my fondest memories are the hours I have spent by his side discussing principles of the gospel and receiving instruction as only he could give it. In this way the foundation for my own knowledge was laid in truth, so that I too can say I know that my Redeemer lives, and that Joseph Smith is, was, and always will be a prophet of the living God."

—Joseph Fielding Smith, in Bryant S. Hinckley, "Greatness in Men: Joseph Fielding Smith," *Improvement Era*, June 1932, 459.

"Father, Now Who's Smarter?"

"[Our horse Junie] was one of the most intelligent animals I ever saw. She seemed almost human in her ability. I couldn't keep her locked in the barn because she would continually undo the strap on the door of her stall. I used to put the strap connected to the half-door of the stall over the top of the post, but she would simply lift it off with her nose and teeth. Then she would go out in the yard.

"There was a water tap in the yard used for filling the water trough for our animals. Junie would turn this on with her teeth and then leave the water running. My father would get after me because I couldn't keep that horse in the barn. She never ran away; she just turned on the water and then walked around the yard or over the lawn or through the garden. In the middle of the night, I would hear the water running and then I would have to get up and shut it off and lock Junie up again.

"My father suggested that the horse seemed smarter than I was. One day he decided that he would lock her in so that she couldn't get out. He took the strap that usually looped over the top of the post and buckled it around the post and under a crossbar, and then he said, 'Young lady, let's see you get out of there now!' My father and I left the barn and started to walk back to the house; and before we reached it, Junie was at our side.

"[I asked,] 'Father, now who's smarter?'"

—Joseph Fielding Smith, in McConkie, *True and Faithful*, 19.

"I Was Trained at My Mother's Knee"

"I was trained at my mother's knee to love the Prophet Joseph Smith and to love my Redeemer. . . . I am grateful for the training that I received and I tried to follow the counsel that was given to me by my father. But I must not give him all the credit. I think a good part of it, a very great part of it, should go to my mother whose knee I used to sit by as a little child and listen to her stories about the pioneers. . . . She used to teach me and put in my hands, when I was old enough to read, things that I could understand. She taught me to pray [and] to be true and faithful to my covenants and obligations, to attend to my duties as a deacon and as a teacher . . . and later as a priest. . . . I had a mother who saw to it that I did read, and I loved to read."

—Joseph Fielding Smith, in Smith and Stewart, *Life of Joseph Fielding Smith*, 56.

"Why Most Babies Had to Be Born at Night"

"Mother was a licensed midwife. When she would get called to a confinement somewhere in the valley, usually in the middle of the night, I would have to get up, take a lantern out to the barn, and hitch Junie [the horse] up to the buggy.

"I was only about ten or eleven years old at the time; and that horse had to be gentle and yet strong enough to take me and Mother all over the valley, in all kinds of weather. One thing I never could understand, however, was why most of the babies had to be born at night and so many of them in winter."

—Joseph Fielding Smith, "My Dear Young Fellow Workers," *New Era*, Jan. 1971, 4–5.

"She Told Me Stories about the Prophet Joseph Smith"

"I never knew my Grandmother [Mary Fielding] Smith. I have always regretted that, because she was one of the most noble women who ever lived, but I did know her good sister, my Aunt Mercy Thompson, and as a boy I used to go and visit her in her home and sit at her knee, where she told me stories about the Prophet Joseph Smith, and, oh, how grateful I am for that experience."

—Joseph Fielding Smith, "An Anchor to Our Souls," in Conference Report, Apr. 1962, 44.

"I Worked Like a Work Horse"

"I worked like a work horse [at Zion's Cooperative Mercantile Institution (ZCMI) in my late teens] all day long and was tired out when night came, carrying sacks of flour and sacks of sugar and hams and bacons on my back. I weighed 150 pounds, but I thought nothing of picking up a 200-pound sack and putting it on my shoulders."

—Joseph Fielding Smith, in Smith and Stewart, *Life of Joseph Fielding Smith*, 65.

"I'D PREFER TO GO TO GERMANY"

"[President Franklin D. Richards, President of the Quorum of the Twelve Apostles] asked me where I'd like to go [on my mission.] I told him I had no choice particularly, only to go where I was sent. But he said, 'You must have some place where you would prefer to go to.' I said, 'Well, I'd prefer to go to Germany.' So they sent me to England!"

—Joseph Fielding Smith, in Smith and Stewart, *Life of Joseph Fielding Smith*, 79.

"I HAVE BEEN OUT TRACTING TODAY"

On the first day of his missionary work in England, Joseph Fielding Smith wrote:

"This has been a very important day in my short life. I came from my home less than a month ago for the purpose of preaching the gospel of our Lord. . . . I have been out tracting today and delivered 25 tracts [pamphlets]. It is the first of this kind of work that I ever tried to do and it did not come to me very easy. . . . I bore my testimony to the world for the first time today, but will be able to do so better. With the help of the Lord I shall do his will as I was called to do."

—Joseph Fielding Smith, in Smith and Stewart, *Life of Joseph Fielding Smith*, 90.

"I HAVE DEPENDED ON THE LORD FOR STRENGTH AND COMFORT"

When his wife Louie Shurtliff Smith died on March 30, 1908, Joseph Fielding Smith wrote:

"During this month which has been one of constant anxiety and worry for me, I have passed through trials and experiences of the deepest and most painful kind. And through it all I have depended on the Lord for strength and comfort. After suffering most excruciating pain for three or four weeks and after an illness covering a period of nearly two months my beloved wife was released from her suffering . . . and departed from me and our precious babies, for a better world, where we patiently and in sorrow await a meeting which shall be most glorious."

—Joseph Fielding Smith, in Smith and Stewart, *Life of Joseph Fielding Smith*, 162.

"He Would Be a Credit to His Calling"

Edith S. Patrick, a sister of Joseph Fielding Smith, recalled:

"I remember mother telling us that in 1910 father [Joseph F. Smith] came home from his temple council meeting and seemed very worried. When asked what was troubling him, he said that Joseph had been chosen as one of the Twelve. He said the brethren had unanimously selected him and he said now he, as the president, would be severely criticized, having his son made an apostle. Mother told him not to worry one minute as to what people might say. She knew the Lord had chosen him and said she knew he would be a credit to his calling."

—Edith S. Patrick, in Smith and Stewart, *Life of Joseph Fielding Smith*, 174–175.

"I Was So Startled and Dumbfounded I Could Hardly Speak"

"As I was going to the tabernacle to attend [general conference on April 6, 1910] . . . Ben E. Rich, who was the president of the mission in the Southern States met me as I crossed the street. . . . He said to me as we went to cross the street to the tabernacle, 'Are you going to take your place up on the stand as one of the Council of the Twelve today?' I said, 'Brother Rich, I have a brother in that council. There is no reason for you or anybody to think that I would be called into that council. I am not looking for it or anything of that kind.'

"As he entered the tabernacle a doorkeeper also bantered with him. 'Well Joseph, who is the new apostle to be?'

"'I don't know,' replied Joseph. 'But it won't be you and it won't be me!'

". . . As Elder [Heber J.] Grant read down through the list of the apostles, just before he reached the new name, the impression swept across Joseph's mind that the name to be read might be his. Yet when he actually heard his name read, 'I was so startled and dumbfounded I could hardly speak.'

"With dozens of well wishers waiting after conference to shake his hand and congratulate him upon his appointment, Joseph was late getting back to his home. He hoped Ethel and the children had not yet heard the good news, for he wished to be the one to tell them—and tell them in his own way: 'I guess we'll have to sell the cow,' he said. 'I haven't time to take care of it anymore!'

—Joseph Fielding Smith, in Smith and Stewart, *Life of Joseph Fielding Smith,* 175–176.

"A Wall of Defense"

Three years after being ordained an Apostle, Joseph Fielding Smith received the following counsel in a priesthood blessing:

"You have been blessed with ability to comprehend, to analyze, and defend the principles of truth above many of your fellows, and the time will come when the accumulative evidence that you have gathered will stand as a wall of defense against those who are seeking and will seek to destroy the evidence of the divinity of the mission of the Prophet Joseph; and in this defense you will never be confounded, and the light of the Spirit will shed its rays upon your heart as gently as the dews that fall from heaven, and it will unfold to your understanding many truths concerning this work."

—Joseph Fielding Smith, in Smith and Stewart, *Life of Joseph Fielding Smith*, 195.

"We Used to Box Once in a While"

Douglas A. Smith said of his father, Joseph Fielding Smith:

"We used to box once in a while, or at least feign the act of boxing. I had too much respect to hit him and he had too much love to hit me. . . . It was more or less shadowboxing. We used to play chess and I rejoiced when I could beat him. Now I look back and feel that maybe it was prearranged."

—Douglas A. Smith, in D. Arthur Haycock, "Exemplary Manhood Award," *Speeches of the Year*, Apr. 18, 1972, 5, in *Teachings of Presidents of the Church: Joseph Fielding Smith*, 74.

"I Wish My Kiddies Would Be Good"

Amelia Smith McConkie wrote of her father, Joseph Fielding Smith:

"He entertained us by playing good music on the old Edison phonograph. To our delight he would dance to the music or march around the room, and even try to sing. . . . He brought us beautiful big, sweet oranges and sat on the bed to peel them, then gave us one segment at a time. He told us stories about his childhood, or how his father took care of him when he was sick. If the occasion warranted he would give us a blessing. . . . If any of us needed to be corrected for some misbehavior he simply put his hands on our shoulders and looking into our eyes with a hurt look in his own, said, 'I wish my kiddies would be good.' No spanking or other punishment could ever have been more effective."

—Amelia Smith McConkie, in "Joseph Fielding Smith," *Church News*, Oct. 30, 1993.

"Worthy of a Glorious Resurrection"

On January 2, 1945, Joseph Fielding Smith received a telegram informing him that his son, Lewis Smith, had been killed in World War II. Of his son's death, Joseph wrote:

"This word came to us as a most severe shock as we had high hopes that soon he would be back in the United States. We had felt that he would be protected as he has escaped several times before from danger. It was hard for us to realize that such a thing could happen. . . . As severe as the blow is, we have the peace and happiness of knowing that he was clean and free from the vices so prevalent in the world and found in the army. He was true to his faith and is worthy of a glorious resurrection, when we shall be reunited again."

—Joseph Fielding Smith, in Gibbons, *Joseph Fielding Smith*, 358–359.

"THAT IS SHOCKING TO ME"

"I have seen two members of the Church sitting together [in sacrament meeting], enter into a conversation, stop long enough for the blessing to be asked on the water or on the bread, then start again on their conversation. . . . That is shocking to me, and I am sure it is to the Lord."

— Joseph Fielding Smith, in Smith, *Seek Ye Earnestly*, 122.

"I AM KEEPING THE WORD OF WISDOM NOW"

"I attended a stake conference a number of years ago and spoke on the Word of Wisdom. . . .

"[As the conference ended] I went to the rear of the building, [and] nearly everybody had left, but a man held out his hand and said:

"'Brother Smith, that is the first discourse on the Word of Wisdom that I ever liked.'

"I said: 'Haven't you heard other discourses on the Word of Wisdom?'

"He said: 'Yes, but this is the first one that I ever enjoyed.'

"I said: 'How is that?'

"He said: 'Well, you see, I am keeping the Word of Wisdom now.'"

—Joseph Fielding Smith, "Scriptural Promises to the Obedient," in Conference Report, Oct. 1935, 12.

"Do I Love the Prophet Joseph Smith?"

"Do I love the Prophet Joseph Smith? Yes, I do, as my father did before me. I love him because he was the servant of God and because of the restoration of the gospel and because of the benefits and blessings that have come to me and mine, and to you and yours, through the blessings that were bestowed upon this man and those who were associated with him."

—Joseph Fielding Smith, in Conference Report, Apr. 1960, 73.

"That's about as Close to Heaven As I Can Get Just Now"

Biographer John J. Stewart recalled:

"I remember my surprise one day when I called at [Joseph Fielding Smith's] office in Salt Lake City. His secretary, Rubie Egbert, said, 'Step to the window here and maybe you can see him.' Curious, I walked to the window. But all that I could see was a jet streaking through the blue sky high above the Great Salt Lake. Its trail of white vapor clearly marked some steep climbs, loops, dives, rolls and turns. 'He's out there fulfilling prophecy,' explained his secretary with a chuckle. 'Scriptures say that in the last days there will be vapors of smoke in the heavens.'

"'You mean he's in that plane?' I asked incredulously.

"'Oh yes, that's him all right. He's very fond of flying. Says it relaxes him. A friend in the National Guard calls him up and says, 'How about a relaxing?' and up they go. Once they get in the air he often takes over the controls. Flew down to Grand Canyon and back last week, 400 miles an hour!'

"I could not resist driving to the airport to be there when he landed. As the two-place T-Bird roared down the runway to a stop, from the rear cockpit, in suit and helmet, climbed this benign old gentleman, then about 80, smiling broadly. 'That was wonderful!' he exclaimed. 'That's about as close to heaven as I can get just now.'"

—Joseph Fielding Smith, in Smith and Stewart, *Life of Joseph Fielding Smith*, 1–2.

Harold B. Lee

BORN: MARCH 28, 1899, CLIFTON, IDAHO
DIED: DECEMBER 26, 1973, SALT LAKE CITY, UTAH
PRESIDENT OF THE CHURCH: JULY 7, 1972, TO DECEMBER 26, 1973

HAROLD B. LEE

HAROLD BINGHAM LEE, SON OF Samuel Lee and Louisa Bingham, was born March 28, 1899, near Clifton, Idaho. Harold's parents set an example for him of hard work, faithfulness, and compassion. He credited his mother's inspiration and gift of healing to the preservation of his life. When Harold was eight years old, he accidently spilled a can of lye on himself. His mother opened a vat of pickled beets and poured cup after cup of red vinegar over his head and body to neutralize the poisonous effects of the lye. When Harold punctured an artery on a broken bottle, his mother stopped the bleeding and cleaned the wound. When the wound festered and became infected, she healed the infection by rubbing the ashes of a black sock in the open wound.[66]

Harold began his educational pursuits at a grammar school in Clifton, Idaho, before enrolling in the Oneida Stake Academy at Preston, Idaho. At age seventeen, he attended Idaho's Albion State Normal School. After two summers (1916 and 1917) at the Normal School, Harold passed the state's fifteen-subject test and received two teaching certificates. By age eighteen, he was a school principal in Oxford, Idaho. While in Oxford, he founded the Oxford Athletic Club, started a women's choir, and served as elders quorum president.

At age twenty-one, Harold served a mission to the western states. There he met Fern Lucinda Tanner, a sister missionary from Utah. Following their missions, Harold and Fern renewed their acquaintance and were married on November 14, 1923, in the Salt Lake Temple. They became the parents of two daughters.

To better his employment opportunities and support his family, Harold enrolled in the University of Utah. After completing coursework that led to graduation, he was hired as a principal in the Granite School District. At the same time, he also served as president of the Salt Lake Pioneer Stake, where he initiated a program of self-help and relief.

On April 10, 1941, Harold was ordained an Apostle of the Lord Jesus Christ by President Heber J. Grant. At age forty-two, he was nearly twenty years younger than any other member of the Twelve. As an Apostle, Harold was assigned to oversee and implement the welfare program of the Church. Under his watchful guidance, Church welfare was extended to needy individuals, families, and communities in many countries throughout the world.

It was President David O. McKay who appointed Harold to be chairman of the Church Correlation Committee. In that capacity, Harold pioneered the worldwide coordination of Church materials and activities. He initiated organizational changes within the Church to improve efficiency and effectiveness of councils, programs, and events to better serve the "one" and teach the rising generation the principles of the gospel of Jesus Christ.

After thirty-one years in the Quorum of the Twelve, Harold was sustained as President of the Church on July 7, 1972. "Never think of me as the head of the Church," he said. "Jesus Christ is the head of this Church. I am only a man, his servant."[67] In his last public address, Harold said, "If it were not for the assurance that I have that the Lord is near to us, guiding, directing, the burden would be almost beyond my strength, but because I know that He is there, and that He can be appealed to, and if we have ears to hear attuned to Him, we will never be left alone."[68]

After only eighteen months as President of the Church, Harold B. Lee died of a fatal pulmonary hemorrhage on December 26, 1973, in Salt Lake City. Although his death at age seventy-four was unexpected by Latter-day Saints, it was not unexpected by his wife Freda, for Harold had told her, "God is very near."[69]

"Some felt that his passing was untimely, but the death of a man of God is never untimely." At his funeral, President Spencer W. Kimball said, "A giant redwood has fallen and left a great space in the forest.'"[70] Harold is remembered for devoting his life to strengthening the Latter-day Saints and building the kingdom of God.

THE LIFE STORY OF HAROLD B. LEE IN HIS OWN WORDS

"I GUESS WE WON'T RING THE PIGS TODAY"

"I remember a little boyhood experience. We had pigs that were tearing up the garden, causing great mischief on the farm. Father sent me two miles to the store to get an instrument so we could ring the noses of the pigs. We had great difficulty rounding them up and getting them in the pen, and I was fooling around with this instrument that I had been sent to purchase, I pressed down too hard and it broke. Father would have been justified in giving me a scolding right there, after all the effort and money wasted, but he just looked at me, smiled, and said, 'Well, son, I guess we won't ring the pigs today. Turn them out and we'll go back tomorrow and try it over again.' How I loved that father, that he didn't scold me for an innocent little mistake that could have made a breach between us."

—Harold B. Lee, in Williams, *Teachings of Harold B. Lee*, 279–280.

"SHE HAD TO TEACH US THE SCRIPTURES"

"In my Primary class, I had a great teacher—not great in the sense that she had gone to school and had received degrees for perfection in the science of teaching, pedagogy, but she had a way of believing . . . that in order for her to build faith in us she had to teach us the scriptures."

— Harold B. Lee, in "How Primary Teachers Can Strengthen Their Testimonies," 47th annual Primary conference, Apr. 3, 1933, 9, Church History Library, in *Teachings of Presidents of the Church: Harold B. Lee*, 66.

"Don't Go Over There!"

"I have a believing heart that started with a simple testimony that came when I was a child—I think maybe I was around ten or eleven years of age. I was with my father out on a farm away from our home, trying to spend the day busying myself until my father was ready to go home. Over the fence from our place were some tumbledown sheds that would attract a curious boy, and I was adventurous. I started to climb through the fence, and I heard a voice as clearly as you are hearing mine, calling me by name and saying, 'Don't go over there!' I turned to look at my father to see if he were talking to me, but he was way up at the other end of the field. There was no person in sight. I realized then, as a child, that there were persons beyond my sight, for I had definitely heard a voice."

—Harold B. Lee, *Stand Ye in Holy Places*, 139.

"We Won the Debate"

"As just a high school boy, I went away on a high school debating team trip. We won the debate. I called mother on the telephone only to have her say, 'Never mind, Son. I know all about it. I will tell you when you get home at the end of the week.' When I came home she took me aside and said, 'When I knew it was just time for this performance to start, I went out among the willows by the creekside, and there, all by myself, I remembered you and prayed [to] God you would not fail.' I have come to know that that kind of love is necessary for every son and daughter who seeks to achieve in this world."

—Harold B. Lee, "A Tribute to Father, Mother and Wife," in Conference Report, Apr. 6, 1941, 120.

"I Received a Most Encouraging Letter from Father"

On August 27, 1922, while a young missionary in the western states, Harold B. Lee wrote:

"I received a most encouraging letter from Father, who told me they would never ask for my release and would only pray God to increase their crops so I can stay until released. I am so appreciative of my people at home. Waldo, my sixteen-year-old brother, just sent me a check for $40, saying he wanted some credit, too, so you see they all consider that they are doing the Lord's work when they help to keep [me] in the mission field. I could cry when I think of it all, and my prayer is that God will make me humble so that I shall not disappoint them when I do go home."

—Harold B. Lee, in Goates, *Harold B. Lee*, 69.

"She Reminded Me of Our Family Prayers"

"We began married life on a borrowed $300. Due to [Fern's] high standards, our present home has all the conveniences possible, and while small and not the most convenient, it has breathed the influence of a charming wife and a loving mother. These sterling qualities were apparent on the first night of our marriage when she reminded me of our family prayers."

— Harold B. Lee, in Goates, *Harold B. Lee*, 87.

"The New President of Pioneer Stake"

"On the Friday preceding the quarterly conference, I was called to the office of President Rudger Clawson, where I was told by President Clawson and Elder George Albert Smith that I had been chosen by the First Presidency and the Twelve as the new president of Pioneer Stake. I told them I would much prefer working as a counselor to Brother Hyde, and was bluntly told by George Albert Smith that I had been invited to meet with them, not to tell them what should be done, but to find out if I was willing to do what the Lord wanted me to do. There followed a discussion on the selection of my counselors. Again I was told when I asked if they had any suggestions on that, 'We have suggestions, but we are not going to tell you—that is your responsibility. If you are guided by the Spirit of the Lord, you will choose those whom we have in mind.'

"I retired that night, or rather early morning, to a fitful sleep. . . . During the few hours I tried to sleep it would seem that I had chosen two counselors and was trying to hold council meetings with them. Disagreements, obstacles, and misunderstandings would arise, and I would awake with a start to realize that my first choices were wrong. This process was repeated with ten or twelve of my brethren until, when morning came, I was certain the Lord had guided me to choose . . . my counselors."

— Harold B. Lee, in Goates, *Harold B. Lee*, 88–89.

"I Was Just a Young Man in My Thirties"

As a stake president in the 1930s, Harold B. Lee recalled:

"We had been wrestling with this question of welfare. There were few government work programs; the finances of the Church were low. . . . And here we were with 4,800 of our 7,300 people [in our stake] who were wholly or partially dependent. We had only one place to go, and that was to apply the Lord's program as set forth in the revelations. . . .

"[T]he First Presidency . . . called me one morning [in 1935] asking if I would come to their office. . . . They wished me now to head up the welfare movement to turn the tide from government relief, direct relief, and help to put the Church in a position where it could take care of its own needy.

"After that morning I rode in my car (spring was just breaking) up to the head of City Creek Canyon into what was then called Rotary Park; and there, all by myself, I offered one of the most humble prayers of my life.

"There I was, just a young man in my thirties. My experience had been limited. I was born in a little country town in Idaho. I had hardly been outside the boundaries of the states of Utah and Idaho. And now to put me in a position where I was to reach out to the entire membership of the Church, worldwide, was one of the most staggering contemplations that I could imagine. How could I do it with my limited understanding?

"As I kneeled down, my petition was, 'What kind of an organization should be set up in order to accomplish what the Presidency has assigned?' And there came to me on that glorious morning one of the most heavenly realizations of the power of the priesthood of God. It was as though something were saying to me, 'There is no new organization necessary to take care of the needs of this people. All that is necessary is to put the priesthood of God to work. There is nothing else that you need as a substitute.' With that understanding, then, and with the simple application of the power of the priesthood, the welfare program has gone forward now by leaps and bounds, overcoming obstacles that seemed impossible, until now it stands as a monument to the power of the priesthood."

—Harold B. Lee, "Admonitions of the Priesthood," in Conference Report, Oct. 1972, 123–124.

"I've Been Awakened and . . . Unable to Sleep"

"Sometimes in the middle of the night I've been awakened and am unable to sleep until I've gotten out of bed and put down on paper the thing that I have been wrestling with. But it takes a lot of courage to act when directed as an answer to prayers."

—Harold B. Lee, "Qualities of Leadership," address to the Latter-day Saint Student Association convention, Aug. 1970, 5, in *Teachings of Presidents of the Church: Harold B. Lee*, 54.

"I Was Awakened in the Wee Hours"

"I was once in a situation where I needed help. The Lord knew I needed help, as I was on an important mission. I was awakened in the wee hours of the morning and was straightened out on something that I had planned to do in a contrary way, and the way was clearly mapped out before me as I lay there that morning, just as surely as though someone had sat on the edge of my bed and told me what to do. Yes, the voice of the Lord comes into our minds and we can be directed thereby."

—Harold B. Lee, *Teachings of Presidents of the Church: Harold B. Lee*, 50.

"The President Was Waiting for Me"

"I was sitting in the audience attending the general priesthood meeting as the managing director of the Church Welfare Program. At the conclusion, President J. Reuben Clark, who was conducting the meeting, called my name out and asked that I come to the stand to meet Bishop Joseph L. Wirthlin. Bishop Wirthlin did have a matter of business to mention to me, but it was really a way to have me meet with President Heber J. Grant.

"When I arrived at the stand, Elder Joseph Anderson said that the President was waiting for me in the General Authorities' room. It amazed me, and I immediately sensed that there was something more than just a social visit that President Grant had in mind. It was then that he announced to me that I had been named to be elevated to the Quorum of the Twelve."

—Harold B. Lee, in Goates, *Harold B. Lee*, 157.

"At the 'Foot of the Ladder'"

"I came to know what it meant to be at the 'foot of the ladder,' as President Clark called it, but I wasn't there for long. I heard Elder John A. Widtsoe tell about when he was called as a junior member. He sat there for fifteen years before there was a vacancy.

"Contrary to that, in thirteen years I had moved from that junior position until I was very near to the president of the Twelve. When called I was twenty years younger than the next youngest member of the quorum, Brother Stephen L Richards. I recall President Grant would look along the line, and noting my dark hair compared to the gray hair of those older brethren, would say that the color line was well marked. My hair, though, began to change pretty rapidly from that point on."

—Harold B. Lee, in Goates, *Harold B. Lee*, 162.

"Truth Was Being Trumpeted in My Ears"

"When I sat in as a younger member of the Council of the Twelve, the first Church reorganization I was permitted to participate in was when President [Heber J.] Grant passed away. . . . As the [new] President named his counselors and they took their places at the head of the room, down inside me I had a witness that these were the men that the Lord wanted to be the Presidency of the Church. It came to me with a conviction that was as though that truth was being trumpeted in my ears."

—Harold B. Lee, in Williams, *Teachings of Harold B. Lee*, 542–543.

"Your Heart Begins to Tell You Things That Your Mind Does Not Know"

"I once had a visit from a young Catholic priest who came with a stake missionary from Colorado. I asked him why he had come, and he replied, 'I came to see you.'

"'Why?' I asked.

"'Well,' he said, 'I have been searching for certain concepts that I have not been able to find. But I think I am finding them now in the Mormon community.'

"That led to a half-hour conversation. I told him, 'Father, when your heart begins to tell you things that your mind does not know, then you are getting the Spirit of the Lord.'

"He smiled and said, 'I think that's happening to me already.'

"'Then don't wait too long,' I said to him.

"A few weeks later I received a telephone call from him. He said, 'Next Saturday I am going to be baptized a member of the Church, because my heart has told me things my mind did not know.'"

—Harold B. Lee, *Stand Ye in Holy Places*, 92–93.

"Never More Beautiful Than in a Storm"

"Some years ago I went to a stake conference where the Manti Temple is located down in southern Utah. It was a dark, stormy night and it was snowing. As we left our meetings and went to the home of the stake president, we stopped there in the car and looked up at the temple situated high on a hill. As we sat impressed by the sight of that beautifully lighted temple shining through the snowy and dark night, the stake president said something to me that was very meaningful. He said, 'That temple, lighted as it is, is never more beautiful than in a storm or when there is a dense fog.' To understand the importance of that, may I say to you that never is the gospel of Jesus Christ more important to you than in a storm or when you are having great difficulty."

—Harold B. Lee, in Williams, *Teachings of Harold B. Lee*, 488.

"I Have Seen the Prophecies of Our Present Leaders Fulfilled"

On December 31, 1941, Harold B. Lee wrote in his journal:

"This page closes the greatest and most important year of my life. During the last twelve months, I have seen the prophecies of our present leaders fulfilled regarding war and economic trends, proving again their divine callings. In my call to [the] apostleship I have experienced the most intensive schooling and preparation of any similar period. I have known the terrors of the evil tempter and in contrast the sublime joy of inspiration and the revelations of the Holy Spirit. My wife and family have been a constant source of encouragement and happiness and despite the terrors of World War, the peace of God seems to be with us."

—Harold B. Lee, in Goates, *Harold B. Lee*, 175.

"If You Want to Learn to Love God"

"[I]n the early morning hours I was given a glorious dream. In that dream it seemed that I was in the company of brethren being instructed by the President of the Church, and while there were others there, it seemed that everything he was saying was just for me. . . . That dream came back to me, today—came back to me with a vividness that was overwhelming, for this was the message: 'If you want to learn to love God, you must learn to love His children and to love serving His children. No person loves God unless he loves service and unless he loves our Heavenly Father's children.'"

—Harold B. Lee, Los Angeles California Temple dedicatory service, 161–163, in *Teachings of Presidents of the Church: Harold B. Lee*, 107.

"I, Too, Had a Personal Witness"

"When I was searching for the Spirit to deliver a talk on the Easter theme, the resurrection of the Lord, I closeted myself, read the four gospels, particularly down to the Crucifixion, the Resurrection, and I had something happen to me. As I read, it was as though I was reliving, almost, the very incident, not just a story. And then I delivered my message and bore testimony that now, as one of the least of my brethren, I, too, had a personal witness of the death and the resurrection of our Lord and Master. Why? Because I had had something burned into my soul that I could speak with a certainty that is beside all doubt."

—Harold B. Lee, "Lectures in Theology: Last Message Series," address given at Salt Lake Institute of Religion, Jan. 15, 1971, 11, as cited in *Teachings of Presidents of the Church: Harold B. Lee*, 45.

"I Have Had to Submit to Some . . . Severe Tests"

"I have had to submit to some tests, some severe tests, before the Lord, I suppose to prove me to see if I would be willing to submit to all things whatsoever the Lord sees fit to inflict upon me, even as a little child does submit to its father."

—Harold B. Lee, in Conference Report, Oct. 1967, 98.

"I'll Never Forget the Look on His Face"

Helen Lee Goates wrote of her father, Harold B. Lee:

"I'll never forget the look on his face [as he spoke on the telephone]. He kept repeating: 'Oh, no. No. Oh, no.' . . . He covered the phone receiver and looked as though all the cares in the world had suddenly settled upon him. He said to us, so gravely, 'President Smith is gone.' . . .

"I went over to him, and put my hand on his arm and said: 'Daddy dear, I guess the day has finally come that you must have thought through the years you would never be prepared for.' He answered: 'Oh, I'm afraid I'm not. I'm afraid I'm not.' . . .

"I had never seen him look so weak and so completely at a loss. All through the years, except for the circumstances of my mother's passing, Daddy was a 'rock of Gibraltar' to all of us—the very epitome of strength and goodness. But at that moment he was completely devastated.

"It was only a moment, however, until he straightened up, squared his shoulders, and began to take charge."

—Harold B. Lee, in Goates, *Harold B. Lee*, 454.

"Go Thou and Do Likewise"

After the death of President Joseph Fielding Smith in July 1972, Harold B. Lee took an occasion to gaze upon the portraits of the ten preceding Presidents of the Church displayed in the Salt Lake Temple. He later said:

"There, in prayerful meditation, I looked upon the paintings of those men of God—true, pure men, God's noblemen—who had preceded me in a similar calling. . . . President Joseph Fielding Smith was there with his smiling face, my beloved prophet-leader who made no compromise with truth. . . . He seemed in that brief moment to be passing to me, as it were, a sceptre of righteousness as though to say to me, 'Go thou and do likewise.'"

—Harold B. Lee, "May the Kingdom of God Go Forth," in Conference Report, Oct. 1972, 18–20.

"What an Overwhelming Training Program!"

"I have a consciousness as I have thought through this responsibility [President of the Church] and have been close enough to the Brethren over the years, that one in this position is under the constant surveillance of Him in whose service we are. Never would He permit one in this position to lead this church astray. You can be sure of that. When I think of the process by which a man comes to a leadership position in the Church, I think of my own experience for thirty-one and a half years, and all the circumstances which have come in my own life— what an overwhelming training program! When the change in the First Presidency came, I contrasted it with the way political parties bring a president of the United States to office, or the inauguration of a king, to see how, by the Lord's plan, these changes are made without rancor, without bickering. The plan is set and the Lord makes no mistakes, so He has told us."

—Harold B. Lee, in Williams, *Teachings of Harold B. Lee*, 535–536.

"Someone Laid His Hand upon My Head"

"On the way across the country, we were sitting in the forward section of the airplane. Some of our Church members were in the next section. As we approached a certain point en route, someone laid his hand upon my head. I looked up; I could see no one. That happened again before we arrived home, again with the same experience. Who it was, by what means or what medium, I may never know, except I knew that I was receiving a blessing that I came a few hours later to know I needed most desperately.

"As soon as we arrived home, my wife very anxiously called the doctor. It was now about eleven o'clock at night. He called me to come to the telephone, and he asked me how I was. I said, 'Well, I am very tired. I think I will be all right.' But shortly thereafter, there came massive hemorrhages, which had they occurred while we were in fight, I wouldn't be here today talking about it. I know that there are powers divine that reach out when all other help is not available. . . . Yes, I know that there are such powers."

—Harold B. Lee, "Stand Ye in Holy Places," in Conference Report, Apr. 1973, 123.

"I Bear You My Solemn Witness"

"I bear you my solemn witness that [the Church] is true, that the Lord is in his heavens; he is closer to us than you have any idea. You ask when the Lord gave the last revelation to this Church? The Lord is giving revelations day by day, and you will witness and look back on this period and see some of the mighty revelations the Lord has given in your day and time. To that I bear you my witness."

—Harold B. Lee, in Goates, *Harold B. Lee*, 501.

"The Advent of the Savior"

"I come to you today with no shadow of doubting in my mind that I know the reality of the person who is presiding over this church, our Lord and Master, Jesus Christ. I know that he is. I know that he is closer to us than many times we have any idea. They are not an absentee Father and Lord. They are concerned about us, helping to prepare us for the advent of the Savior, whose coming certainly isn't too far away because of the signs that are becoming apparent."

—Harold B. Lee, "Stand Ye in Holy Places," in Conference Report, Apr. 8, 1973, 124.

Spencer W. Kimball

Born: March 28, 1895, Salt Lake City, Utah
Died: November 5, 1985, Salt Lake City, Utah
President of the Church: December 30, 1973, to November 5, 1985

SPENCER W. KIMBALL

SPENCER WOOLLEY KIMBALL, SON OF Andrew Kimball and Olive Woolley, was born March 28, 1895, in Salt Lake City. When Spencer was three years old, his family moved to Thatcher, Arizona. Spencer worked hard as a child to tame the desert on the family farm in Thatcher. His hardest experience, however, was the death of his mother in 1906, when he was eleven years old.

In his youth, Spencer excelled in sports and music and was president of his class each year at the Gila Academy. After graduating from the academy, Spencer accepted a mission call to serve in the Swiss-German Mission. Due to the outbreak of World War I, his mission call was changed to the Central States Mission.[71]

After completing an honorable mission, Spencer returned to Thatcher, where he met Camilla Eyring, a home-economics teacher at the Gila Academy. Thirty-one days after meeting Camilla, Spencer asked her father if he would approve of their marriage. Spencer and Camilla were married on November 16, 1917, in Thatcher. At that time, Spencer had only ten dollars to his name and Camilla owed fifty dollars for her schooling. In June 1918 Spencer and Camilla were sealed for eternity in the Salt Lake Temple.

Spencer supported Camilla and their growing family as a bank clerk until 1927. In that year, he invested $150 in the Kimball-Greenhalgh Insurance Agency and went to work for the agency as an insurance salesman. Within the first month of his employment, Spencer had doubled his investment. Due to the hours Spencer kept in the office, coworkers joked that he would die with his shoes on.

In 1943, while serving as president of the Mount Graham Stake, Spencer was called to the Quorum of the Twelve Apostles. He felt inadequate to accept such a calling and "wrestled" with the Lord for a witness that he was worthy to serve. "There was one great desire, to get a testimony of my calling," he said. "How I prayed! How I suffered! How I wept! How I struggled." After eighty-five days of praying for an answer, Spencer received a spiritual confirmation that it was the will of the Lord for him to be an Apostle.[72]

During his apostolic service, Spencer suffered from debilitating illnesses and afflictions—heart attacks, throat cancer, boils, deafness, Bell's palsy, and brain tumors. Any of these maladies would have stunted the work of most men, but Spencer refused to let physical limitations prevent him from fulfilling his responsibilities. He wrote several books, the most quoted being *The Miracle of Forgiveness*. Spencer worked tirelessly in behalf of Father Lehi's descendants. Whether the descendants were residing in North or South America or living on the isles of the sea, Spencer sought them out and shared with them the gospel of Jesus Christ.

In 1973 Spencer was sustained as the twelfth President of The Church of Jesus Christ of Latter-day Saints. During his administration, he encouraged members to "lengthen your stride" and "do it." Under his direction, a new LDS edition of the scriptures was published, worthy nineteen-year-old men were called to serve missions, genealogical research was expanded, and temple building progressed at a rate never before seen. No other event in his administration, however, was more groundbreaking than his remarkable revelation in June 1978 that extended the priesthood to all worthy males.

Spencer died on November 5, 1985, in Salt Lake City.

THE LIFE STORY OF SPENCER W. KIMBALL IN HIS OWN WORDS

"WHY DO WE TAKE THE EGGS TO THE BISHOP?"

"I remember as a youth, walking with my mother up the dusty road to the bishop's house in a day when we often paid tithing from our animals and produce. As we walked, I said, 'Why do we take the eggs to the bishop?' She answered, 'Because they are tithing eggs and the bishop receives the tithing for Heavenly Father.' My mother then recounted how each evening when the eggs were brought in, the first one went into a small basket and the next nine went into a large basket."

—Spencer W. Kimball, "He Did It with All His Heart, and Prospered," *Ensign*, March 1981, 4.

"THE HABIT OF 'GOING TO MEETING'"

"When I was a very small boy, I was taught the habit of going to sacrament meetings. Mother always took me with her. Those warm afternoons I soon became drowsy and leaned over on her lap to sleep. I may not have learned much from the sermons, but I learned the habit of 'going to meeting.' The habit stayed with me through my life."

—Spencer W. Kimball, "A Testimony of the Truth Comes through Righteous Living," in Conference Report, Oct. 1944, 43.

"I Was Thrilled to Hear All the Brethren Speak"

"I remember coming to this [Salt Lake] tabernacle as a boy from Arizona, with my father, to attend general conference. I was thrilled to hear all the Brethren speak. . . . I was thrilled at their utterances and took their warnings seriously, even as a young man. These men are among the prophets of God, just as were the prophets of the Book of Mormon and of the Bible."

—Spencer W. Kimball, "Listen to the Prophets," *Ensign*, May 1978, 76.

"Until I Knew Them by Heart"

"When I was nine years old, I milked nine cows each day at my home in Thatcher, Arizona. I thought, 'What a waste of time, to sit on a three-legged stool. Maybe there is something else I could do while I am milking.' So I sang the songs of Zion until I knew all the well-known hymns that are generally sung. Then I said, 'Well, I have got to have something more!'

"So I got a copy of the Articles of Faith and put it on the ground right beside me and I went through them, over and over again, a thousand times. Then I got a copy of the Ten Commandments. I typed them up on cards and took them out with me where I milked and repeated them over and over until I knew them by heart.

"Then, as I got a little closer to my mission, I typed scriptures that I thought would be helpful to me and I learned them . . . so that when I went on my mission I would be prepared for it. If every Latter-day Saint would do this, I think it would be a wonderful thing."

—Spencer W. Kimball, in Lamanite Conference, San Diego North Stake, May 3, 1975, in Kimball, *Teachings of Spencer W. Kimball*, 131.

"My Eleven-Year-Old Heart Seemed to Burst"

"[News of mother's death] came as a thunderbolt. I ran from the house out in the backyard to be alone in my deluge of tears. Out of sight and sound, away from everybody, I sobbed and sobbed. Each time I said the word 'Ma' fresh floods of tears gushed forth until I was drained dry. Ma—dead! But she couldn't be! Life couldn't go on for us. . . . My eleven-year-old heart seemed to burst."

—Spencer W. Kimball, in Kimball and Kimball, *Spencer W. Kimball*, 46.

"A Sympathetic Heart for the Sons and Daughters of Lehi"

"I do not know when I began to love the children of Lehi. It may have come to me at birth, because those years preceding and after I was born, were spent by my father on missions among the Indians in Indian territory. He was president of the mission. This love may have come in those first years of my childhood, when my father used to sing the Indian chants to us children and show us souvenirs from and pictures of, his Indian friends. It may have come from my patriarchal blessing which was given to me by Patriarch Samuel Claridge, when I was nine years of age. One line of the blessing reads:

"'You will preach the gospel to many people, but more especially to the Lamanites, for the Lord will bless you with the gift of language and power to portray before that people, the gospel in great plainness. You will see them organized and be prepared to stand as the bulwark 'round this people.'"

"I do not know when my appreciation for them came, but I have always had a sympathetic heart for the sons and daughters of Lehi."

—Spencer W. Kimball, "Appreciation for the Descendants of Lehi," in Conference Report, Apr. 6, 1947, 144.

"You Have Never Read That Holy Book"

"[Susan Young Gates, daughter of Brigham Young,] gave a rousing talk on the reading of the scriptures and making them our own; then she stopped her dissertation to ask this mixed congregation, about a thousand of us, 'How many of you have read the Bible through?'

". . . An accusing guilt complex spread over me. [At age fourteen,] I had read many books by that time, the funny papers, and light books, but my accusing heart said to me, 'You, Spencer Kimball, you have never read that holy book. Why?' I looked around me at the people in front and on both sides of the hall to see if I was alone in my failure to read the sacred book. Of the thousand people, there were perhaps a half dozen who proudly raised their hands. I slumped down in my seat. I had no thought for the others who had also failed, but only a deep accusing thought for myself. I don't know what other people were doing and thinking, but I heard no more of the sermon. It had accomplished its work. When the meeting closed, I sought the large double exit door and rushed to my home a block east of the chapel; and I was gritting my teeth and saying to myself, 'I will. I will. I will.'

"Entering the back door of our family home, I went to the kitchen shelf where we kept the coal oil lamps, selected one that was full of oil and had a newly trimmed wick, and climbed the stairs to my attic room. There I opened my Bible and began [with] Genesis, first chapter and first verse, and I read well into the night with Adam and Eve and Cain and Abel, and Enoch and Noah and through the flood even to Abraham."

About a year later he had finished reading the bible:

"What a satisfaction it was to me to realize I had read the Bible through from beginning to end! And what exultation of spirit! And what joy in the over-all picture I had received of its contents!"

—Spencer W. Kimball, "What I Read as a Boy," *Children's Friend*, Nov. 1943, 508.

"With a Wife Like Camilla Eyring"

Speaking of his wife, Camilla Eyring Kimball, Spencer W. Kimball said:

"Camilla has been by my side in every experience. We have buried our parents and other loved ones, and have given up our own little children prematurely born. We have been in the depths and soared to the heights.

"She has trembled and prayed through many hours of heart and throat and brain surgery for me, and through the hours of surgery on the legs of our youngest. She showed her character and strength through those agonizing days of wonder and fear at the hospitals and then those tiring, never-ending days and nights of uncomplaining care. For the little fellow she changed his day braces to night splints, and she rubbed and massaged his limbs and bathed and rubbed and bound them. For me she constantly helped and encouraged in every illness. . . .

"We have wept together and we have laughed together. . . . Our life has been full of fun in spite of all the sad and serious things. We have danced; we have sung; we have entertained; we have loved and been loved. With a wife like Camilla Eyring, life becomes inclusive, full, and abundant."

—Spencer W. Kimball, in Miner and Kimball, *Camilla*, viii.

"Heaven Was in Our Home"

"As a youth, and with my wife and children in our home, I remember our beloved family activities. Heaven was in our home. When each person did something, whether it was sing a song, lead a game, recite an article of faith, tell a story, share a talent, or perform an assignment, there was growth and good feeling."

—Spencer W. Kimball, "Therefore I Was Taught," *Ensign*, Jan. 1982, 3.

"Couldn't Pay at the End of the Month"

"All my life from childhood I have heard the Brethren saying, 'get out of debt and stay out of debt.' I was employed for some years in the banks and I saw the terrible situation that many people were in because they had ignored that important counsel. . . .

". . . One of the shocking things of my life was to find on the books the accounts of many of the people in the community that I knew. I knew them. I knew approximately what their income was, and then I saw them wear it away. In other words, I saw they were buying their clothes, their shoes, everything they had 'on time.'

"And I found that it was my duty to make the bills at the end of the month from them. And many of them couldn't pay at the end of the month. They couldn't pay even the installments that were arranged for them. And having been reared in a home that took care of its funds, I couldn't understand it. I could understand how a person could buy a home on time or perhaps could even buy an automobile on time. But I never could quite understand how anybody would wear clothes they didn't own. Or eat food that they had to buy 'on time.'"

—Spencer W. Kimball, "Law of Consecration," in Conference Report, Apr. 1975, 166–167.

"THE SEVEN GOBLETS WERE STILL FULL"

"When I was district governor of the Rotary Clubs of Arizona . . . , I went to Nice, France, to the international convention. As a part of that celebration there was a sumptuous banquet for the district governors, and the large building was set for an elegant meal. When we came to our places, I noted that at every place there were seven goblets, along with numerous items of silverware and dishes; and everything was the best that Europe could furnish.

"As the meal got underway, an army of waiters came to wait on us, seven waiters at each place, and they poured wine and liquor. Seven glass goblets were filled at every plate. The drinks were colorful. I was a long way from home; I knew many of the district governors; they knew me. But they probably did not know my religion nor of my stand on the Word of Wisdom. At any rate, the evil one seemed to whisper to me, 'This is your chance. You are thousands of miles from home. There is no one here to watch you. No one will ever know if you drink the content of those goblets. This is your chance!' And then a sweeter spirit seemed to whisper, 'You have a covenant with yourself; you promised yourself you would never do it; and with your Heavenly Father you made a covenant, and you have gone these years without breaking it, and you would be stupid to break this covenant after all these years.' Suffice it to say that when I got up from the table an hour later, the seven goblets were still full."

—Spencer W. Kimball, "Obedience to Word of Wisdom," in Conference Report, Apr. 1974, 127–128.

"It Is So Good to See You"

"Of the thousand [of dreams] through the years, most have passed out of mind with the dawn, but this was different. I stood in the room with other people around me, then I saw him. Father was a handsome person, tall, with dark piercing eyes and a commanding appearance. And there he was, not as a vague apparition, but so real and so like himself. I called out 'Oh! Father, Father, it is so good to see you.' He had a radiant smile such as he had had in real life. It warmed me. I was pulsating with gladness. I could not understand why others could not see him, he was so clear and distinct and pleasing. 'Oh, my beloved father!' Then he seemed to be moving away. He had been only an arm's length from me. He faded out of the picture and was gone. I awakened and lay reliving the dream or vision again and again. I did not want it to pass from my memory. I went to my desk and wrote it in my journal and went back to bed, lying quietly in the darkness musing, reliving the hallowed experience. So vivid it was that I felt sure it had some meaning. . . . If it did nothing more for me than to more completely connect mortality with the life beyond, it served a good purpose. . . .

"There settled down over me a comfort and a peace which, except in a few weak moments has never left me."

—Spencer W. Kimball, in Kimball, *Teachings of Spencer W. Kimball*, 42–43.

"Ye Ought to Forgive One Another"

"I was struggling with a community problem in a small ward . . . where two prominent men, leaders of the people, were deadlocked in a long and unrelenting feud. Some misunderstanding between them had driven them far apart with enmity. As the days, weeks, and months passed, the breach became wider. The families of each conflicting party began to take up the issue and finally nearly all the people of the ward were involved. Rumors spread and differences were aired and gossip became tongues of fire until the little community was divided by a deep gulf. I was sent to clear up the matter. . . . I arrived at the frustrated community about 6 p.m., Sunday night, and immediately went into session with the principal combatants.

"How we struggled! How I pleaded and warned and begged and urged! Nothing seemed to be moving them. Each antagonist was so sure that he was right and justified that it was impossible to budge him.

"The hours were passing—it was now long after midnight, and despair seemed to enshroud the place; the atmosphere was still one of ill temper and ugliness. Stubborn resistance would not give way. Then it happened. I aimlessly opened my Doctrine and Covenants again and there before me it was. I had read it many times in past years and it had had no special meaning then. But tonight it was the very answer. It was an appeal and an imploring and a threat and seemed to be coming direct from the Lord. I read [section 64] from the seventh verse on, but the quarreling participants yielded not an inch until I came to the ninth verse. Then I saw them flinch, startled, wondering. Could that be right? The Lord was saying to us—to all of us—'Wherefore, I say unto you, that ye ought to forgive one another.' . . .

"This was an obligation. They had heard it before. They had said it in repeating the Lord's Prayer. But now: '. . . for he that forgiveth not his brother his trespasses standeth condemned before the Lord. . . .'

"'. . . For there remaineth in him the greater sin.' . . ."

"Shocked, the two men sat up, listened, pondered a minute, then began to yield. This scripture added to all the others read brought them to their knees. Two a.m. and two bitter adversaries were shaking hands, smiling and forgiving and asking forgiveness. Two men were in a meaningful embrace. This hour was holy. Old grievances were forgiven and forgotten, and enemies became friends again. No reference was ever made again to the differences. The skeletons were buried, the closet of dry bones was locked and the key was thrown away, and peace was restored."

—Spencer W. Kimball, *Miracle of Forgiveness*, 281–282.

"I Felt It [Was] True of Him"

"I spoke at the funeral service of a young Brigham Young University student who died during World War II. There had been hundreds of thousands of young men rushed prematurely into eternity through the ravages of that war, and I made the statement that I believed this righteous youth had been called to the spirit world to preach the gospel to those deprived souls. This may not be true of all who die, but I felt it true of him."

—Spencer W. Kimball, *Faith Precedes the Miracle*, 101.

"I Have Read That Book More Than Seventy-Six Times"

Elder Richard G. Scott wrote:

"Elder Spencer W. Kimball supervised our area [South America,] when I was mission president. I observed how well he understood and used the Book of Mormon in his inspiring messages to members and missionaries alike. . . .

"At a missionary zone meeting on one occasion, he said, 'Richard, you used a scripture from the Book of Mormon today that I had never thought of using in that way.' That was the careful preparation for a very significant lesson he wanted me to learn. He then added, 'And to think that I have read that book more than seventy-six times.'"

—Richard G. Scott, "The Power of the Book of Mormon in My Life," *Ensign*, Oct. 1984, 9.

"WE JUST COULDN'T LET THEM DOWN"

"We held an evening general meeting in Santo Domingo, the capital city of the Dominican Republic. Nearly 1,600 souls were present.

"About an hour after the close of the general meeting, a busload of one hundred members from the Puerto Plata Branch arrived at the meeting place. They had been delayed because their bus broke down. Under ordinary circumstances, they could have made the trip in about four hours, but they finally arrived after 10:00 P.M. to find the hall dark and empty. Many wept because they were so disappointed. All were converts, some for a few months and others only weeks or days.

"Sister Kimball and I had gone to bed after a long and tiring day. Upon learning of the plight of these faithful souls, my secretary knocked on the door of our hotel room and woke us up. He apologized for disturbing us but thought that I would want to know about the late arrivals and perhaps dictate a personal message to them. However, I felt that wouldn't be good enough and not fair to those who had come so far under such trying circumstances—one hundred people jammed into one bus. I got out of bed and dressed and went downstairs to see the members who had made such an effort only to be disappointed because of engine trouble. The Saints were still weeping as we entered the hall, so I spent more than an hour visiting with them.

"They then seemed relieved and satisfied and got back on the bus for the long ride home. They had to get back by morning to go to work and to school. Those good people seemed so appreciative of a brief visit together that I felt we just couldn't let them down. As I returned to my bed, I did so with a sense of peace and contentment in my soul."

—Spencer W. Kimball, "Rendering Service to Others," *Ensign*, May 1981, 45–46.

"MAKE THE GOSPEL UNIVERSAL TO ALL WORTHY PEOPLE"

"As you know, on the ninth of June a policy was changed that affects great numbers of people throughout the world. Millions and millions of people will be affected by the revelation which came. I remember very vividly that day I walked to the temple and ascended to the fourth floor where we have our solemn assemblies and where we have out meetings of the Twelve and the First Presidency. After everybody had gone out of the temple, I knelt and prayed. I prayed with much fervency. I knew that something was before us that was extremely important to many of the children of God. I knew that we could receive the revelations of the Lord only by being worthy and ready for them and ready to accept them and put them into place. Day after day I went alone and with great solemnity and seriousness in the upper rooms of the temple, and there I offered my soul and offered my efforts to go forward with the program. I wanted to do what he wanted. I talked about it to him and said, 'Lord, I want only what is right. We are not making any plans to be spectacularly moving. We want only the thing that thou dost want, and we want it when you want it and not until.'

"We met with the Council of the Twelve Apostles, time after time, in the holy room where there is a picture of the Savior in many different moods and also pictures of all the Presidents of the Church. Finally we had the feeling and the impression from the Lord, who made it very clear to us, that this was the thing to do to make the gospel universal to all worthy people. You will meet this situation undoubtedly as you bring the gospel to them on condition that their lives can be changed.

"I anticipate the day when the gospel, that has come to you and your families and has transformed your lives, will begin to transform their lives and make new people out of them. They will become people who will love the Lord and who will make the same sacrifices that you make."

—Spencer W. Kimball, in Kimball, *Teachings of Spencer W. Kimball*, 450–451.

"That Is My Lord Whose Names You Revile"

"In the hospital one day I was wheeled out of the operating room by an attendant who stumbled, and there issued from his angry lips vicious cursing with a combination of the names of the Savior. Even half-conscious, I recoiled and implored: 'Please! Please! That is my Lord whose names you revile.'

"There was a deathly silence, then a subdued voice whispered, 'I am sorry.' He had forgotten for the moment that the Lord had forcefully commanded all his people, 'Thou shalt not take the name of the Lord thy God in vain; for the Lord will not hold him guiltless that taketh his name in vain.'"

—Spencer W. Kimball, "President Kimball Speaks Out on Profanity," *Ensign*, Feb. 1981, 3.

"I FELT ABSOLUTELY CERTAIN THAT I WOULD DIE"

"I felt absolutely certain that I would die, when my time came, as president of the Twelve. . . .

"I said at President Lee's funeral that no one had prayed harder than Sister Kimball and I for his restoration when he was ill and for his continuation while he was well."

—Spencer W. Kimball, "When the World Will Be Converted," *Ensign*, Oct. 1974, 3.

"THE LORD KNOWS WHAT HE IS DOING"

"Recently a prominent doctor, knowing of my surgery and cancer treatments, exhibited a little surprise at my assuming the great responsibility of the church presidency. He was not a member of the Church and evidently had never known the pull and the pressure one feels when one has a positive assurance that the Lord is not playing games, but rather has a serious program for man and for his glory. The Lord knows what he is doing, and all his moves are appropriate and right."

—Spencer W. Kimball, "A Program for Man," *Ensign*, Nov. 1976, 110.

"The Lord Called Me to This Position"

"I know that the Lord called me to this position. I know that there are greater prophets, perhaps, than I, but I wish to do all I can to carry forward the work of the Lord as he wants it done. Every night and morning I kneel and pray with deep sincerity that the Lord will inspire me and reveal to me the direction I should go and what I should tell the people of this Church."

—Spencer W. Kimball, in Conference Report, Guatemala City Guatemala Area Conference 1977, 24, in *Teachings of Presidents of the Church: Spencer W. Kimball*, 237–238.

"I Always Have Very Tender Feelings about Prayers"

"I always have very tender feelings about prayers and the power and blessings of prayer. In my lifetime I have received more blessings than I can ever adequately give thanks for. The Lord has been so good to me. I have had so many experiences in sickness and in health that leave me with no shadow of doubt in my heart and mind that there is a God in heaven, that he is our Father, and that he hears and answers our prayers."

—Spencer W. Kimball, "We Need a Listening Ear," *Ensign*, Nov. 1979, 5.

Ezra Taft Benson

Born: August 4, 1899, Whitney, Idaho
Died: May 30, 1994, Salt Lake City, Utah
President of the Church: November 10, 1985, to May 30, 1994

EZRA TAFT BENSON

EZRA TAFT BENSON, SON OF George Taft Benson Jr. and Sarah B. Dunkley, was born August 4, 1899, in Whitney, Idaho, the eldest of eleven children. Ezra was named for his great-grandfather Ezra Taft Benson, the first man called to the apostleship after the martyrdom of Joseph Smith.

Ezra was raised on the family farm in Whitney, Idaho. He attended the Oneida Stake Academy, a Church-run school in Preston, Idaho, and later Utah State Agriculture College (now Utah State University), where he met his wife, Flora Smith Amussen. During World War I, he served in the U.S. military. At the end of the war, Ezra served a mission to Great Britain, where he presided over the Newcastle area in 1923. Ezra and Flora were married September 10, 1926, in the Salt Lake Temple.

After his mission, Ezra enrolled in Brigham Young University and was named in the yearbook "the most popular man."[73] In 1927 he attended Iowa State College, graduating with a master's degree in agricultural science. He was employed as a county farm agent and as an extension specialist for the University of Idaho (at the same time serving as president of the Boise Idaho Stake). He pursued additional graduate work at the University of California at Berkeley until being named executive secretary of the National Council of Farmer Cooperatives in Washington, D.C. While working in the nation's capital, he also served as president of the Washington D.C. Stake.

On October 7, 1943, Ezra was called to be an Apostle of the Lord Jesus Christ. As a member of the Quorum of the Twelve Apostles, he served as president of the European Mission and supervised the distribution of welfare aid to Europeans after World War II. From 1953 to 1961, he was the secretary of agriculture in the Dwight D. Eisenhower cabinet. In this capacity, he was featured on the covers of *U.S. News and World Report*, *Newsweek*, *Business Week*, and twice on the cover of *Time* magazine. He wrote more than a dozen books, including *Crossfire: The Eight Years with Eisenhower*; *The Constitution: A Heavenly Banner*; and *God, Family, Country: Our Three Great Loyalties*. Universities from Maine to Hawaii awarded him honorary doctoral degrees. President David O. McKay said that Ezra's service to the nation will "stand for all time—as a credit to the Church."[74]

In 1973 Ezra became President of the Quorum of the Twelve Apostles and on November 10, 1985, the thirteenth President of The Church of Jesus Christ of Latter-day Saints. During his administration, temples were dedicated in North and South America, Europe, and Asia, and missionary work was extended to fifty additional countries. He delivered eight major addresses on the cycles of pride and addresses titled "Beware of Pride" and "Cleansing the Inner Vessel." He was tireless in exhorting Latter-day Saints to read the Book of Mormon.

Ezra died of heart failure on Memorial Day, May 30, 1994, in Salt Lake City at the age of ninety-four.

The Life Story of Ezra Taft Benson in His Own Words

"I Cannot Recall a Time That I Did Not Believe in Jesus Christ"

"I cannot recall a time that I did not believe in Jesus Christ. It seems that the reality of His life, death, and resurrection has always been a part of me. I was reared in a home by faithful parents who earnestly believed in and testified of Christ, for which I am most grateful."

—Ezra Taft Benson, "The Meaning of Easter," *Ensign*, Apr. 1992, 2.

"A Spirit of Missionary Work"

"When my own father went on a mission, I remember, as the eldest son, the letters that he wrote from the mission field in the Midwest. There came into that home a spirit of missionary work that has never left it, for which I am humbly grateful."

—Ezra Taft Benson, "Our Responsibility to Share the Gospel," *Ensign*, May 1985, 8.

"Ward Teachers Are Here"

"I can remember, as if it were yesterday, growing up as a young boy in Whitney, Idaho. We were a farm family, and when we boys were out working in the field, I remember Father calling to us in a shrill voice from the barnyard: 'Tie up your teams, boys, and come on in. The ward teachers are here.' Regardless of what we were doing, that was the signal to assemble in the sitting room to hear the ward teachers.

"These two faithful priesthood bearers would come each month either by foot or by horseback. We always knew they would come. I can't remember one miss. And we would have a great visit. They would stand behind a chair and talk to the family. They would go around the circle and ask each child how he or she was doing and if we were doing our duty. Sometimes Mother and Father would prime us before the ward teachers came so we would have the right answers. But it was an important time for us as a family. They always had a message, and it was always a good one."

—Ezra Taft Benson, "To the Home Teachers of the Church," *Ensign*, May 1987, 51.

"Tithing Settlement the Following Day"

"On one occasion when I was a teenager, I overheard Father and Mother talking about their finances in preparation for tithing settlement the following day. Father [owed] twenty-five dollars at the bank, which was due during the week. In figuring their tithing, he owed twenty-five dollars more. He also had a hay derrick [something used to lift hay onto a haystack] which he had built. He . . . was trying to sell it, but had met with no success.

"What were they to do—[pay] the bank, pay their tithing later, or pay their tithing and hope that they could [pay the bank] in just a few days? After discussing the matter, and I am sure praying together before they retired, Father decided next day to go to tithing settlement and pay the twenty-five dollars, which would make him a full-tithe payer. As he rode home by horseback, one of his neighbors stopped him and said, 'George, I understand you have a derrick for sale. How much are you asking for it?'

"Father said, 'Twenty-five dollars.' The neighbor said, 'I haven't seen it, but knowing the way you build, I am sure it is worth twenty-five dollars. Just a minute and I will go in the house and make out a check for it. I need it.' This is a lesson I have not forgotten."

—Ezra Taft Benson, *The Teachings of Ezra Taft Benson*, 471–472.

"My Temple Memories Extend Back—Even to Young Boyhood"

"I am grateful to the Lord that my temple memories extend back—even to young boyhood. I remember so well, as a little boy, coming in from the field and approaching the old farm house in Whitney, Idaho. I could hear my mother singing 'Have I Done Any Good in the World Today?'

"I can still see her in my mind's eye bending over the ironing board with newspapers on the floor, ironing long strips of white cloth, with beads of perspiration on her forehead. When I asked her what she was doing, she said, 'These are temple robes, my son. Your father and I are going to the temple. . . .'

"Then she put the old flatiron on the stove, drew a chair close to mine, and told me about temple work—how important it is to be able to go to the temple and participate in the sacred ordinances performed there. She also expressed her fervent hope that some day her children and grandchildren and great-grandchildren would have the opportunity to enjoy these priceless blessings.

"These sweet memories about the spirit of temple work were a blessing in our farm home."

—Ezra Taft Benson, "What I Hope You Will Teach Your Children about the Temple," *Ensign*, Aug. 1985, 8.

"Character Is Shaped in Just Such Crucibles"

"One day in the middle of an important examination in high school, the point of my lead pencil broke. In those days, we used pocketknives to sharpen our pencils. I had forgotten my penknife, and turned to ask a neighbor for his. The teacher saw this; he accused me of cheating. When I tried to explain, he gave me a tongue-lashing for lying; worse, he forbade me to play on the basketball team in the upcoming big game.

"I could see that the more I protested the angrier he seemed to become. But, again and again, I stubbornly told what had happened. Even when the coach pleaded my cause, the teacher refused to budge.

The disgrace was almost more than I could bear. Then, just minutes before the game, he had a change of heart, and I was permitted to play. But there was no joy in it. We lost the game; and though that hurt, by far the deeper pain was being branded a cheat and a liar.

"Looking back, I know that lesson was God-sent. Character is shaped in just such crucibles.

"My parents believed me; they were understanding and encouraging. Supported by them, Uncle Serge's lessons in courage, and a clear conscience, I began to realize that when you are at peace with your Maker you can, if not ignore human criticism, at least rise above it. And I learned something else—the importance of avoiding even the appearance of evil. Though I was innocent, circumstance made me look guilty. Since this could so easily be true in many of life's situations, I made a resolution to keep even the appearance of my actions above question. . . . And it struck me, too, that if this injustice happened to me, it could happen to others, and I must not judge their actions simply on appearances."

—Ezra Taft Benson, in *Teachings of the Presidents of the Church Student Manual*, 216.

"Who Is That Girl?"

"'Who is that girl?' [Ezra] asked.

"'Why, that's Flora Amussen,' his cousin replied.

"'When I come here, I'm going to "step" her.'

"'You'll never make it; she's too popular for a farm boy.'

"'That makes it all the more interesting.'"

Recalling his first date with Flora, Ezra wrote:

"As we left the house and she kissed her mother tenderly, I knew I was the escort of a choice girl.

"Nothing in Flora's life impressed me more deeply than her reverent kindness to and deep love for her mother. Their companionship was an inspiration—one of the sweetest relationships I have ever known between a parent and child."

—Ezra Taft Benson, in Derin Head Rodriguez, "Flora Amussen Benson: Handmaiden of the Lord, Helpmeet of a Prophet, Mother in Zion," *Ensign*, Mar. 1987, 16–17.

"The Veil Is Very Thin"

"When I was a freshman at Utah State, living in the home of my grandmother, Louise Ballif Benson, who spent most of her time working on genealogical research and temple work, I remember coming home from a party about midnight. As I entered the door, I could hear someone speaking in Grandmother's room and I wondered who could be there at that time of the night. As I got closer and heard her voice, I realized that she was praying, thanking the Lord that He had extended her life for a few years after her husband had gone on so that she could complete the family temple work. She also prayed that she might see the last of her thirteen children married in the temple. This had now been accomplished and she would now like to go to her husband if it was pleasing to the Lord.

"As I left for a mission a few months later and as I shook her hand, I had the distinct impression I would not see her again in mortal life. A few months later in England, I got an impression that Grandmother had passed away. I mentioned it to my companion. He said, 'She has been ill, you are just worried about it.' 'No, she has not been sick,' I replied. Ten days later I received a letter from Father saying that she had passed peacefully away. As near as I could tell, it was the same day on which I received that impression."

—Ezra Taft Benson, "Temple Memories," Ogden Utah Temple dedication, Jan. 18, 1972.

"We Sailed Right into Salt Lake Port"

"I was a young missionary in northern England in 1922. Opposition to the Church became very intense. It became so strong that the mission president asked that we discontinue all street meetings, and in some places tracting was also discontinued. The opposition started largely among the ministers, and it became very, very severe. They didn't know anything about us to speak of. I remember tracting one day when a lovely lady came to the door.

We were having a nice conversation and the name Mormon was mentioned by my companion. Her husband came to the door in a Navy uniform, and he said, 'Oh, you can't tell me anything about those old Mormons. I've been in the British Navy for twenty years. We sailed right into Salt Lake port, and they wouldn't even let us land.' That was so typical of what they knew about us in those days."

—Ezra Taft Benson, "Our Commission to Take the Gospel to All the World," in Conference Report, Apr. 1984, 44.

"DISCONTINUE ALL STREET MEETINGS"

"In 1923 I was serving a mission in Great Britain. At that time there was great opposition to the Church. It began with the ministers and then spread through the press. Many anti-Mormon articles appeared in the daily press. A number of anti-Mormon movies were shown, and derogatory plays were produced on the stage. The general theme was the same—that Mormon missionaries were in England to lure away British girls and make slaves of them on Utah farms. . . .

"One time we received a letter from mission headquarters instructing us that we should discontinue all street meetings. At that time I was serving as the conference president, and my companion was the conference clerk. When this instruction arrived, we already had a meeting scheduled for the following Sunday night. So we reasoned that we would hold that meeting and then discontinue street meetings thereafter. That's where we made our mistake!

"The next Sunday evening we held our street meeting down near the railway station as scheduled. The crowd was large and unruly. In our efforts to preach to them, my companion and I stood back to back. He spoke in one direction, and I faced the other half of the crowd.

"When the saloons closed, the rougher, coarser element came out on the streets, many under the influence of liquor. The crowd became noisy, and those on the outside were not able to hear too well.

"Some yelled, 'What's the excitement?'

"Others yelled back, 'It's those dreadful Mormons.'

"To this, others responded, 'Let's get them and throw them in the river.'

"Soon an attempt was made to trample us under their feet. But since we were taller than the average man there, we put our hands on their shoulders and prevented them from getting us under their feet.

"During the excitement, my companion and I became separated. . . .

"When I arrived at the lodge, I found that my companion was not yet there. I worried and then prayed and waited. I became so concerned about him that I decided to disguise my appearance by putting on an old American cap and taking off my topcoat. Then I went out to try to find him.

"As I neared the place of the meeting, a man recognized me and asked, 'Have you seen your companion?'

"I said, 'No. Where is he?'

"He responded, 'He's down on the other side of the railway station with one side of his head mashed in.'

"This frightened me greatly, and I sprinted to the site as fast as I could. Before I reached the railway station, however, I met [a policeman who had previously escorted me home]. He said, 'I thought I told you to stay in and not come out on the street again tonight.'

"I replied, 'You did, officer. But I'm concerned about my companion. Do you know where he is?'

"He replied, 'Yes, he got a nasty blow on the side of his head, but he's gone to the lodge now. I walked partway with him as I did earlier with you. Now you get back there and don't come out anymore tonight.'

"So I went back to the lodge and found my companion disguising himself in order to go out and look for me. We threw our arms around each other and knelt together in prayer. From that experience I learned always to follow counsel, and that lesson has followed me all the days of my life."

—Ezra Taft Benson, "Preparing Yourselves for Missionary Service," in Conference Report, Apr. 1985, 36–37.

"Tonight We Received a Witness"

"My companion and I had been invited to travel over to South Shields, on the northwest coast, and speak in the sacrament meeting.

"In the letter of invitation, we were promised there would be a number of nonmembers present. They said, 'Many of our friends do not believe the lies that are printed about the Church.'

"We fasted and prayed sincerely and went to the sacrament meeting. The hall was filled. My companion had planned to talk on the first principles, and I had studied hard in preparation for a talk on the Apostasy. There was a wonderful spirit in the meeting. My companion spoke first and gave an excellent inspirational message. I followed and talked with a freedom I had never before experienced in my life.

"When I sat down, I realized that I had not mentioned the Apostasy. I had talked about the Prophet Joseph Smith and had borne my witness of his divine mission and of the truthfulness of the Book of Mormon. I couldn't hold back the tears.

"After the meeting ended, many people came forward, several of whom were nonmembers, and said to us, 'Tonight we received a witness that Mormonism is true. We are now ready to consider baptism.'

"This was an answer to our prayers, for we had prayed to say only those things which would touch the hearts of the investigators."

—Ezra Taft Benson, "Our Commission to Take the Gospel to All the World," in Conference Report, Apr. 1984, 44.

"I'm Willing to Square My Life"

"At a stake presidency's meeting in Boise, Idaho, years ago, we were trying to select a president for the weakest and smallest elders quorum in the stake. Our clerk had brought a list of all the elders of that quorum, and on the list was the name of a man whom I had known for some years. He came from a strong Latter-day Saint family, but he wasn't doing much in the Church. . . .

"I said to the stake president, 'Would you authorize me to go out and meet this man and challenge him to square his life with the standards of the Church and take the leadership of his quorum? I know there is some hazard in it, but he has the ability.'

"The stake president said, 'You go ahead, and the Lord bless you.'

"After Sunday School I went to this man's house. I'll never forget the look on his face as he opened the door and saw a member of his stake presidency standing there. He hesitantly invited me in; his wife was preparing dinner, and I could smell the aroma of coffee coming from the kitchen. I asked him to have his wife join us, and when we were seated, I told him why I had come. 'I'm not going to ask you for your answer today,' I told him. 'All I want you to do is to promise me that you will think about it, pray about it, and think about it in terms of what it will mean to your family, and then I'll be back to see you next week. If you decide not to accept, we'll go on loving you,' I added.

"The next Sunday, as soon as he opened the door I saw there had been a change. He was glad to see me, and he quickly invited me in and called to his wife to join us. He said, 'Brother Benson, we have done as you said. We've thought about it and we've prayed about it, and we've decided to accept the call. If you brethren have that much confidence in me, I'm willing to square my life with the standards of the Church, a thing I should have done long ago. . . .

"He was set apart as elders quorum president, and attendance in his quorum began going up—and it kept going up. He went out, put his arm around the less-active elders, and brought them up."

—Ezra Taft Benson, "Feed My Sheep," *Ensign*, Sept. 1987, 4–5.

"Oh, President Grant, That Can't Be!"

"The announcement [of Ezra's call to the Twelve] seemed unbelievable and overwhelming. . . . For several minutes [I] could only say, 'Oh, President [Heber J.] Grant, that can't be!' which I must have repeated several times before I was able to collect my [thoughts] enough to realize what had happened. . . . He held my hand for a long time as we both shed tears. . . .

"I felt so utterly weak and unworthy that his words of comfort and reassurance which followed were doubly appreciated. Among other things he stated, 'The Lord has a way of magnifying men who are called to positions of leadership.' When in my weakness I was able to state that I loved the Church he said, 'We know that, and the Lord wants men who will give everything for His work.'

"He told of the action taken in a special meeting of the First Presidency and the Twelve two weeks before and that the discussion regarding me had been enthusiastically unanimous."

—Ezra Taft Benson, in Dew, *Ezra Taft Benson*, 174–175.

"The Light of Faith in Their Eyes"

"I well remember our first meeting at Karlsruhe. After we had made visits through Belgium, Holland, and the Scandinavian countries, we went into occupied Germany. We finally found our way to the meeting place, a partially bombed-out building located in the interior of a block. The Saints had been in session for some two hours waiting for us, hoping that we would come because the word had reached them that we might be there for the conference. And then for the first time in my life I saw almost an entire audience in tears as we walked up onto the platform, and they realized that at last, after six or seven long years, representatives from Zion, as they put it, had finally come back to them. Then as the meeting closed, prolonged at their request, they insisted we go to the door and shake hands with each one of them as [they] left the bombed-out building. And we noted that many of them, after they had passed through the line went back and came through the second and third time, so happy were they to grasp our hands. As I looked into their upturned faces, pale, thin, many of these Saints dressed in rags, some of them barefooted, I could see the light of faith in their eyes as they bore testimony to the divinity of this great latter-day work, and expressed their gratitude for the blessings of the Lord.

"That is what a testimony does. We saw it in many countries. I say there is no greater faith, to my knowledge, anywhere in the Church than we found among those good people in Europe."

—Ezra Taft Benson, "The Faithfulness of the European Saints," in Conference Report, Apr. 1947, 154.

"Karl G. Maeser Stood Before Me"

"Soon after retiring I had this impressive dream: Karl G. Maeser stood before me. He was tall, dignified yet pleasing, dressed in a dark suit and white shirt, clean shaven with ruddy face and clear blue eyes. He said to me, 'Brother Benson, what are you doing to promote the sacred work in the temples for my people of Europe? They are a choice people who have played a major role in building up the Kingdom of God in these last days. The sacred ordinances must be performed for them in the temples in order to permit their progress in the spirit world. Will you please do all you can to help bring this about? They are a choice people of our Heavenly Father.' These were his words as nearly as I can recall them. He smiled kindly as he nodded goodbye without further words. The brief message impressed me deeply."

—Ezra Taft Benson, in Dew, *Ezra Taft Benson*, 381.

"I Realized the Fulfillment of a Dream"

"Shortly after President Spencer W. Kimball became President of the Church, he assigned me to go into the vault of the St. George Temple and check the early records. As I did so, I realized the fulfillment of a dream I had had ever since learning of the visit of the Founding Fathers to the St. George Temple. I saw with my own eyes the record of the work which was done for the Founding Fathers of this great nation, beginning with George Washington.

"Think of it: the Founding Fathers of this nation, those great men, appeared within those sacred walls and had their vicarious work done for them. . . .

"Unfortunately, we as a nation have apostatized in various degrees from different Constitutional principles as proclaimed by the inspired founders. We are fast approaching that moment prophesied by Joseph Smith when he said: 'Even this nation will be on the very verge of crumbling to pieces and tumbling to the ground, and when the Constitution is upon the brink of ruin, this people will be the staff upon which the nation shall lean, and they shall bear the Constitution away from the very verge of destruction.'"

—Ezra Taft Benson, "Our Divine Constitution," in Conference Report, Oct. 1987, 5–6.

"WE ARE RICHLY BLESSED"

"I have sometimes said to my wife, as I returned from visiting in the stakes, that I do not know exactly what heaven is going to be like, but I could ask nothing finer over there than to have the pleasure and joy of associating with the type of men and women I meet in the leadership of the stakes and wards of Zion and the missions of the earth. Truly we are richly blessed."

—Ezra Taft Benson, "Faith of the Latter-day Saints," in Conference Report, Oct. 1948, 98.

"I NEITHER DESIRED NOR INTENDED TO MAKE A CHANGE"

When U.S. President Dwight D. Eisenhower invited Ezra Taft Benson to serve as his secretary of agriculture. Ezra recalled:

"I didn't want the job. . . . Nobody in his right mind, I told myself, would seek to be Secretary of Agriculture in times like these. . . . I knew something of what the post entailed: the splintering cross fires, the intense pressures, the tangled problems. . . .

"Most of all, however, I was more than satisfied with the work I was already doing as one of the Council of the Twelve. . . . I neither desired nor intended to make a change. . . .

"Even though I felt I had already received from my Church what in my eyes was a greater honor than government could bestow, and

I told him [President Eisenhower] so, I accepted the responsibility of becoming Secretary of Agriculture to serve for not less than two years—if he wanted me that long."

—Ezra Taft Benson, *Cross Fire*, 3–4, 12.

"OUR GLORIOUS LOS ANGELES TEMPLE"

"At a party at the Beverly Hills Hilton Hotel in Los Angeles, I had been asked by the President of the United States to greet the president of one of our newer republics, the president of eighty-eight million people scattered on some 3,000 islands a thousand miles long, a nation that had been in existence only a few years. As we sat there at this dinner, which was sponsored in large measure by the motion picture industry and at which many movie stars were present, I could look out a beautiful bay window. Down the avenue, on the elevation, I could see the soft floodlights around our glorious Los Angeles Temple, and I had the joy of pointing it out to my guests and to friends at our table and other tables. I thought, as we sat there, 'Much of what goes on tonight is simply the froth of life. The things that endure, the things that are real, the things that are important are those things represented in the temple of God."

—Ezra Taft Benson, *God, Family, Country*, 85.

"THE LORD HAS SPOKEN, WE WILL DO OUR BEST"

Of becoming President of The Church of Jesus Christ of Latter-day Saints, Ezra Taft Benson said at a press conference:

"This is a day I have not anticipated. My wife, Flora, and I have prayed continually that President Kimball's days would be prolonged on this earth, and another miracle performed on his behalf. Now that the Lord has spoken, we will do our best, under His guiding direction, to move the work forward in the earth."

—Ezra Taft Benson, in Don L. Searle, "President Ezra Taft Benson Ordained Thirteenth President of the Church," *Ensign*, Dec. 1985, 5.

"Move the Book of Mormon Forward"

"I do not know fully why God has preserved my life to this age, but I do know this: That for the present hour He has revealed to me the absolute need for us to move the Book of Mormon forward now in a marvelous manner. You must help with this burden and with this blessing which He has placed on the whole Church, even all the children of Zion."

—Ezra Taft Benson, "Flooding the Earth with the Book of Mormon," *Ensign*, Nov. 1988, 6.

"I Have a Vision"

"I have a vision of homes alerted, of classes alive, and of pulpits aflame with the spirit of Book of Mormon messages.

"I have a vision of home teachers and visiting teachers, ward and branch officers, and stake and mission leaders counseling our people out of the most correct of any book on earth—the Book of Mormon.

"I have a vision of artists putting into film, drama, literature, music, and paintings great themes and great characters from the Book of Mormon.

"I have a vision of thousands of missionaries going into the mission field with hundreds of passages memorized from the Book of Mormon so that they might feed the needs of a spiritually famished world.

"I have a vision of the whole Church getting nearer to God by abiding by the precepts of the Book of Mormon.

"Indeed, I have a vision of flooding the earth with the Book of Mormon."

—Ezra Taft Benson, "Flooding the Earth with the Book of Mormon," *Ensign*, Nov. 1988, 4–6.

Howard W. Hunter

Born: November 14, 1907, Boise, Idaho
Died: March 3, 1995, Salt Lake City, Utah
President of the Church: June 5, 1994, to March 3, 1995

HOWARD W. HUNTER

HOWARD W. HUNTER, SON OF John William Hunter and Nellie Marie Rasmussen, was born November 14, 1907, in Boise, Idaho. Howard gained a testimony of the gospel of Jesus Christ in his childhood, but his father, a nonmember, asked him to wait to be baptized. Five months after his twelfth birthday, with his father's consent, Howard was baptized at an indoor swimming pool complex in Boise.

In his youth, Howard excelled in school, music, and Scouts, becoming the second teenager in Idaho to achieve the rank of Eagle Scout. After graduating from high school, he organized Hunter's Croonaders band and performed on weekends in Idaho and for two months aboard a cruise ship in the Pacific. With the hope of furthering his musical career, Howard moved to Southern California.

In California, Howard met Clara (Claire) May Jeffs. Howard and Claire were married on June 10, 1931, in the Salt Lake Temple. After their marriage, Howard decided to forgo his music career for a stable family life. He supported his family by working in the title department of the Los Angeles County Flood Control District. At night, he attended evening courses offered by the Southwestern University Law School. After five years of taking law courses, Howard graduated cum laude from the Southwestern University Law School and opened a law practice in Los Angeles.

Although Howard was busy with family and career responsibilities, he never turned down an opportunity to serve in the Church. He was a Scoutmaster, bishop, and high priest group leader before becoming president of the Pasadena Stake. On October 9, 1959, Howard was called to be an Apostle of the Lord Jesus Christ. He served in the Quorum of the Twelve Apostles for thirty-four years, including ten years as President. He became the fourteenth President of The Church of Jesus Christ of Latter-day Saints on June 5, 1994.

Howard's presidency lasted only a few months, the shortest tenure of any President in the history of the Church. Among the many hallmarks of his administration was a focus on Christlike living and temple worthiness. President Hunter encouraged Latter-day Saints to study the life of the Savior and follow the Savior's example of love, compassion, and forgiveness. He asked adult members to "hasten to the temple as frequently as time and means and personal circumstances allow. Let us go not only for our kindred dead, but let us also go for the personal blessing of temple worship."[75]

Like many prophets, President Hunter was no stranger to adversity and pain. Yet he acknowledged that the Lord has "repeatedly spared my life and restored my strength, has repeatedly brought me back from the edge of eternity, and has allowed me to continue in my mortal ministry for another season."[76]

After enduring the pain of cancer, his last words were "'thank you' to those about him; his spirit left his pain-racked body and stepped across that threshold into a better world" on March 3, 1995.[77]

The Life Story of Howard W. Hunter in His Own Words

"My Mother Had Taught Me to Pray"

"My mother had taught me to pray and to thank Heavenly Father for all the things that I enjoyed. I often thanked Him for the beauty of the earth and for the wonderful times that I had at the ranch and by the river and with the Scouts. I also learned to ask Him for the things that I wanted or needed."

—Howard W. Hunter, in Kellene Ricks, "Friend to Friend," *Friend*, Apr. 1990, 6.

"The Serious Burn Did Not Hinder"

After Howard W. Hunter scalded his hand in boiling water, his mother called ". . . the doctor and he recommended that my arm be packed in mashed potatoes and bandaged. Some of the neighbor ladies came in to help. I can remember sitting on the drain board in the kitchen while boiled potatoes were mashed and packed around my arm and cloths were torn into strips to make a bandage. Fortunately the serious burn did not hinder the growth of my arm, but I have carried the scar all my life."

—Howard W. Hunter, in Knowles, *Howard W. Hunter*, 18.

"I Heard a Cannon Go Off"

"I was dreaming away when I heard a cannon go of[f] twice. I woke up and was so scared I couldn't move. Then Mr. Harvey holer'd 'The wars over' [World War I]. Then all us kids got up and celebrated. John Henry had four battery. We hooked my motor up to them and was run[n]ing it when Mrs. Harvey came over and said there was going to be a parade up town. John and I went up [to the town center] on my wheel and watched the parade. Finaly we joined in. Their was t[w]o Chinaman in back of us that had about 100 boxes of fire crackers. Theyed shoot them of[f] under us. Then we went up to the Capatal and hear[d] some speaking. Then we came home. After dark we built a big fire and beat big tin cans and had a good time."

—Howard W. Hunter, in Knowles, *Howard W. Hunter*, 25.

"The Court of Honor Was Held"

"By the time the court of honor was held, I had qualified for fifteen merit badges and for the Life Scout and Star Scout awards. Only six more were required for the rank of Eagle Scout. The scouting magazine had carried stories of boys who had gained the rank of Eagle, but we were told there had not yet been one in Idaho. The race was on between Edwin Phipps of Troop 6 and me."

The *Idaho Statesman* on May 12, 1923, reported:

"Howard Hunter of troop 22, Boise council, Boy Scouts of America, having qualified for merit badges in 32 subjects, was honored Friday at the city hall by the court of honor of the Boise council, with the degree of 'eagle scout.' Hunter was given awards for athletics, civics, first aid to animals, camping, poultry keeping, physical development, pathfinding, horsemanship, marksmanship, cooking and painting. The honor attained by Scout Hunter is the highest in scouting, and he is the second Boise scout to reach this rank. The first eagle badge was awarded to Edwin Phipps some months ago."

—Howard W. Hunter, in Knowles, *Howard W. Hunter*, 40–41.

"It Would Be Better for Us to Get Married"

"I had not given up the hope of going on a mission and I had saved some money with that in mind. Claire [Jeffs, his girlfriend] offered to help support me and wait for me until I returned. Even though I appreciated the offer, I could not accept the proposal of having her work and support me. We finally decided that it would be better for us to get married and at a later time, as soon as conditions might permit, we would go on a mission together.

"One beautiful spring evening, we drove to Palos Verdes and parked on the cliffs where we could watch the waves roll in from the Pacific and break over the rocks in the light of a full moon. We talked about our plans and I put a diamond ring on her finger. We made many decisions that night and some strong resolutions regarding our lives. The moon was setting in the west and dawn was just commencing to break when we got home."

—Howard W. Hunter, in Knowles, *Howard W. Hunter*, 79–80.

"Tithing Would Come First"

"Because my father had not been a member of the Church during my years at home, tithing had never been discussed in our family and I had never considered its importance. As we talked, I realized that the bishop did not intend to give me a temple recommendation. In his kindly way he taught me the importance of the law and when I told him I would henceforth be a full tithe payer, he continued the interview and relieved my anxiety by filling out and signing a recommendation form. . . . [Claire and I] resolved that we would live this law throughout our marriage and tithing would come first."

—Howard W. Hunter, in Knowles, *Howard W. Hunter*, 81.

"The Pounding Surf Was a Lullaby"

The first home of Howard and Claire Hunter was an apartment at Hermosa Beach. Howard recalled:

"[W]e were up early. I put on my swimming trunks, ran across the beach, and dived into the breakers. After a vigorous swim and a warm shower, breakfast was ready. It took only fifteen minutes to drive to the bank in Hawthorne and I was ready for the day's work. We often went swimming together in the evening after I got home, and we usually walked down the beach under the stars before we went to bed. Even though the days were warm, the sea breeze made the evenings cool and comfortable, and the pounding surf was a lullaby."

—Howard W. Hunter, in Knowles, *Howard W. Hunter*, 83.

"I Had Always Thought of a Bishop as Being an Older Man"

"I had always thought of a bishop as being an older man and I asked how I could be the father of [the newly created El Serento Ward] at the young age of thirty-two. They said I would be the youngest bishop that had been called in Southern California to that time, but they knew I could be equal to the assignment. I expressed my appreciation for their confidence and told them I would do my best."

—Howard W. Hunter, in Knowles, *Howard W. Hunter*, 94.

"Because of My Calling as a Bishop"

"We knew there was a possibility that the United States would be drawn into the conflict [World War II]. In such an event the reserves would be the first to be called up. On the other hand all men might be called and there would be an advantage in having a commission. As the time approached we were more inclined to forfeit the commission, and my thirty-second birthday came and passed without the application being filed—so did my privilege of becoming a reserve officer. . . .

". . . There were black-out restrictions, economic changes, shortages, rationing, and other emergency measures. All men over the age of eighteen were required to register for the draft. Because of my calling as a bishop, I was given a 4D classification as a minister with a deferment from the draft until the conclusion of the war. If I had taken out the commission as a reserve officer, which I almost did, I would have been called into service immediately."

—Howard W. Hunter, in Knowles, *Howard W. Hunter*, 96–97.

"Conducting My First Stake Conference"

"I was nervous and fearful about conducting my first stake conference. Claire, too, was nervous. We had never before had a General Authority in our home, and she was anxious to have everything just right. Brother [Marion G.] Romney came by train, and I went to [the] East Los Angeles Station to meet him. As soon as we were in the car and commenced to talk, he made me feel at ease with his kindly manner. . . . I felt I had found a friend with understanding."

—Howard W. Hunter, in Knowles, *Howard W. Hunter*, 124.

"I Was Impressed by the Great Change"

"I recall a young man in our stake when I served as a stake president. He traveled around with a crowd which thought it was smart to do things that were not right. On a few occasions he was caught in some minor violations. One day I got a call from the police station and was told he was being held because of a traffic violation. He had been caught speeding, as he had on a few other occasions prior to this time. Knowing the things he was doing might prevent him from going on a mission, he straightened up, and when he was 19 years of age he received his call.

"I shall never forget the talk we had when he returned. He told me that while he was in the mission field he had often thought of the trouble he had caused by the mistaken belief that the violation of little things was not important. But a great change had come into his life. He had come to the realization that there was no happiness or pleasure in violation of the law, whether it be God's law or whether it be the laws which society imposes upon us.

"He said to me, 'When I drive a car now and the speed limit is 55 miles an hour, I feel it is morally wrong to drive a single mile faster.'

"I was impressed by the great change that had come over this young man while he served on his mission and studied moral principles. How unfortunate it is that he had to learn his lesson the hard way, but what a great blessing comes when there is the realization that one cannot be in violation and feel good about that conduct."

—Howard W. Hunter, "Basic Concepts of Honesty," *New Era*, Feb. 1978, 4–5.

"PRAY FOR HIM EVERY MORNING AND EVERY NIGHT"

"I was interested in the story told today about the one who prayed and prayed for another and eventually a good feeling and a good spirit came. As it was told, I thought about an occasion when I was a bishop. One of the brethren in the ward came to me with bitterness in his soul toward another man. I said to him, 'My brother, if you will go home and pray for him every morning and every night, I'll meet you two weeks from today at this same time and then we will decide what should be done.' You already know his conclusion when he came back in two weeks. He said, 'He needs some help.' I said, 'Are you willing to help him?' His answer was, 'Yes, of course.' All the venom was gone and all the bitterness was gone. This is the way it is when we pray for one another."

—Howard W. Hunter, Williams, *Teachings of Howard W. Hunter*, 39–40.

"I HAVE NEVER BEEN ON A GLOOMY WELFARE PROJECT"

"I have never been on a gloomy welfare project. I have climbed trees and picked lemons, peeled fruit, tended a boiler, carried boxes, unloaded trucks, cleaned the cannery, and a thousand and one other things, but the things I remember most are the laughing and the singing and the good fellowship of people engaged in the service of the Lord."

—Howard W. Hunter, "Welfare and the Relief Society," *Relief Society Magazine*, Apr. 1962, 238, in Williams, *Teachings of Howard W. Hunter*, 159.

"This Was a Birthday I Have Never Forgotten"

"While I was speaking to the congregation [in the chapel of the Mesa Arizona Temple], my father and mother came into the chapel dressed in white. I had no idea my father was prepared for his temple blessings, although Mother had been anxious about it for some time. I was so overcome with emotion that I was unable to continue to speak. President Pierce came to my side and explained the reason for the interruption. When my father and mother came to the temple that morning they asked the president not to mention to me that they were there because they wanted it to be a birthday surprise. This was a birthday I have never forgotten because on that day they were endowed and I had the privilege of witnessing their sealing, following which I was sealed to them."

—Howard W. Hunter, in Knowles, *Howard W. Hunter*, 135.

"You Are Called to Be One of His Special Witnesses"

"President McKay greeted me with a pleasant smile and a warm handshake and then said to me, 'Sit down, President Hunter, I want to talk with you. The Lord has spoken. You are called to be one of his special witnesses, and tomorrow you will be sustained as a member of the Council of the Twelve.'

"I cannot attempt to explain the feeling that came over me. Tears came to my eyes and I could not speak. I have never felt so completely humbled as when I sat in the presence of this great, sweet, kindly man—the prophet of the Lord. He told me what a great joy this would bring into my life, the wonderful association with the brethren, and that hereafter my life and time would be devoted as a servant of the Lord and that I would hereafter belong to the Church and the whole world. He said other things to me but I was so overcome I can't remember the details, but I do remember he put his arms around me and assured me that the Lord would love me and I would have the sustaining confidence of the First Presidency and the Council of the Twelve.

"The interview lasted only a few minutes, and as I left I told him I loved the Church, that I sustained him and the other members of the First Presidency and the Council of the Twelve, and I would gladly give my time, my life, and all that I possessed to this service. He told me I could call Sister Hunter and tell her. . . . I went back to the Hotel Utah and called Claire in Provo, but when she answered the phone I could hardly talk."

—Howard W. Hunter, in Knowles, *Howard W. Hunter*, 144–145.

"I Accept, Without Reservation, the Call"

"I do not apologize for the tears that come to my eyes on this occasion [first time Howard spoke in the Tabernacle] because I believe that I face friends, my brethren and sisters in the Church, whose hearts beat the same as mine today in the thrill of the gospel and in service to others. President McKay, I want you to know, and all of the membership of the Church to know, that I accept, without reservation, the call which you have made of me, and I am willing to devote my life and all that I have in this service. Sister Hunter joins me in this pledge."

—Howard W. Hunter, in Knowles, *Howard W. Hunter*, 146–147.

"My Practice of Law Was Now at an End"

"Today [July 2, 1960] I finished most of my work at the office. Nearly all of the pending matters are completed. I was alone in the office today with the realization that my practice of law was now at an end. I made notes on a number of files and left them on the desk for Gordon [Lund]. I had a sick feeling as I left the office. I have enjoyed the practice of law and it has been my life for the last number of years, but in spite of this I am pleased and happy to respond to the great call which has come to me in the Church."

—Howard W. Hunter, in Knowles, *Howard W. Hunter*, 153.

"A Resolution to Try Harder"

"Sitting with this group of my brethren makes me feel my inadequacies, but always brings a resolution to try harder. Times like these make me feel my own insignificance and unworthiness to be allowed such privileges and blessings. These meetings are highlights in my life and always leave me with the question as to why I was selected and why I am privileged to sit in this council. I left the temple today, as I have on previous occasions, feeling my inadequacies and wondering why I was selected for this association. I always resolve to attempt to do better and strive to be the example of what is expected."

—Howard W. Hunter, in Knowles, *Howard W. Hunter*, 226–227.

"Now It Is Too Late"

"I was in the mission home in San Francisco when the mission president received a telephone call and said, 'I must cross the bay and take a message to an elder that his father has just passed away.' I went with him. We crossed over the Bay Bridge, up to Berkeley, and stopped at an apartment building. A fine-looking elder came to the door. He was excited to see his mission president and said, 'Oh, president, come in; we want to tell you what happened this morning.' The president said, 'Elder, sit down with us for a moment; we have a sad message to deliver to you.'

"I will never forget that occasion as the young man's head fell into his arms and he commenced to sob. After we had comforted him he said, 'My father was the greatest man I have ever known. I have never told him that. I don't believe I realized it in my years of growing up, but since I have come into the mission field a maturity has come to me to make me appreciate my father and my mother. I decided last week I was going to sit down and write my father a letter and tell him how much I loved him and how much he has meant to me, but now it is too late.'"

—Howard W. Hunter, in Williams, *Teachings of Howard W. Hunter*, 94.

"Things Have Been Worse and They Will Always Get Better"

"In my lifetime I have seen two world wars plus Korea plus Vietnam and all that you are currently witnessing. I have worked my way through the depression and managed to go to law school while starting a young family at the same time. I have seen stock markets and world economics go crazy and have seen a few despots and tyrants go crazy, all of which causes quite a bit of trouble around the world in the process.

"So I am frank to say tonight that I hope you won't believe all the world's difficulties have been wedged into your decade or that things have never been worse than they are for you personally, or that they will never get better. I reassure you that things have been worse and they will always get better. They always do—especially when we live and love the gospel of Jesus Christ and give it a chance in our lives."

—Howard W. Hunter, in "An Anchor to the Souls of Men," CES Fireside for Young Adults, Feb. 7, 1993, in Williams, *Teachings of Howard W. Hunter*, 202.

"Children Love Primary"

"As I travel about in the stakes and the missions and review their reports and the statistics, I am always pleased to note that the percentage of attendance at Primary is higher than any of the other organizations in the Church. Children love Primary. Teachers love to teach children. This is a choice organization, and our calls to serve are great blessings to us."

—Howard W. Hunter, in Williams, *Teachings of Howard W. Hunter*, 206.

"It Is Simple If We Have a Little Faith"

"As I travel about the Church and see the results of the payment of tithes, I come to the conclusion that it is not a burden, but a great blessing. Like all of the Lord's commandments and laws, it is simple if we have a little faith. The Lord said in effect, 'Take out the decimal point and move it over one place.' That is the law of tithing. It's just that simple."

—Howard W. Hunter, in Williams, *Teachings of Howard W. Hunter*, 105.

"I've Felt to Pour Out My Soul in Thanksgiving"

"I have stood in the Garden of Gethsemane on many occasions. I've contemplated in my mind the suffering, the agony of the Savior. That agony that was experienced when our Heavenly Father permitted him, in a way our minds cannot even comprehend, to take upon himself the pain and sins of all mankind. My soul was filled with sorrow as I've thought of his great sacrifice for mankind.

"I've stood beneath Golgotha, the place of the skull, and contemplated the humiliation of the crucifixion which led to our Savior's mortal death, but which brought to pass his and all mankind's immortality. And again my soul has been subdued.

"And I've stood in front of the garden tomb and imagined that glorious day of resurrection when the Savior emerged from the tomb alive, resurrected, immortal. In that contemplation my heart has swelled with joy.

"Through these experiences I've felt to pour out my soul in thanksgiving and appreciation to our Heavenly Father for the love which he and his Son have given to us through the glorious atoning sacrifice."

—Howard W. Hunter, in "The Atonement of Jesus Christ," address given at mission presidents' seminar, June 24, 1988, 2–3, 7, Church History Library, Salt Lake City; Williams, *Teachings of Howard W. Hunter*, 8–9.

"We Must Not Walk on Our Lower Lip"

"I am here tonight to tell you that despair, doom, and discouragement are not an acceptable view of life for a Latter-day Saint. However high on the charts they are on the hit parade of contemporary news, we must not walk on our lower lip every time a few difficult moments happen to confront us.

"I am just a couple of years older than most of you [university students], and in those few extra months I have seen a bit more of life than you have. I want you to know that there have always been some difficulties in mortal life and there always will be. But knowing what we know, and living as we are supposed to live, there really is no place, no excuse, for pessimism and despair."

—Howard W. Hunter, "An Anchor to the Souls of Men," *Speeches of the Year*, Feb. 7, 1993; see also Williams, *Teachings of Howard W. Hunter*, 199.

"I Lost My Balance and Fell Backwards"

"I got along well today until about the middle of my talk [in the Salt Lake Tabernacle on April 1, 1988] when I lost my balance and fell backwards into an arrangement of flowers and landed on my back on the podium of the [choir] conductor. President Monson, Boyd Packer, and Dale Springer [a Church security guard] quickly lifted me up on my feet and I continued my talk."

—Howard W. Hunter, in Knowles, *Howard W. Hunter*, 285.

"Forgive Me if I Remain Seated"

"I had great apprehension about being able to fill the assignment [speak in the Salt Lake Tabernacle], but my brethren encouraged me to try. Boyd Packer and Russell Ballard had made arrangements to have casters put on my tabernacle chair and to have a shelf-like pulpit built which was hinged on the top and attached to the rail of the stand near the pulpit so it could be lifted up when used and then lowered. I was the second speaker in the first session. Brother Packer and Brother Ballard pushed me up to the rail and raised the hinged pulpit so I could speak seated in the wheelchair. I spoke on the subject of 'The Opening and Closing of Doors,' the effect of adversity in our lives. The fear I had seemed to leave me and I felt I had overcome my disability."

Howard W. Hunter began his address by saying:

"Forgive me if I remain seated while I present these few remarks. It is not by choice that I speak from a wheelchair. I notice that the rest of you seem to enjoy the conference sitting down, so I will follow your example."

—From the journal of Howard W. Hunter, in Knowles, *Howard W. Hunter*, 280–281.

"One of the Greatest Events in All History"

"My testimony of its divinity hinges upon the simple story of the lad under the trees kneeling and receiving heavenly visitors. If it is not true, Mormonism falls. If it is true—and I bear witness that it is—it is one of the greatest events in all history."

—"Joseph Smith the Seer," Joseph Smith memorial service address, Dec. 15, 1960, Logan, Utah, in Williams, *Teachings of Howard W. Hunter*, 189.

Gordon B. Hinckley

Born: June 23, 1910, Salt Lake City, Utah
Died: January 27, 2008, Salt Lake City, Utah
President of the Church: March 12, 1995, to January 27, 2008

GORDON B. HINCKLEY

GORDON BITNER HINCKLEY, SON OF Bryant S. Hinckley and Ada Bitner, was born June 23, 1910, in Salt Lake City. Gordon descended from a long line of faithful progenitors such as his father, Bryant Hinckley, who presided over a stake in Salt Lake City, served on the YMMIA General Board, and as president of the Northern States Mission.

As a child Gordon suffered from allergies, asthma, hay fever, and whooping cough aggravated by the number of coal-burning stoves in Salt Lake City. Although he described himself as "a shy and bashful boy—freckle-faced and awkward," Gordon was destined for greatness.[78] In his youth, he attended public schools and the University of Utah. On a mission to Great Britain, he wrote to his father about being discouraged. Instead of sympathizing with him, his father penned, "Forget yourself and go to work."[79] This wise counsel set the stage for the rest of Gordon's life.

On April 29, 1937, Gordon married Marjorie Pay in the Salt Lake Temple. Theirs was an exemplary sixty-seven-year marriage of love, loyalty, and good humor. To support his family, Gordon was employed as the executive secretary of the Church Radio, Publicity, and Literature Committee. He was serving as president of the Salt Lake East Millcreek Stake when President David O. McKay called him to be an Assistant to the Quorum of the Twelve Apostles. At the October 1961 general conference, Gordon was sustained as a member of the Twelve. From 1981 to 1995, he served in the First Presidency as a counselor to Spencer W. Kimball, Ezra Taft Benson, and Howard W. Hunter.

On March 12, 1995, Gordon B. Hinckley was sustained as the fifteenth President of The Church of Jesus Christ of Latter-day Saints. As President, he exhibited an inexhaustible desire for work, a quick wit, a keen mind, and an uncompromising testimony of restored truths.[80] He encouraged members to reach out to neighbors and those who had strayed from the faith. He traveled the world and spoke to Latter-day Saints in more than sixty countries. Through television interviews and national press publications, such as *60 Minutes* and *Larry King Live*, and hundreds of newspaper and magazine articles, President Hinckley increased media attention and improved the public image of the Church. He addressed the National Press Club in Washington, D.C., the Religion News Writers Association, the U.S. Conference of Mayors, and twice the Los Angeles World Affairs Council.

Some of the notable hallmarks of his administration were the construction of the Conference Center in Salt Lake City, the release of "The Family: A Proclamation to the World," the Perpetual Education Fund, and the expansion of Quorums of the Seventy. In addition, President Hinckley wrote and edited several manuals, pamphlets, scripts, and books, including bestselling *Standing for Something.* Wanting to extend temple blessings to members worldwide, President Hinckley began the most extensive temple-building program in the history of the Church.

On January 27, 2008, President Hinckley died at age ninety-seven in Salt Lake City.

The Life Story of Gordon B. Hinckley in His Own Words

"I Was about Five Years of Age"

"The earliest instance of which I have recollection of spiritual feelings was when I was about five years of age, a very small boy. I was crying from the pain of an earache. There were no wonder drugs at the time. That was 85 years ago. My mother prepared a bag of table salt and put it on the stove to warm. My father softly put his hands upon my head and gave me a blessing, rebuking the pain and the illness by authority of the holy priesthood and in the name of Jesus Christ. He then took me tenderly in his arms and placed the bag of warm salt at my ear. The pain subsided and left. I fell asleep in my father's secure embrace. As I was falling asleep, the words of his administration floated through my mind. That is the earliest remembrance I have of the exercise of the authority of the priesthood in the name of the Lord."

—Gordon B. Hinckley, "My Testimony," *Ensign*, May 2000, 70.

"Lingering Peace and Security in Communing with the Heavens"

"My brother and I slept in an unheated bedroom in the winter. People thought that was good for you. Before falling into a warm bed, we knelt to say our prayers. There were expressions of simple gratitude. They concluded in the name of Jesus. The distinctive title of Christ was not used very much when we prayed in those days.

"I recall jumping into my bed after I had said amen, pulling the covers up around my neck, and thinking of what I had just done in speaking to my Father in Heaven in the name of His Son. I did not have great knowledge of the gospel. But there was some kind of lingering peace and security in communing with the heavens in and through the Lord Jesus."

—Gordon B. Hinckley, "My Testimony," *Ensign*, May 2000, 70.

"A Great Surge of Love for and Belief in the Mighty Prophet"

"When at the age of twelve I was ordained a deacon, my father, who was president of our stake, took me to my first stake priesthood meeting. In those days these meetings were held on a week night. I recall that we went to the Tenth Ward building in Salt Lake City, Utah. He walked up to the stand, and I sat on the back row, feeling a little alone and uncomfortable in that hall filled with strong men who had been ordained to the priesthood of God. The meeting was called to order, the opening song was announced, and—as was then the custom—we all stood to sing. There were perhaps as many as four hundred there. Together these men lifted their strong voices, some with the accents of the European lands from which they had come as converts, all singing these words with a great spirit of conviction and testimony:

"'Praise to the man who communed with Jehovah!

Jesus anointed that Prophet and Seer.

Blessed to open the last dispensation,

Kings shall extol him, and nations revere.' (*Hymns*, no. 147)

"They were singing of the Prophet Joseph Smith, and as they did so there came into my heart a great surge of love for and belief in the mighty Prophet of this dispensation. In my childhood I had been taught much of him in meetings and classes in our ward as well as in our home; but my experience in that stake priesthood meeting was different. I knew then, by the power of the Holy Ghost, that Joseph Smith was indeed a prophet of God."

—Gordon B. Hinckley, "Praise to the Man," *Ensign*, Aug. 1983, 2.

"The Most Stinging Rebuke She Ever Gave Me"

"We enrolled in junior high school. But the building could not accommodate all the students, so our class of the seventh grade was sent back to the Hamilton School. We were insulted. We were furious. We'd spent six unhappy years in that building, and we felt we deserved something better. The boys of the class all met after school. We decided we wouldn't tolerate this kind of treatment. We were determined we'd go on strike.

"The next day we did not show up. But we had no place to go. We couldn't stay home, because our mothers would ask questions. We didn't think of going downtown to a show. We had no money for that. We didn't think of going to the park. We were afraid we might be seen by Mr. Clayton, the truant officer. We didn't think of going out behind the school fence and telling shady stories because we didn't know any. We'd never heard of such things as drugs or anything of the kind. We just wandered about and wasted the day.

"The next morning, the principal, Mr. Stearns, was at the front door of the school to greet us. His demeanor matched his name. He said some pretty straightforward things and then told us that we could not come back to school until we brought a note from our parents. That was my first experience with a lockout. Striking, he said, was not the way to settle a problem. We were expected to be responsible citizens, and if we had a complaint, we could come to the principal's office and discuss it.

"There was only one thing to do, and that was to go home and get the note.

"I remember walking sheepishly into the house. My mother asked what was wrong. I told her. I said that I needed a note. She wrote a note. It was very brief. It was the most stinging rebuke she ever gave me. It reads as follows:

"'Dear Mr. Stearns, Please excuse Gordon's absence yesterday. His action was simply an impulse to follow the crowd.'

"She signed it and handed it to me.

"I walked back over to school and got there about the same time a few other boys did. We all handed our notes to Mr. Stearns. I do not know whether he read them, but I have never forgotten my mother's note. Though I had been an active party to the action we had taken, I resolved then and there that I would never do anything on the basis of simply following the crowd."

—Gordon B. Hinckley, "Some Lessons I Learned as a Boy," *Ensign*, May 1993, 53.

"FORGET YOURSELF AND GO TO WORK"

"I was not well when I arrived [in England on a mission]. Those first few weeks, because of illness and the opposition which we felt, I was discouraged. I wrote a letter home to my good father and said that I felt I was wasting my time and his money. He was my father and my stake president, and he was a wise and inspired man. He wrote a very short letter to me which said, 'Dear Gordon, I have your recent letter. I have only one suggestion: forget yourself and go to work.' Earlier that morning in our scripture class my companion and I had read these words of the Lord: 'Whosoever will save his life shall lose it; but whosoever shall lose his life for my sake and the gospel's, the same shall save it.' (Mark 8:35.)

"Those words of the Master, followed by my father's letter with his counsel to forget myself and go to work, went into my very being. With my father's letter in hand, I went into our bedroom in the house at 15 Wadham Road, where we lived, and got on my knees and made a pledge with the Lord, I covenanted that I would try to forget myself and lose myself in His service.

"That July day in 1933 was my day of decision. A new light came into my life and a new joy into my heart. The fog of England seemed to lift, and I saw the sunlight. I had a rich and wonderful mission experience, for which I shall ever be grateful."

—Gordon B. Hinckley, "Taking the Gospel to Britain: A Declaration of Vision, Faith, Courage, and Truth," *Ensign*, July 1987, 7.

"In a Most Unlikely Place, Began a Career"

Elder Boyd K. Packer wrote of Gordon B. Hinckley:

"[Gordon B. Hinckley] returned with an assignment from his mission president to report to the First Presidency a condition that could not adequately be conveyed in writing. He was to spend just a few minutes with President Heber J. Grant and his counselors. He was there for the duration of the meeting. As it turned out in the months ahead, that report was a job interview as well.

"A new committee of the Twelve was organized to bring to missionary work the power of the latest means of communication. Brother Hinckley was to serve as producer and secretary for the Church Radio, Publicity, and Mission Literature Committee. This was, in fact, the beginning of the Public Communications Office in the Church. . . . The committee included six members of the Twelve with Elder Stephen L. Richards as chairman.

"There was an empty office available, but no furniture at the moment. He went downstairs to the main office to ask for a ream of paper. 'A whole ream?' What did he intend to do, write a book? Did he know how many pages were in a ream? He did.

"Being resourceful, he went to a former missionary companion whose father dealt in office furniture and came away with a rickety reject table. One leg was short; that could be fixed with a block of wood. The top was warped and split a little; that could be ignored. He brought his typewriter from home and, in a most unlikely place, began a career that would take him to the ordination of an Apostle and to the First Presidency of the Church."

—Boyd K. Packer, "President Gordon B. Hinckley: First Counselor," *Ensign*, Feb. 1986, 5.

"I've Only Got $150 to My Name"

Marjorie Peay, wife of Gordon B. Hinckley, recalled:

"I remember [Gordon] calling me one day before we were married and saying, 'We have got to call this off. I've only got $150 to my name.' And I said, 'I get a husband plus $150. We are in good shape!'"

—"A husband plus $150: 'We Are in Good Shape!'" *Church News*, June 24, 2000.

"Moved a Small Piece of Steel Three Inches"

"Many years ago I worked for a railroad in the central offices in Denver. I was in charge of what is called head-end traffic. That was in the days when nearly everyone rode passenger trains. One morning I received a call from my counterpart in Newark, New Jersey. He said, 'Train number such-and-such has arrived, but it has no baggage car. Somewhere, 300 passengers have lost their baggage, and they are mad.'

"I went immediately to work to find out where it may have gone. I found it had been properly loaded and properly trained in Oakland, California. It had been moved to our railroad in Salt Lake City, been carried to Denver, down to Pueblo, put on another line, and moved to St. Louis. There it was to be handled by another railroad which would take it to Newark, New Jersey. But some thoughtless switchman in the St. Louis yards moved a small piece of steel just three inches, a switch point, then pulled the lever to uncouple the car. We discovered that a baggage car that belonged in Newark, New Jersey, was in fact in New Orleans, Louisiana—1,500 miles from its destination. Just the three-inch movement of the switch in the St. Louis yard by a careless employee had started it on the wrong track, and the distance from its true destination increased dramatically. That is the way it is with our lives. Instead of following a steady course, we are pulled by some mistaken idea in another direction. The movement away from our original destination may be ever so small, but, if continued, that very small movement becomes a great gap and we find ourselves far from where we intended to go."

—Gordon B. Hinckley, "A Prophet's Counsel and Prayer for Youth," *Ensign*, Jan. 2001, 5–7.

"He Decided to Stay at His Post with the Church"

Elder Wendell J. Ashton wrote of Gordon B. Hinckley:

"During World War II, there came an event which could have drastically altered the course of [Gordon B. Hinckley's] life. Shortly after the attack on Pearl Harbor plunged America into war late in 1941, he applied at the United States Navy recruiting office for officer training, but he was rejected because of a history of allergies. So to assist otherwise with the war effort he went to work with the Denver & Rio Grande Western Railroad Company, and as a stationmaster, he called the trains.

"The railroad company promoted him to assistant manager of mail, baggage, and express for the entire system. This took him and his family to Denver. With the end of the war, Elder Stephen L Richards asked him to return to the Church office. Railroad officials asked him to take a ninety-day leave and return if he wished. About a year later, Elder Hinckley received a call from Denver. He decided to stay at his post with the Church. 'This is the Lord's work,' he told a friend. 'I felt I would make my best contribution in life by continuing to do my humble part to further the cause.'"

—Wendell J. Ashton, "Gordon B. Hinckley of the Council of the Twelve," *Improvement Era*, Dec. 1961, 978.

"We Had to Come to the Land of Miracles"

"On that trip [to the Holy Land in September 1972] President [Harold B.] Lee became quite ill. Late one evening Sister Lee rang our room and asked if I would give her husband a blessing. President Edwin Q. Cannon of the Swiss Mission was traveling with us on this assignment, so I asked him to join me in administering to the President. We did so, and then, with a good deal of concern about President Lee's health, I went to bed.

"Later in the night President Lee began to cough. It was a deep, terrible cough, and it went on for some time. Situated as we were in adjoining hotel rooms, I could hear him. He coughed and coughed and coughed. Finally all of that stopped and I went off to sleep, grateful he had been given some relief.

"Brother Lee said nothing at all of the matter the next day, but on the following day he said to me, 'We had to come to the land of miracles to witness a miracle within ourselves!' He then told me how in the most violent of the coughing, he had coughed up a very large clot of blood. Just a little more than one year later, he died from what was spoken of as a pleural embolism."

—Gordon B. Hinckley, in Jeffrey R. Holland, "President Gordon B. Hinckley: Stalwart and Brave He Stands," *Ensign*, June 1995, 12.

"Reverence and Respect for the House of the Lord"

President Thomas S. Monson said of Gordon B. Hinckley:

"Each Thursday morning the members of the First Presidency and the Quorum of the Twelve Apostles have a meeting in the temple. We are driven in carts underground from the Church office parking lot to the temple. During the cold winter months, President Hinckley always wore a coat and a hat during the brief ride. As our cart passed under Main Street, President Hinckley knew that we were then within the confines of the temple rather than under the street and, without a word, would remove his hat and place it on his lap. He seemed to know instinctively when that moment arrived. It was such a simple yet profound expression of reverence and respect for the house of the Lord, and it made a deep impression on me."

—Thomas S. Monson, "God be with You Till We Meet Again," *Ensign*, Mar. 2008, 30.

"Be Still and Know That I Am God"

"When I accepted President Kimball's call to join [the First Presidency in 1981], I did not know exactly how I would function or fit in, and perhaps they did not at the time. But the circumstances called for additional help, and I was more than willing to give it. I did not know whether it would be for a few days or a few months. . . .

"That was a very heavy and overwhelming responsibility. It was an almost terrifying load at times. Of course, I consulted with our brethren of the Twelve.

"I recall on one particular occasion getting on my knees before the Lord and asking for help in the midst of that very difficult situation. And there came into my mind those reassuring words, 'Be still and know that I am God' (D&C 101:16). I knew again that this was His work, that He would not let it fail, that all I had to do was work at it and do my very best, and that the work would move forward without . . . hindrance of any kind."

—Gordon B. Hinckley, in Jeffrey R. Holland, "President Gordon B. Hinckley: Stalwart and Brave He Stands," *Ensign*, June 1995, 12.

"The Painting Grew in Beauty and Value"

"There came to my office a man from Las Vegas, Nevada. His wife and married daughter were with him. When we had accomplished the purpose of his visit, the younger woman asked if I would accept something from her thirteen-year-old daughter. She unwrapped a painting of two butterflies around a flowering shrub.

"The mother explained that her daughter had been struck by a car in a terrible accident when she was four years of age. Her body was badly broken. She was left paralyzed from the shoulders down, a quadriplegic without the use of arms or legs. She had painted this picture holding a brush between her teeth and moving her head.

"As I listened to that story, the painting grew in beauty and value before my eyes. It became more than a portrayal of butterflies. It represented remarkable courage in the face of blinding adversity; tenacious practice in holding and moving the brush; pleading prayers for help; faith—the faith of a child, nurtured by loving parents, that she could create beauty notwithstanding her handicap.

"Some might say that this is not a masterpiece. Without knowledge of its origin, that could be the judgment. But what is the test of art? Is it not the inspiration which comes from looking at it? I will hang this small painting in my study so that during occasional hours of struggle there will come into my mind the picture of a beautiful little girl, robbed of the use of her feet and hands, gripping the handle of a paintbrush in her teeth to create a thing of beauty. Thank you, Krystal, for what you have done for me."

—Gordon B. Hinckley, "Bring Up a Child in the Way He Should Go," in Conference Report, Oct. 1993, 54.

"I Paid Little Attention to It as the Years Passed"

"The first of many trees that I planted was a thornless honey locust. Envisioning the day when its filtered shade would assist in cooling the house in the summertime, I put it in a place at the corner where the wind from the canyon to the east blew the hardest. I dug a hole, put in the bare root, put soil around it, poured on water, and largely forgot it. It was only a wisp of a tree, perhaps three-quarters of an inch in diameter. It was so supple that I could bend it with ease in any direction. I paid little attention to it as the years passed.

"Then one winter day, when the tree was barren of leaves, I chanced to look out the window at it. I noticed that it was leaning to the west, misshapen and out of balance. I could scarcely believe it. I went out and braced myself against it as if to push it upright. But the trunk was now nearly a foot in diameter. My strength was as nothing against it. I took from my toolshed a block and tackle. Attaching one end to the tree and another to a well-set post, I pulled the rope. The pulleys moved a little, and the trunk of the tree trembled slightly. But that was all. It seemed to say, 'You can't straighten me. It's too late. I've grown this way because of your neglect, and I will not bend.'

"Finally in desperation I took my saw and cut off the great heavy branch on the west side. The saw left an ugly scar, more than eight inches across. I stepped back and surveyed what I had done. I had cut off the major part of the tree, leaving only one branch growing skyward. More than half a century has passed since I planted that tree. My daughter and her family live there now. The other day I looked again at the tree. It is large. Its shape is better. It is a great asset to the home. But how serious was the trauma of its youth and how brutal the treatment I used to straighten it.

"When it was first planted, a piece of string would have held it in place against the forces of the wind. I could have and should have supplied that string with ever so little effort. But I did not, and it bent to the forces that came against it.

"I have seen a similar thing, many times, in children whose lives I have observed. The parents who brought them into the world seem almost to have abdicated their responsibility. The results have been tragic. A few simple anchors would have given them the strength to withstand the forces that have shaped their lives. Now it appears it is too late."

—Gordon B. Hinckley, "Bring Up a Child in the Way He Should Go," in Conference Report, Oct. 1993, 59.

"The Concept of These Smaller Temples"

"As we were riding to El Paso [after attending the centennial observance of the Juarez Academy in Colonia Juarez, Mexico, in June 1997], I reflected on what we could do to help these people in the Church colonies in Mexico. . . . They've been so very faithful over the years. They've kept the faith. They've gone on missions in large numbers. These stakes have produced very many mission presidents who served faithfully and well. They've been the very epitome of faithfulness.

"And yet, they've had to travel all the way to Mesa, Ariz. to go to a temple. . . .

"I thought of these things and what could be done. The concept of these smaller temples came into my mind. . . .

"[On the airplane,] I took a piece of paper and sketched out the floor plan, and turned it over to the architects to refine it.

"The concept is beautiful."

—Gordon B. Hinckley, in "Reflecting on a Need Led to New Concept," *Church News*, June 24, 2000.

"THE GIRL OF MY DREAMS"

"My brethren and sisters, at the outset, if you will bear with me, I wish to exercise a personal privilege. Six months ago, at the close of our conference, I stated that my beloved companion of 67 years was seriously ill. She passed away two days later. It was April 6, a significant day to all of us in this Church. I wish to thank publicly the dedicated doctors and wonderful nurses who attended her during her final illness.

"My children and I were at her bedside as she slipped peacefully into eternity. As I held her hand and saw mortal life drain from her fingers, I confess I was overcome. Before I married her, she had been the girl of my dreams, to use the words of a song then popular. She was my dear companion for more than two-thirds of a century, my equal before the Lord, really my superior. And now in my old age, she has again become the girl of my dreams."

—Gordon B. Hinckley, "The Women in Our Lives," in Conference Report, Oct. 2004, 82.

"HE PUT ON HIS SHOES AND WENT BACK TO WORK"

Virginia H. Pierce said of her father, Gordon B. Hinckley:
"Following the death of Mother, his grief was almost overwhelming. Characteristically, he acknowledged it—felt it, wept, and mourned deeply. He went to the Lord with his tears, thus allowing the loss to carve out an even deeper place in his heart for compassion and dig an even deeper well of faith and trust in God. Then, with that increase in compassion and faith, he put on his shoes and went back to work—in every sense of the word."

—Virginia H. Pearce, "A Daughter's Tribute," *Ensign*, Mar. 2008, 18.

"A SMALL TOUCH OF MINE IN THIS GREAT HALL"

"I love trees. When I was a boy we lived on a farm in the summer, a fruit farm. Every year at this season we planted trees. I think I have never missed a spring since I was married, except for two or three years when we were absent from the city, that I have not planted trees, at least one or two—fruit trees, shade trees, ornamental trees, and spruce, fir, and pine among the conifers. I love trees.

"Well, some 36 years ago I planted a black walnut. It was in a crowded area where it grew straight and tall to get the sunlight. A year ago, for some reason it died. But walnut is a precious furniture wood. I called Brother Ben Banks of the Seventy, who, before giving his full time to the Church, was in the business of hardwood lumber. He brought his two sons, one a bishop and the other recently released as a bishop and who now run the business, to look at the tree. From all they could tell it was solid, good, and beautiful wood. One of them suggested that it would make a pulpit for this hall. The idea excited me. The tree was cut down and then cut into two heavy logs. Then followed the long process of drying, first naturally and then kiln drying. The logs were cut into boards at a sawmill in Salem, Utah. The boards were then taken to Fetzer's woodworking plant, where expert craftsmen designed and built this magnificent pulpit with that wood. The end product is beautiful. I wish all of you could examine it closely. It represents superb workmanship, and here I am speaking to you from the tree I grew in my backyard, where my children played and also grew.

"It is an emotional thing for me. I have planted another black walnut or two. I will be long gone before they mature. When that day comes and this beautiful pulpit has grown old, perhaps one of them will do to make a replacement. To Elder Banks and his sons, Ben and Bradley, and to the skilled workers who have designed and built this, I offer my profound thanks for making it possible to have a small touch of mine in this great hall [the Conference Center in Salt Lake City] where the voices of prophets will go out to all the world in testimony of the Redeemer of Mankind."

—Gordon B. Hinckley, "To All the World in Testimony," in Conference Report, April 2000, 6.

Thomas S. Monson

BORN: AUGUST 21, 1927, SALT LAKE CITY, UTAH
PRESIDENT OF THE CHURCH: FEBRUARY 3, 2008, TO PRESENT

Thomas S. Monson

Thomas Spencer Monson, son of G. Spencer Monson and Gladys Condie, was born August 21, 1927, in Salt Lake City. Tom spent many carefree summers at a family cabin in Vivian Park in Provo Canyon. When he was twelve years old, he saved a girl from drowning in the Provo River. He said of the incident, "I just happened to be in the right place at the right time in order to provide assistance."[81]

Although his family didn't have many luxuries, the example of his parents' selfless giving and young Tom's tender heart led him to seek out the less fortunate in his neighborhood. For example, when Tom learned that the family of a childhood friend was having no Christmas dinner, Tom gave them his two pet rabbits—beautiful New Zealand white rabbits—saying, "It isn't turkey, but they will make you a good Christmas dinner."[82]

At the end of World War II, Tom enlisted in the United States Navy. After his military stint, he enrolled in the University of Utah, graduating cum laude in business. He married Frances Beverly Johnson on October 7, 1948, in the Salt Lake Temple. Of his wife, Tom said, "I could not have asked for a more loyal, loving, and understanding companion."[83] After sixty-four years of marriage, Frances passed away on May 17, 2013.

Elder Harold B. Lee took special interest in young Tom Monson. Elder Lee ordained Tom a high priest and set him apart as a counselor in a bishopric. Later Tom sought Elder Lee's advice about being commissioned an ensign in the Naval Reserve. Elder Lee advised

Tom to decline the commission and request a discharge. Tom expressed concern that such a request would not be granted given tensions in Asia. "Have more faith, Brother Monson," said Elder Lee. "Your future is not with the military."[84] Tom followed Elder Lee's advice and was discharged from the Naval Reserve in the last group processed before the outbreak of the Korean War. His headquarters outfit was activated, and six weeks later he was called to serve as a counselor in his ward bishopric.

At age twenty-two Tom was called to be the bishop of the Sixth-Seventh Ward in Salt Lake City. At the time, membership in the ward numbered 1,080, of which eighty-five were widows. Tom visited each widow on a regular basis, making sure her spiritual and temporal needs were met. Five years later, Tom was set apart as a counselor in the Temple View Stake presidency in Salt Lake City. He served as president of the Canadian Mission from 1959 to 1962. Although he and his family had moved from the Sixth-Seventh Ward, Tom continued his visits to each of the widows at Christmastime until 2009, when the last one passed away.

After completing his mission assignment, Tom worked for the Deseret News Press, one of the largest commercial printing firms in the western United States. Both before and after his service as a mission president, he had a distinguished career, including as an advertising executive with the *Deseret News* and as general manager of the Deseret News Press.

At age thirty-six, Tom was called to be an Apostle—one of the youngest men called to the Quorum of the Twelve Apostles in the twentieth century. At age fifty-eight, he was called to the First Presidency of the Church—the youngest man to hold that position in more than eighty years. He served as a counselor to Presidents Ezra Taft Benson, Howard W. Hunter, and Gordon B. Hinckley.

On February 3, 2008, Thomas S. Monson became the sixteenth President of The Church of Jesus Christ of Latter-day Saints. President Boyd K. Packer said of him, "[Tom] is more Christlike than the rest of us. He's known for emphasizing and elevating things that are most important, the ordinary things. He is the one for whom the widow and the orphan are not just statements in a book."

The Life Story of Thomas S. Monson in His Own Words

"We'll Just Burn a Circle in the Weeds"

"When I was growing up, each summer from early July until early September, my family stayed at our cabin at Vivian Park in Provo Canyon in Utah.

"One of my best friends during those carefree days in the canyon was Danny Larsen, whose family also owned a cabin at Vivian Park. . . .

"One morning Danny and I [age eight] decided we wanted to have a campfire that evening with all our canyon friends. We just needed to clear an area in a nearby field where all could gather. The June grass which covered the field had become dry and prickly, making the field unsuitable for our purposes. . . .

". . . I said to Danny, 'All we need is to set these weeds on fire. We'll just burn a circle in the weeds!' He readily agreed. . . .

". . . Without so much as a second thought, I ran to our cabin and grabbed a few matchsticks, making certain no one was watching. I hid them quickly in one of my pockets.

"Back to Danny I ran, excited that in my pocket I had the solution to our problem. I recall thinking that the fire would burn only as far as we wanted and then would somehow magically extinguish itself.

"I struck a match on a rock and set the parched June grass ablaze. It ignited as though it had been drenched in gasoline. . . . The menacing flames began to follow the wild grass up the mountainside, endangering the pine trees and everything else in their path.

"Finally we had no option but to run for help. Soon all available men and women at Vivian Park were dashing back and forth with wet burlap bags, beating at the flames in an attempt to extinguish them. After several hours the last remaining embers were smothered. The ages-old pine trees had been saved, as were the homes the flames would eventually have reached.

"Danny and I learned several difficult but important lessons that day—not the least of which was the importance of obedience."

—Thomas S. Monson, "Obedience Brings Blessings," *Ensign*, May 2013, 89–90.

"It Was a Memorable Christmas"

"Again Christmastime had come. We were preparing for the oven a gigantic turkey and anticipating the savory feast that awaited. A neighborhood pal of mine asked a startling question: 'What does turkey taste like?'

"I responded, 'Oh, about like chicken tastes.'

"Again a question: 'What does chicken taste like?'

"It was then that I realized my friend had never eaten chicken or turkey. I asked what his family was going to have for Christmas dinner. There was no prompt response, just a downcast glance and the comment, 'I dunno. There's nothing in the house.'

"I pondered a solution. There was none. I had no turkeys, no chicken, no money. Then I remembered I did have two pet rabbits. Immediately I took them to my friend and handed the box to him with the comment, 'Here, take these two rabbits. They're good to eat—just like chicken.'

"He took the box, climbed the fence, and headed for home—a Christmas dinner safely assured. Tears came easily to me as I closed the door to the empty rabbit hutch. But I was not sad. A warmth, a feeling of indescribable joy, filled my heart. It was a memorable Christmas."

—Thomas S. Monson, "Christmas Gifts, Christmas Blessings," *Ensign*, Dec. 1995, 4.

"If You Need It More Than Mark, You Take It"

"As Christmas approached, I yearned as only a [ten-year-old] boy can yearn for an electric train. My desire was not to receive the economical and everywhere-to-be-found windup model train; rather, I wanted one that operated through the miracle of electricity. The times were those of economic depression; yet Mother and Dad, through some sacrifice I am sure, presented to me on Christmas morning a beautiful electric train.

"For hours I operated the transformer, watching the engine first pull its cars forward, then push them backward around the track. Mother entered the living room and said to me that she had purchased a windup train for Mrs. Hansen's son, Mark, who lived down the lane. I asked if I could see the train. The engine was short and blocky, not long and sleek like the expensive model I had received. However, I did take notice of an oil tanker car that was part of his inexpensive set. My train had no such car, and pangs of envy began to be felt. I put up such a fuss that Mother succumbed to my pleadings and handed me the oil tanker car. She said, 'If you need it more than Mark, you take it.' I put it with my train set and felt pleased with the result.

"Mother and I took the remaining cars and the engine down to Mark Hansen. The young boy was a year or two older than I. He had never anticipated such a gift and was thrilled beyond words. He wound the key in his engine, it not being electric like mine, and was overjoyed as the engine and two cars, plus a caboose, went around the track.

"Then Mother wisely asked, 'What do you think of Mark's train, Tommy?'

"I felt a keen sense of guilt and became very much aware of my selfishness. I said to Mother, 'Wait just a moment. I'll be right back.'

"As swiftly as my legs could carry me, I ran home, picked up the oil tanker plus an additional car from my train set, and ran back down the lane to the Hansen home, joyfully saying to Mark, 'We forgot to bring two cars that belong to your train.' Mark coupled the two extra cars to his set. I watched the engine make its labored way around the track and felt supreme joy, difficult to describe and impossible to forget. The spirit of Christmas had filled my very soul."

—Thomas S. Monson, "Christmas Gifts, Christmas Blessings," *Ensign*, Dec. 1995, 3–4.

"She Was Our Nemesis, the Destroyer of Our Fun"

"When I was a deacon, I loved baseball; in fact, I still do. I had a fielder's glove inscribed with the name 'Mel Ott.' He was the Darryl Strawberry of my day. My friends and I would play ball in a small alleyway behind the houses where we lived. The quarters were cramped but all right, provided you hit straight away to center field. However, if you hit the ball to the right of center, disaster was at the door. Here lived a lady who would watch us play, and as soon as the ball rolled to her porch her English setter would retrieve the ball and present it to Mrs. Shinas as she opened the door. Into her house Mrs. Shinas would return and add the ball to the many she had previously confiscated. She was our nemesis, the destroyer of our fun—even the bane of our existence. . . .

"This private war continued for some time—perhaps two years—and then an inspired thaw melted the ice of winter and brought a springtime of good feelings to the stalemate. One night as I performed my daily task of hand-watering our front lawn, holding the nozzle of the hose in hand as was the style at that time, I noticed that Mrs. Shinas's lawn was dry and turning brown. I honestly don't know what came over me, but I took a few more minutes and, with our hose, watered her lawn. This I did each night, and then when autumn came, I hosed her lawn free of leaves as I did ours and stacked the leaves in piles at the street's edge to be burned or gathered. During the entire summer I had not seen Mrs. Shinas. We had long since given up playing ball in the alley. We had run out of baseballs and had no money to buy more.

"Then early one evening, her front door opened, and Mrs. Shinas beckoned for me to jump the small fence and come to her front porch. This I did, and as I approached her, Mrs. Shinas invited me into her living room, where I was asked to sit in a comfortable chair.

She went to the kitchen and returned with a large box filled with baseballs and softballs, representing several seasons of her confiscation efforts. The filled box was presented to me; however, the treasure was not to be found in the gift, but rather in her voice. I saw for the first time a smile come across the face of Mrs. Shinas, and she said, 'Tommy, I want you to have these baseballs, and I want to thank you for being kind to me.' I expressed my own gratitude to her and walked from her home a better boy than when I entered. No longer were we enemies. Now we were friends."

—Thomas S. Monson, "A Royal Priesthood," *Ensign*, May 1991, 49–50.

"You're Tommy Monson, My Primary Boy"

"When Melissa Georgell was in her nineties, she lived in a nursing facility in the northwest part of Salt Lake City. One year just before Christmas, I determined to visit my beloved Primary president. Over the car radio I heard the music of familiar Christmas carols: 'Hark! the Herald Angels Sing,' 'O Little Town of Bethlehem,' and many others. I reflected on the visit made by wise men those long years ago and the visit made by us boys when we portrayed the wise men in the pageant. The wise men brought precious gifts to the Christ child. I brought to Melissa only the gift of love and a desire to say 'Thank you.'

"I found her in the lunch room. She was staring at her plate of food, teasing it with the fork she held in her aged hand. Not a bite did she eat. As I spoke to her, my words were met by a benign but blank stare. I gently took her fork from her and began to feed her, talking all the time I did so about her service to boys and girls as a Primary worker and the joy which was mine to have later served as her bishop. You know, there wasn't even a glimmer of recognition, far less a spoken word. . . .

". . . My one-sided conversation wound down. I stood to leave. I held her frail hand in mine and gazed down into her wrinkled but beautiful countenance and said, 'God bless you, Melissa, and merry Christmas.'

"Without warning, she spoke the words, 'I know you. You're Tommy Monson, my Primary boy. How I love you.'

"She pressed my hand to her lips and bestowed on it the kiss of love. Tears coursed down her cheeks and bathed our clasped hands. Those hands, that day, were hallowed by heaven and graced by God. The herald angels did sing, for I heard them in my heart."

—Thomas S. Monson, "Primary Days," *Ensign*, Apr. 1994, 68.

"Through the Net It Went"

"As a young teenager, I participated in a Church basketball game. When the outcome was in doubt, the coach sent me onto the playing floor right after the second half began. I took an inbounds pass, dribbled the ball toward the key, and let the shot fly. Just as the ball left my fingertips, I realized why the opposing guards did not attempt to stop my drive: I was shooting for the wrong basket! I offered a silent prayer: 'Please, Father, don't let that ball go in.' The ball rimmed the hoop and fell out.

"From the bleachers came the call: 'We want Monson, we want Monson, we want Monson—out!' The coach obliged.

"Many years later, as a member of the Council of the Twelve, I joined other General Authorities in visiting a newly completed chapel where, as an experiment, we were trying out a tightly woven carpet on the gymnasium floor.

"While several of us were examining the floor, Bishop J. Richard Clarke, who was then in the Presiding Bishopric, suddenly threw the basketball to me with a challenge: 'I don't believe you can hit the basket, standing where you are!'

"I was some distance behind what is now the professional three-point line. I had never made such a basket in my entire life. Elder Mark E. Petersen of the Twelve called out to the others, 'I think he can!'

"My thoughts returned to my embarrassment of years before, shooting toward the wrong basket. Nevertheless, I aimed and let that ball fly. Through the net it went!

"Throwing the ball in my direction, Bishop Clarke once more issued the challenge: 'I know you can't do that again!'

"Elder Petersen spoke up, 'Of course, he can!'

"The words of the poet echoed in my heart: 'Lead us, O lead us, / Great Molder of men, / Out of the shadow / To strive once again.' I shot the ball. It soared toward the basket and went right through.

"That ended the inspection visit.

"At lunchtime Elder Petersen [not knowing how lucky the shots had been] said to me, 'You know, you could have been a starter in the NBA.'"

—Thomas S. Monson, "The Call for Courage," *Ensign*, May 2004, 56–57.

"I Have Never Forgotten the Interview"

"As I approached my 18th birthday and prepared to enter military service in World War II, I was recommended to receive the Melchizedek Priesthood. Mine was the task to telephone President Paul C. Child, my stake president, for an interview. He was one who loved and understood the holy scriptures. It was his intent that all others should similarly love and understand them. Since I knew from others of his rather detailed and searching interviews, our telephone conversation went something like this:

"'Hello, President Child. This is Brother Monson. I have been asked by the bishop to visit with you relative to being ordained an elder.'

"'Fine, Brother Monson. When can you see me?'

"Knowing that his sacrament meeting was at six o'clock, and desiring minimum exposure of my scriptural knowledge to his review, I suggested, 'How would five o'clock be?'

"His response: 'Oh, Brother Monson, that would not provide us sufficient time to peruse the scriptures. Could you please come at two o'clock, and bring with you your personally marked and referenced set of scriptures.'

"Sunday finally arrived, and I visited President Child's home on Indiana Avenue. I was greeted warmly, and then the interview began. He said, 'Brother Monson, you hold the Aaronic Priesthood. Have you ever had angels minister to you?'

"My reply was, 'No, President Child.'

"'Do you know,' said he, 'that you are entitled to such?'

"Again came my response, 'No.'

"Then he instructed, 'Brother Monson, repeat from memory the 13th section of the Doctrine and Covenants.'

"I began, 'Upon you my fellow servants, in the name of Messiah I confer the Priesthood of Aaron, which holds the keys of the ministering of angels . . .'

"'Stop,' President Child directed. Then in a calm, kindly tone he counseled, 'Brother Monson, never forget that as a holder of the Aaronic Priesthood you are entitled to the ministering of angels.'

"It was almost as though an angel were in the room that day. I have never forgotten the interview. I yet feel the spirit of that solemn occasion. I revere the priesthood of Almighty God. I have witnessed its power. I have seen its strength. I have marveled at the miracles it has wrought."

—Thomas S. Monson, "Priesthood Profiles," *New Era*, June 1987, 4–6.

"Monson, I'm Glad You Hold the Priesthood"

"When I departed for active duty with the navy, a member of my ward bishopric was at the train station to bid me farewell. Just before train time, he placed in my hand a book titled Missionary Handbook. I laughed and commented, 'I'm not going on a mission.' He answered, 'Take it anyway. It may come in handy.'

"It did. During basic training our company commander instructed us concerning how we might best pack our clothing in a large sea bag. He advised, 'If you have a hard, rectangular object you can place in the bottom of the bag, your clothes will stay more firm.' I suddenly remembered just the right rectangular object—the Missionary Handbook. Thus it served for 12 weeks.

"The night preceding our Christmas leave our thoughts were, as always, on home. The barracks were quiet. Suddenly I became aware that my buddy in the adjoining bunk—a Mormon boy, Leland Merrill—was moaning with pain. I asked, 'What's the matter, Merrill?'

"He replied, 'I'm sick. I'm really sick.'

"I advised him to go to the base dispensary, but he answered knowingly that such a course would prevent him from being home for Christmas.

"The hours lengthened; his groans grew louder. Then, in desperation, he whispered, 'Monson, Monson, aren't you an elder?' I acknowledged this to be so, whereupon he said, 'Give me a blessing.'

"I became very much aware that I had never given a blessing. I had never received such a blessing, and I had never witnessed a blessing being given. My prayer to God was a plea for help. The answer came: 'Look in the bottom of the sea bag.' Thus, at 2:00 A.M. I emptied on the deck the contents of the bag. I then took to the night light that hard, rectangular object, the Missionary Handbook, and read how one blesses the sick. With about 120 curious sailors looking on, I proceeded with the blessing. Before I could stow my gear, Leland Merrill was sleeping like a child.

"The next morning Merrill smilingly turned to me and said, 'Monson, I'm glad you hold the priesthood.' His gladness was only surpassed by my gratitude."

—Thomas S. Monson, "Priesthood Profiles," *New Era*, June 1987, 6.

"There Was a Young Lady I Wanted to Meet"

"As a student at the University of Utah, I was attending a dance on campus in the old union building. I was dancing with my date, a girl from West High School, when a young lady from East High School danced by with her partner. Her name was Frances Johnson, although I didn't know it at the time. I just took one look and decided that there was a young lady I wanted to meet. But she danced away. I might never have seen her again.

"About two months later I did. One day while waiting for the streetcar in Salt Lake City, I looked across the way and couldn't believe my eyes. There was the young lady I had seen dancing across the floor. She was standing with another young lady and a young man whom I remembered from grade school days. Unfortunately, I couldn't remember his name. I had a decision to make. What should

I do? I found in my heart an appreciation of the phrase: 'When the time for decision arrives, the time for preparation is past.' I squared my shoulders and plunged toward my opportunity. I walked up to that young man and said, 'Hello, my old friend from grade school days.'

"He looked at me blankly and said, 'I can't quite remember your name.' I told him my name. He told me his name, and then he introduced me to the girl who later became my wife. That day I made a note in my student directory to call on Frances Beverly Johnson, and I did. That decision, I believe, was perhaps the most important that I have ever made.

—Thomas S. Monson, "Whom Shall I Marry?" *New Era*, Oct. 2004, 4.

"He's My Grandfather's Brother"

"I asked [Frances Johnson] to go out with me. I went to her home to call on her. She introduced me, and her father said, 'Monson—that's a Swedish name, isn't it?'

"I said, 'Yes.'

"He said, 'Good.'

"Then he went into another room and brought out a picture of two missionaries with their top hats and their copies of the Book of Mormon.

"'Are you related to this Monson,' he said, 'Elias Monson?'

"I said, 'Yes, he's my grandfather's brother. He . . . was a missionary in Sweden.'

"Her father wept. He wept easily. He said, 'He and his companion were the missionaries who taught the gospel to my mother and my father and all of my brothers and sisters and to me.' He kissed me on the cheek. And then her mother cried, and she kissed me on the other cheek. And then I looked around for Frances. She said, 'I'll go get my coat.'"

—Thomas S. Monson, "Abundantly Blessed," *New Era*, May 2008, 111.

"A Fast Offering Envelope"

"One Sunday afternoon I received a phone call from the proprietor of a drugstore located within our ward boundaries. He indicated that earlier that morning, a young boy had come into his store and had purchased an ice-cream sundae from the soda fountain. He had paid for the purchase with money he took from an envelope, and then when he left, he had forgotten the envelope. When the proprietor had a chance to examine it, he found that it was a fast-offering envelope with the name and telephone number of our ward printed on it. As he described to me the boy who had been in his store, I immediately identified the individual—a young deacon from our ward who came from a less-active family.

"My first reaction was one of shock and disappointment to think that any of our deacons would take fast-offering funds intended for those in need and would go to a store on a Sunday and buy a treat with the money. I determined to visit the boy that afternoon in order to teach him about the sacred funds of the Church and his duty as a deacon to gather and to protect those funds.

"As I drove to the home, I offered a silent prayer for direction in what I should say to compose the situation. I arrived and knocked on the door. It was opened by the boy's mother, and I was invited into the living room. Although the room was barely lighted, I could see how small and run-down it was. The few pieces of furniture were threadbare. The mother herself looked worn out.

"My indignation at her son's actions that morning disappeared from my thoughts as I realized that here was a family in real need. I felt impressed to ask the mother if there was any food in the house. Tearfully she admitted that there was none. She told me that her husband had been out of work for some time and that they were in desperate need not only of food but also of money with which to pay the rent so that they wouldn't be evicted from the tiny house.

"I never did bring up the matter of the fast-offering donations, for I realized that the boy had most likely been desperately hungry when he stopped at the drugstore. Rather, I immediately arranged for assistance for the family, that they might have food to eat and a roof over their heads. In addition, with the help of the priesthood leaders in the ward, we were able to arrange employment for the husband so that he could provide for his family in the future."

—Thomas S. Monson, "Heavenly Homes, Forever Families," *Ensign*, June 2006, 101.

"I Worried about Any Members Who Were Inactive"

"As a bishop, I worried about any members who were inactive, not attending, not serving. Such was my thought one day as I drove down the street where Ben and Emily Fullmer lived. Aches and pains of advancing years caused them to withdraw from activity to the shelter of their home—isolated, detached, shut out from the mainstream of daily life and association. Ben and Emily had not been in our sacrament meeting for many years. Ben, a former bishop, would sit constantly in his front room reading and memorizing the New Testament. . . .

". . . I approached the door to their home and knocked. I heard the tiny fox terrier dog bark at my approach. Emily welcomed me in. Upon seeing me, she exclaimed, 'All day long I have waited for my phone to ring. It has been silent. I hoped the postman would deliver a letter. He brought only bills. Bishop, how did you know today is my birthday?'

"I answered, 'God knows, Emily, for He loves you.'

"In the quiet of their living room, I said to Ben and Emily, 'I really don't know why I was directed here today, but I was. Our Heavenly Father knows. Let's kneel in prayer and ask Him why.' This we did, and the answer came. As we arose from our knees, I said to Brother Fullmer, 'Ben, would you come to priesthood meeting when we meet with all the priesthood and relate to our Aaronic Priesthood boys the story you once told me when I was a boy, how you and a group of boys were en route to the Jordan River to swim one Sunday, but you felt the Spirit direct you to attend Sunday School. And you did. One of the boys who failed to respond to that Spirit drowned that Sunday. Our boys would like to hear your testimony.'

"'I'll do it,' he responded.

"I then said to Sister Fullmer, 'Emily, I know you have a beautiful voice. My mother has told me so. Our ward conference is a few weeks away, and our choir will sing. Would you join the choir and attend our ward conference and perhaps sing a solo?'

"'What will the number be?' she inquired.

"'I don't know,' I said, 'but I'd like you to sing it.'

"She sang. He spoke to the Aaronic Priesthood. Hearts were gladdened by the return to activity of Ben and Emily. They rarely missed a sacrament meeting from that day forward. The language of the Spirit had been spoken. It had been heard. It had been understood. Hearts were touched and souls saved. Ben and Emily Fullmer had come home."

—Thomas S. Monson, "Bring Him Home," *Ensign*, Nov. 2003, 58–59.

"You Found Me, Bishop!"

"I noted one Sunday morning that Richard, one of our priests who seldom attended, was again missing from priesthood meeting. I left the quorum in the care of the adviser and visited Richard's home. His mother said he was working at a local garage servicing automobiles. I drove to the garage in search of Richard and looked everywhere but could not find him. Suddenly, I had the inspiration to gaze down into the old-fashioned grease pit situated at the side of the building. From the darkness I could see two shining eyes. I heard Richard say, 'You found me, Bishop! I'll come up.' As Richard and I visited, I told him how much we missed him and needed him. I elicited a commitment from him to attend his meetings.

"His activity improved dramatically. He and his family eventually moved away, but two years later I received an invitation to speak in Richard's ward before he left on a mission. In his remarks that day, Richard said that the turning point in his life was when his bishop found him hiding in a grease pit and helped him to return to activity.

"Through the years I have received yearly progress reports from Richard, telling of his testimony, his family, and his faithful service in the Church, including his service as a bishop himself—twice."

—Thomas S. Monson, "Sugar Beets and the Worth of a Soul," *Ensign*, July 2009, 6–7.

"OUR WARD HAD 23 MEN IN UNIFORM"

"An assignment came from Church headquarters for all bishops . . . to write a personal, monthly letter to each serviceman from his ward. Our ward had 23 men in uniform. . . .

"One evening I handed to a sister in the ward the stack of 23 letters for the current month. Her assignment was to handle the mailing and to maintain the constantly changing address list. She glanced at one envelope and, with a smile, asked, 'Bishop, don't you ever get discouraged? Here is another letter to Brother Bryson. This is the 17th letter you have sent to him without a reply.'

"I responded, 'Well, maybe this will be the month.' As it turned out, that was the month. For the first time, he responded to my letter. His reply was a keepsake, a treasure. He was serving far away on a distant shore, isolated, homesick, alone. He wrote, 'Dear Bishop, I ain't much at writin' letters.' (I could have told him that several months earlier.) His letter continued, 'Thank you . . . for the personal letters. I have turned over a new leaf. I have been ordained a priest in the Aaronic Priesthood. My heart is full. I am a happy man.'

"Brother Bryson was no happier than was his bishop. I had learned the practical application of the adage 'Do [your] duty; that is best; leave unto [the] Lord the rest.'

"Years later, while attending the Salt Lake Cottonwood Stake when James E. Faust served as its president, I related that account in an effort to encourage attention to our servicemen. After the meeting, a fine-looking young man came forward. He took my hand in his and asked, 'Bishop Monson, do you remember me?'

"I suddenly realized who he was. 'Brother Bryson!' I exclaimed. 'How are you? What are you doing in the Church?'

"With warmth and obvious pride, he responded, 'I'm fine. I serve in the presidency of my elders quorum. Thank you again for your concern for me and the personal letters which you sent and which I treasure.'"

—Thomas S. Monson, "Willing and Worthy to Serve," *Ensign*, May 2012, 68–69.

"He Completed an Honorable Mission"

"As a mission president, I was afforded the privilege of guiding the activities of precious young men and women.

"Some had problems, others required motivation; but one came to me in utter despair. He had made his decision to leave the mission field when but at the halfway mark. His bags were packed, his return ticket purchased. He came by to bid me farewell. We talked; we listened; we prayed. There remained hidden the actual reason for his decision to quit.

"As we arose from our knees in the quiet of my office, the missionary began to weep. Flexing the muscle in his strong right arm, he blurted out, 'This is my problem. All through school my muscle power qualified me for honors in football and track, but my mental power was neglected. President Monson, I'm ashamed of my school record. It reveals that "with effort" I have the capacity to read at but the level of the fourth grade. I can't even read the Book of Mormon. How then can I understand its contents and teach others its truths?'

"The silence of the room was broken by my young nine-year-old son, who, without knocking, opened the door and, with surprise, apologetically said, 'Excuse me. I just wanted to put this book back on the shelf.'

"He handed me the book. Its title: *A Child's Story of the Book of Mormon*, by Dr. Deta P. Neeley. I turned to the foreword and read these words: 'This book has been written with a scientifically controlled vocabulary to the level of the fourth grade.' A sincere prayer from an honest heart had been dramatically answered.

"My missionary accepted the challenge to read the book. Half laughing, half crying, he declared, 'It will be good to read something I can understand.' Clouds of despair were dispelled by the sunshine of hope. He completed an honorable mission. He became a finisher."

[Through the years, he has served in many positions of responsibility in the Church.]

—Thomas S. Monson, "Finishers Wanted," *Ensign*, July 1972, 70.

"This Is the Building We Need Here in St. Thomas"

"[An] evidence of faith took place when I first visited the St. Thomas Branch of the Canadian Mission, situated about one hundred and twenty miles from Toronto. My wife and I had been invited to attend the branch sacrament meeting and to speak to the members there. . . .

". . . Our branch met in the basement of the lodge hall and was comprised of perhaps twenty-five members, twelve of whom were in attendance. The same individuals conducted the meeting, blessed and passed the sacrament, offered the prayers, and sang the songs.

"At the conclusion of the services, the branch president, Irving Wilson, asked if he could meet with me. At this meeting, he handed to me a copy of the *Improvement Era*, forerunner of today's *Ensign*. Pointing to a picture of one of our new chapels in Australia, President Wilson declared, 'This is the building we need here in St. Thomas.'

"I provided encouragement for them to grow in numbers by their personal efforts to fellowship and teach. The outcome is a classic example of faith, coupled with effort and crowned with testimony.

"President Wilson requested six additional missionaries to be assigned to St. Thomas. When this was accomplished, he called the missionaries to a meeting in the back room of his small jewelry store, where they knelt in prayer. He then asked one elder to hand to him the yellow-pages of the telephone directory, which was on a nearby table. President Wilson took the book in hand and observed, 'If we are ever to have our dream building in St. Thomas, we will need a Latter-day Saint to design it. Since we do not have a member who is an architect, we will simply have to convert one.' With his finger moving down the column of listed architects, he paused at one name and said, 'This is the one we will invite to my home to hear the message of the Restoration.'

"President Wilson followed the same procedure with regard to plumbers, electricians, and craftsmen of every description. Nor did he neglect other professions, feeling a desire for a well-balanced branch. The individuals were invited to his home to meet the missionaries, the truth was taught, testimonies were borne and conversion resulted. Those newly baptized then repeated the procedure themselves, inviting others to listen, week after week and month after month.

"The St. Thomas Branch experienced marvelous growth. Within two and one-half years, a site was obtained, a beautiful building was constructed, and an inspired dream became a living reality. That branch is now a thriving ward in a stake of Zion."

—Thomas S. Monson, "Days Never to Be Forgotten," *Ensign*, Nov. 1990, 68–69.

"Heavenly Father Does Hear Our Prayers"

"[B]efore leaving the United States [on a planned visit to Dresden in East Germany], I felt the prompting to buy three cartons of chewing gum. I purchased three flavors: Doublemint, Spearmint, and Juicy Fruit. Now, as the gathering of the youth was concluded, I distributed carefully to each youth two sticks of gum—something they had never before tasted. They received the gift with joy.

"The years went by. I returned to Dresden—the site of our earlier conference. Now we had chapels; now the people had freedom. They had a temple. Germany was no longer separated by political boundaries but had become one nation. The youth were now adults with children of their own.

"Following a large and inspirational conference, a mother and her daughter sought me out to speak to me. The daughter, who was [an older teenager] and who spoke some English, said to me, 'President Monson, do you remember long ago holding a brief gathering of youth following a district conference, where you gave to each boy and each girl two sticks of chewing gum?'

"I responded, 'Oh, yes, I surely do remember.'

"She continued, 'My mother was one to whom you gave that gift. She told me that she rationed in little pieces one stick of gum. She mentioned how sweet to the taste it was and so precious to her.' Then, under the approving smile of her dear mother, she handed to me a small box. As I opened the lid of the box, there I beheld the other stick of gum, still with its wrapper after nearly 20 years. And then she said, 'My mother and I want you to have this.'

"The tears flowed; embraces followed.

"The mother then spoke to me: 'Before you came to our conference so many years ago, I had prayed to my Heavenly Father to know that He indeed cared about me. I saved that gift so that I might remember and teach my [future children] that Heavenly Father does hear our prayers.'

"I [still have] that gift—even a symbol of faith and assurance of the heavenly help our Father and His Son, Jesus Christ, will provide you."

—Thomas S. Monson, "Pathways to Perfection," *Ensign*, May 2002, 101.

"EVERY BLESSING ANY MEMBER OF THE CHURCH ENJOYS"

"On a cloudy and rain-filled day [in 1968] I journeyed to the city of Görlitz, situated deep in the German Democratic Republic [East Germany] near the Polish and Czech borders. I attended my first meeting with the Saints. We assembled in a small and ancient building. As the members sang the hymns of Zion, they literally filled the hall with their faith and devotion. . . .

"I stood at the pulpit, and with tear-filled eyes and a voice choked with emotion, I made a promise to the people: 'If you will remain true and faithful to the commandments of God, every blessing any member of the Church enjoys in any country will be yours.' Then I realized what I had said. That night [when I returned to my hotel], I dropped to my knees and pleaded with my Heavenly Father, 'Father, I'm on Thy errand; this is Thy Church. I have spoken words that came not from me but from Thee and Thy Son. Wilt Thou fulfill the promise in the lives of this noble people.' Thus concluded my first visit to the German Democratic Republic. . . .

"On a Sunday morning, April 27, 1975, I stood on an outcropping of rock situated between the cities of Dresden and Meissen, high above the Elbe River, and offered a prayer on the land and its people. That prayer noted the faith of the members. It emphasized the tender feelings of many hearts filled with an overwhelming desire to obtain temple blessings. A plea for peace was expressed. Divine help was requested. I spoke the words: 'Dear Father, let this be the beginning of a new day for the members of Thy Church in this land.'

"Suddenly, from far below in the valley, a bell in a church steeple began to chime and the shrill crow of a rooster broke the morning silence, each heralding the commencement of a new day. Though my eyes were closed, I felt a warmth from the sun's rays reaching my face, my hands, my arms. How could this be? An incessant rain had been falling all morning.

"At the conclusion of the prayer, I gazed heavenward. I noted a ray of sunshine which streamed from an opening in the heavy clouds, a ray which engulfed the spot where our small group stood. From that moment I knew divine help was at hand."

—Thomas S. Monson, "Thanks Be to God," *Ensign*, May 1989, 50–52.

"Do You Believe In Miracles?"

Ann M. Dibb said of her father, Thomas S. Monson:

"A powerful example of my father's faith took place after my mother experienced a severe injury. She had fallen, hit her head, and was in a coma for three weeks. My father was very concerned and prayed continually. He was given a small room at the hospital, called a Comfort Room, and had all of his work sent to him. He visited my mother every hour and spoke to her. His faith and prayers were answered. She awoke from the coma.

"Not long afterwards, her doctor started explaining to my father and me what we could expect in terms of a recovery. He was not very optimistic. My father interrupted the doctor in mid-sentence and asked, 'Doctor, do you have faith? Do you believe in miracles?' The doctor stammered and did not know how to respond. Then my father continued, 'Well, I do. We're going to continue in our faith. We are going to pray. Frances will be in the Lord's hands, and along with all the capable medical help, we believe the Lord will help her recover.'

"With diligent care, therapy and time, my mother did make a remarkable recovery. Seeing this, several medical professionals acknowledged that my mother's recovery was a miracle. My father has great faith."

—Ann M. Dibb, "My Father Is a Prophet," BYU–Idaho devotional, Feb. 19, 2008.

BIBLIOGRAPHY

BOOKS

Bennett, Frances Grant. *Glimpses of a Mormon Family*. Salt Lake City: Deseret Book, 1968.

Benson, Ezra Taft. *Cross Fire: The Eight Years with Eisenhower*. Garden City, NY: Doubleday, 1962.

_____. *God, Family, Country: Our Three Great Loyalties*. Salt Lake City: Deseret Book, 1974.

_____. *The Teachings of Ezra Taft Benson*. Salt Lake City: Deseret Book, 1988.

Cowan, Richard O., Donald Q. Cannon, and Arnold K. Garr. *Encyclopedia of Latter-day Saint History*. Salt Lake City: Deseret Book, 2001.

Cowley, Matthias F. *Wilford Woodruff, Fourth President of The Church of Jesus Christ of Latter-day Saints: History of His Life and Labors as Recorded in His Daily Journals*. Salt Lake City: Bookcraft, 1964.

Dew, Sheri L. *Ezra Taft Benson: A Biography*. Salt Lake City: Deseret Book, 1987.

_____. *Go Forward with Faith: The Biography of Gordon B. Hinckley.* Salt Lake City: Deseret Book, 1996.

Gibbons, Francis M. *Joseph F. Smith: Patriarch and Preacher, Prophet of God.* Salt Lake City: Deseret Book, 1984.

_____. *Joseph Fielding Smith: Gospel Scholar, Prophet of God.* Salt Lake City: Deseret Book, 1992.

_____. *Lorenzo Snow: Spiritual Giant, Prophet of God.* Salt Lake City: Deseret Book, 1982.

Goates, L. Brent. *Harold B. Lee: Prophet & Seer.* Salt Lake City: Deseret Book, 2002.

Grant, Heber J. *Gospel Standards: Selections from the Sermons and Writings of Heber J. Grant.* Edited by G. Homer Durham. Salt Lake City: Deseret Book, 1976.

Hinckley, Bryant S. *The Faith of Our Pioneer Fathers.* Salt Lake City: Deseret Book, 1956.

_____. *Heber J. Grant: Highlights in the Life of a Great Leader.* Salt Lake City: Deseret Book, 1951.

Holzapfel, Richard Neitzel and R. Q. Shupe. *Joseph F. Smith: Portrait of a Prophet.* Salt Lake City: Deseret Book, 2000.

Hunter, Howard W. *The Teachings of Howard W. Hunter: Fourteenth President of The Church of Jesus Christ of Latter-day Saints.* Eduted by Clyde J. Williams. Salt Lake City: Bookcraft, 1997.

Jenson, Andrew. *Latter-day Saint Biographical Encyclopedia: A Compilation of Biographical Sketches of Prominent Men and Women in The Church of Jesus Christ of Latter-day Saints,* 4 vols. Salt Lake City: Andrew Jenson History Company, 1920.

Journal of Discourses, 26 vols. Liverpool: Latter Day Saints' Book Depot, 1854–1886.

Kimball, Edward L. and Andrew E. Kimball Jr. *Spencer W. Kimball: Twelfth President of The Church of Jesus Christ of Latter-day Saints.* Salt Lake City: Bookcraft, 1977.

Kimball, Spencer W. *Faith Precedes the Miracle*. Salt Lake City: Deseret Book, 1972.

————. *The Miracle of Forgiveness*. Salt Lake City: Bookcraft, 1969.

Kimball, Spencer W. *The Teachings of Spencer W. Kimball*. Edited by Edward L. Kimball. Salt Lake City: Bookcraft, 1982.

Knowles, Eleanor. *Howard W. Hunter*. Salt Lake City, Deseret Book, 1994.

Lee, Harold B. *Stand Ye in Holy Places*. Salt Lake City: Deseret Book, 1974.

Lee, Harold B. *The Teachings of Harold B. Lee: Eleventh President of The Church of Jesus Christ of Latter-day Saints.* Edited by Clyde J. Williams. Salt Lake City: Bookcraft, 1996.

Madsen, Susan Arrington. *The Lord Needed a Prophet*. Salt Lake City: Deseret Book, 1996.

Manuscript History of Brigham Young, 1801–1844. Edited by Elden Jay Watson. Salt Lake City: Elden Jay Watson, 1968.

Manscill, Craig, Robert Freeman, and Dennis Wright, eds. *Presidents of the Church: The Lives and Teachings of the Modern Prophets*. Springville, UT: Cedar Fort, 2008.

McConkie, Joseph F. *True and Faithful: The Life Story of Joseph Fielding Smith.* Salt Lake City: Bookcraft, 1971.

McKay, David Lawrence. *My Father, David O. McKay.* Edited by Lavina Fielding Anderson. Salt Lake City: Deseret Book, 1989.

McKay, David O. *Treasures of Life.* Salt Lake City: Deseret Book, 1962.

McKay, Llewelyn R. *Home Memories.* Salt Lake City: Deseret Book, 1956.

Middlemiss, Clare. *Cherished Experiences from the Writings of President David O. McKay.* Salt Lake City: Deseret Book, 1976.

Miner, Caroline Eyring and Edward L. Kimball. *Camilla: A Biography of Camilla Eyring Kimball.* Salt Lake City: Deseret Book, 1980.

Monson, Thomas S. *On the Lord's Errand: Memoirs of Thomas S. Monson.* Salt Lake City: Deseret Book, 1985.

Nibley, Preston. *The Presidents of the Church.* Salt Lake City: Deseret Book, 1977.

Presidents of the Church Student Manual. Salt Lake City: The Church of Jesus Christ of Latter-day Saints, 2003.

Roberts, B. H. *Comprehensive History of The Church of Jesus Christ of Latter-day Saints,* 7 vols. Provo, UT: Brigham Young University Press, 1965.

_____. *The Life of John Taylor.* Salt Lake City: Bookcraft, 1963.

Romney, Thomas C. *The Life of Lorenzo Snow: Fifth President of the Church of Jesus Christ of Latter-day Saints.* Salt Lake City: S.U.P. Memorial Foundation, 1955.

Smith, Joseph. *History of the Church of Jesus Christ of Latter-day Saints*, 7 vols. Salt Lake City: Deseret Book, 1957.

Smith, Joseph F. *Gospel Doctrine: Selections from the Sermons and Writings of Joseph F. Smith, Sixth President of The Church of Jesus Christ of Latter-day Saints*. Salt Lake City: Deseret Book, 1939.

Smith, Joseph Fielding. *Life of Joseph F. Smith: Sixth President of The Church of Jesus Christ of Latter-day Saints*. Salt Lake City: Deseret News Press, 1938.

————. *Seek Ye Earnestly*. Salt Lake City: Deseret Book, 1970.

Smith, Joseph Fielding Jr. and John J. Stewart. *The Life of Joseph Fielding Smith*. Salt Lake City: Deseret Book, 1972.

Snow, Eliza R. *Biography and Family Record of Lorenzo Snow*. Salt Lake City: Deseret News, 1884.

Swinton, Heidi S. *To the Rescue: The Biography of Thomas S. Monson*. Salt Lake City: Deseret Book, 2010.

Taylor, John. *The Gospel Kingdom: Selections from the Writings and Discourses of John Taylor, Third President of The Church of Jesus Christ of Latter-day Saints*. Edited by G. Homer Durham. Salt Lake City: Bookcraft, 1987.

The Teachings of George Albert Smith: Eighth President of The Church of Jesus Christ of Latter-day Saints. Salt Lake City: Bookcraft, Inc., 1996.

Teachings of Presidents of the Church: George Albert Smith. Salt Lake City: The Church of Jesus Christ of Latter-day Saints, 2011.

Teachings of Presidents of the Church: Harold B. Lee. Salt Lake City: The Church of Jesus Christ of Latter-day Saints, 2000.

Teachings of Presidents of the Church: Heber J. Grant. Salt Lake City: The Church of Jesus Christ of Latter-day Saints, 2013.

Teachings of Presidents of the Church: John Taylor. Salt Lake City: The Church of Jesus Christ of Latter-day Saints, 2001.

Teachings of Presidents of the Church: Joseph Smith. Salt Lake City: The Church of Jesus Christ of Latter-day Saints, 2007.

Teachings of Presidents of the Church: Joseph F. Smith. Salt Lake City: The Church of Jesus Christ of Latter-day Saints, 1998.

Teachings of Presidents of the Church: Joseph Fielding Smith. Salt Lake City: The Church of Jesus Christ of Latter-day Saints, 2013.

Teachings of Presidents of the Church: Lorenzo Snow. Salt Lake City: The Church of Jesus Christ of Latter-day Saints, 2012.

Teachings of Presidents of the Church: Spencer W. Kimball. Salt Lake City: The Church of Jesus Christ of Latter-day Saints, 2006.

West, Emerson R. *Profiles of the Presidents.* Salt Lake City: Deseret Book, 1977.

Wilson, Lycurgus A. *Life of David W. Patten, the First Apostolic Martyr.* Harleysville, PA: Silva Solutions, 2014.

Young, Brigham. *Discourses of Brigham Young: Second President of The Church of Jesus Christ of Latter-day Saints.* Selected by John A. Widtsoe. Salt Lake City: Deseret Book, 1954.

Articles

Ashton, Wendell J. "Elder Gordon B. Hinckley of the Council of the Twelve," *Improvement Era*, Dec. 1961, 978.

Benson, Ezra Taft. "Feed My Sheep." *Ensign*, Sept. 1987, 4–5.

_____. "Flooding the Earth with the Book of Mormon." *Ensign*, Nov. 1988, 4–6.

_____. "The Meaning of Easter." *Ensign*, Apr. 1992, 2.

_____. "Our Responsibility to Share the Gospel." *Ensign*, May 1985, 8.

_____. "To the Home Teachers of the Church." *Ensign*, May 1987, 51.

_____. "What I Hope You Will Teach Your Children about the Temple." *Ensign*, Aug. 1985, 8.

Cannon, Lucy Grant. "A Father Who Is Loved and Honored." *Improvement Era*, Nov. 1936, 682.

Faust, James E. "Howard W. Hunter: Man of God." *Ensign*, Apr. 1995, 26.

Gibbons, Francis M. "President Thomas S. Monson." *Ensign*, July 1995, 10.

Grant, Heber J. "Beginning Life Together." *Improvement Era*, Apr. 1936, 198–199.

_____. "The Nobility of Labor." *Improvement Era*, Dec. 1899, 82–84.

Green, Doyle L. "Tributes Paid President George Albert Smith." *Improvement Era*, June 1951, 404–405.

Hinckley, Bryant S. "Greatness in Men: Joseph Fielding Smith." *Improvement Era*, June 1932, 459.

_____. "Greatness in Men: Superintendent George Albert Smith." *Improvement Era*, Mar. 1932, 295.

Hinckley, Gordon B. "My Testimony." *Ensign*, May 2000, 70.

_____. "Praise to the Man." *Ensign*, Aug. 1983, 2.

_____. "A Prophet Polished and Refined." *Ensign*, Apr. 1995, 33.

_____. "A Prophet's Counsel and Prayer for Youth." *Ensign*, Jan. 2001, 5–7.

_____. "Taking the Gospel to Britain: A Declaration of Vision, Faith, Courage, and Truth." *Ensign*, July 1987, 7.

Holland, Jeffrey R. "President Gordon B. Hinckley: Stalwart and Brave He Stands." *Ensign*, June 1995, 12.

_____. "President Thomas S. Monson: In the Footsteps of the Master." *Ensign*, June 2008, 6.

_____. "President Thomas S. Monson: Man of Action, Man of Faith." *Ensign*, Feb. 1986, 12, 17.

Hull, Thomas. "Instructions to Missionaries." *Improvement Era*, Dec. 1899, 128.

Hunter, Howard W. "Basic Concepts of Honesty." *New Era*, Feb. 1978, 4–5.

_____. "Exceeding Great and Precious Promises." *Ensign*, Nov. 1994, 7.

"Joseph Smith, the Prophet." *Juvenile Instructor*, Nov. 26, 1870, 186.

Kimball, Spencer W. "He Did It with All His Heart, and Prospered." *Ensign*, Mar. 1981, 4.

_____. "Listen to the Prophets." *Ensign*, May 1978, 76.

_____. "President Kimball Speaks Out on Profanity." *Ensign*, Feb. 1981, 3.

_____. "A Program for Man." *Ensign*, Nov. 1976, 110.

_____. "Rendering Service to Others." *Ensign*, May 1981, 45.

_____. "Therefore I Was Taught." *Ensign*, Jan. 1982, 3.

_____. "We Need a Listening Ear." *Ensign*, Nov. 1979, 5.

_____. "What I Read as a Boy." *Children's Friend*, Nov. 1943, 508.

_____. "When the World Will Be Converted." *Ensign*, Oct. 1974, 3.

Lee, Harold B. "Admonitions for the Priesthood of God." *Ensign*, Jan. 1973, 104.

_____. "May the Kingdom of God Go Forth." *Ensign*, Jan. 1973, 23–25.

_____. "Meeting the Needs of a Growing Church." *Improvement Era*, Jan. 1968, 26.

"Memories of a Prophet." *Improvement Era*, Feb. 19, 1970, 72.

Monson, Leland H. "David O. McKay Was a Deacon, Too." *Instructor*, Sept. 1962, 298–299.

Monson, Thomas S. "Abundantly Blessed." *New Era*, Apr. 2008, 111.

_____. "Bring Him Home." *Ensign*, Nov. 2003, 58–59.

_____. "The Call for Courage." *Ensign*, May 2004, 54–57.

_____. "Christmas Gifts, Christmas Blessings." *Ensign*, Dec. 1995, 4.

_____. "Days Never to Be Forgotten." *Ensign*, Nov. 1990, 68–69.

_____. "Finishers Wanted." *Ensign*, July 1972, 70.

_____. "God Be with You Till We Meet Again." *Ensign*, Mar. 2008, 30.

_____. "Heavenly Homes, Forever Families." *Ensign*, June 2006, 101.

_____. "My Brother's Keeper." *Ensign*, May 1990, 47.

_____. "Obedience Brings Blessings." *Ensign*, May 2013, 89–90.

_____. "Pathways to Perfection." *Ensign*, May 2002, 101.

_____. "Primary Days." *Ensign*, April 1994, 68.

_____. "A Royal Priesthood." *Ensign*, May 1991, 49–50.

_____. "Sugar Beets and the Worth of a Soul." *Ensign*, July 2009, 6–7.

_____. "Thanks Be to God." *Ensign*, May 1989, 50–52.

_____. "Whom Shall I Marry?" *New Era*, Oct. 2004, 4.

_____. "Willing and Worthy to Serve." *Ensign*, May 2012, 68–69.

Morrell, Jeanette McKay. "Boyhood of President David O. McKay." *Relief Society Magazine*, Oct. 1953, 656.

Packer, Boyd K. "President Gordon B. Hinckley: First Counselor." *Ensign*, Feb. 1986, 5.

Park, Babzanne and Preston Heiselt. "President Spencer W. Kimball: The Arizona Years." *New Era*, March 1978.

Pearce, Virginia H. "A Daughter's Tribute." *Ensign*, March 2008, 18.

"The Place of the Young Men's Mutual Improvement Associations in the Church." *Improvement Era*, Aug. 1912, 872.

"President Harold B. Lee's Closing Remarks." *Ensign*, Jan. 1972, 129.

"President Heber J. Grant." *Improvement Era*, June 1945, 332.

"Priesthood Profiles." Priesthood commemoration satellite broadcast, May 17, 1987, cited in Thomas S. Monson, "Priesthood Profiles," *New Era*, June 1987, 4–6.

Ricks, Kellene. "Friend to Friend." *Friend*, Apr. 1990, 6.

Rodriguez, Derin Head. "Flora Amussen Benson: Handmaiden of the Lord, Helpmeet of a Prophet, Mother in Zion." *Ensign*, March 1987, 16–17.

Searle, Don L. "President Ezra Taft Benson Ordained Thirteenth President of the Church." *Ensign*, Dec. 1985.

Scott, Richard G. "The Power of the Book of Mormon in My Life." *Ensign*, Oct. 1984, 9.

"Significant Counsel to the Young People of the Church." *Improvement Era*, Aug. 1921, 871–872.

Simpson, Robert L. "The Power and Responsibilities of the Priesthood." *Speeches of the Year*, Mar. 31, 1964, 8.

Smith, George Albert. "Boyhood Experiences." *Juvenile Instructor*, Feb. 1943, 73.

_____. "Freely Have Ye Received, Freely Give." *Ensign*, June 1972, 33–34.

_____. "On Searching for Family Records." *Improvement Era*, Aug. 1946, 491.

_____. "The Pathway of Righteousness." *Improvement Era*, Apr. 1950, 362, 410.

_____. "Your Good Name." *Improvement Era*, March 1947, 139.

Smith, Joseph Fielding. "My Dear Young Fellow Workers." *New Era*, Jan. 1971, 4–5.

_____. "A Prophet's Blessing." *Ensign*, July 1972, 130.

Snow, LeRoi C. "Devotion to a Divine Inspiration." *Young Woman's Journal*, June 1919, 304.

_____. "An Experience of My Father's." *Improvement Era*, Sept. 1933, 677.

_____. "Raised from the Dead." *Improvement Era*, Sept. 1929, 884–886.

Taylor, Moses W. "Stories and Counsel of Prest. Taylor." *Young Woman's Journal*, May 1905, 218–219.

"Three Nights' Public Discussion . . ." In *A Series of Pamphlets, by Orson Pratt . . . (1851)*, 17–18.

Tullidge, Edward W. "Chapters from the Life of Pres. Brigham Young." *Millennial Star*, Apr. 9, 1877, 226.

Wallis, James H. "President Grant—Defender of the Word of Wisdom." *Improvement Era*, Nov. 1936, 698.

"Welfare and the Relief Society." *Relief Society Magazine*, Apr. 1962, 238.

Newspapers

"Accused of Cheating, He Learned of Inner Peace." *Church News*, June 4, 1994.

Benson, Ezra Taft. "Press Conference." *Church News*, Nov. 17, 1985.

"Brigham Young's Reply to the New York Herald." *Millennial Star*, May 6, 1873, 286–287.

Call, Terry W. "David O. McKay." *Deseret News*, Sept. 25, 1993.

"Cultivate Forbearance." *Millennial Star*, July 11, 1892, 441–442.

Deseret News, Deseret News Weekly, Deseret News Semi-Weekly, 1856–1901.

"Discourse by President Wilford Woodruff." *Millennial Star*, May 14, 1896, 310.

"Discourse by President Wilford Woodruff." *Millennial Star*, Nov. 21, 1895, 741.

"Discourse by President Woodruff." *Millennial Star*, Oct. 1, 1891, 628.

"Extract from the Private Journal of Joseph Smith Jr." *Times and Seasons*, Nov. 1839, 7–8.

Heslop, J. M. "Hard Work and Responsibility Bring Success." *Church News*, Feb. 8, 1975.

"History of Brigham Young." *Millennial Star*, July 11, 1863, 439.

"History of Wilford Woodruff (From His Own Pen): Chapter of Accidents." *Millennial Star*, June 24, 1865, 359–360, 392.

"A husband plus $150: 'We Are in Good Shape!'" *Church News*, June 24, 2000.

"Joseph Fielding Smith." *Church News*, Oct. 30, 1993.

"Letter from Joseph Smith to Isaac Galland, March 22, 1839, Liberty Jail, Liberty, Missouri." *Times and Seasons*, Feb. 1840, 55–56.

"Mormonism in Salt Lake." *Millennial Star*, Sept. 14, 1899, 579.

"Organization of the Church in Italy." *Millennial Star*, Dec. 15, 1850, 373.

"Reflecting on a Need Led to New Concept." *Church News*, June 24, 2000.

Smith, George Albert. "Pres. Smith's Leadership Address." *Deseret News*, Feb. 16, 1946.

Smith, Joseph. "Church History." *Times and Seasons*, March 1, 1842, 706–709.

Smith, Joseph. "To the Elders of the Church of Latter Day Saints." *Messenger and Advocate*, Sept. 1835, 179–180.

Snow, Lorenzo. "Discourse." *Millennial Star*, Apr. 18, 1887, 242–243.

"South Sea Islands Members Pay Devotions to Leader,. *Church News*, Jan. 29, 1955.

Van Leer, Twila. "Pres. Hunter is Longtime Family Man, Church Servant." *Deseret News*, June 6, 1994.

CONFERENCE REPORTS

Benson, Ezra Taft. "Faith of the Latter-day Saints." Conference Report, Oct. 1948, 98.

_____. "The Faithfulness of the European Saints." Conference Report, Apr. 1947, 154.

_____. "Our Commission to Take the Gospel to the World." Conference Report, Apr. 1984, 44.

_____. "Our Divine Constitution." Conference Report, Oct. 1987, 5.

_____. "Preparing Yourselves for Missionary Service." Conference Report, Apr. 1985, 48–49.

Grant, Heber J. "Criticism Shows Failure to Observe Law." Conference Report, Apr. 1937, 13.

_____. "The Destroyer Rebuked." Conference Report, Apr. 1925, 9–10.

_____. "Gifts Promised and Bestowed." Conference Report, Oct. 1919, 32.

_____. "His Father." Conference Report, Oct. 1934, 4.

_____. "My Call to the Apostleship." Conference Report, Oct. 3, 1942, 24–25

_____. "My Soul Delighteth in the Song of the Heart." Conference Report, Apr. 1900, 61–62.

Hinckley, Gordon B. "Bring Up a Child in the Way He Should Go." Conference Report, Oct. 1993, 75–78.

_____. "Some Lessons I Learned as a Boy." Conference Report, Apr. 1993, 69–70.

_____. "To All the World in Testimony." Conference Report, Apr. 2000, 5.

_____. "The Women in Our Lives." Conference Report, Oct. 2004, 85.

Kimball, Spencer W. "Appreciation for the Descendants of Lehi." Conference Report, Apr. 6, 1947, 144.

_____. "Law of Consecration." Conference Report, Apr. 1975, 114.

_____. "Obedience to Word of Wisdom." Conference Report, Apr. 1974, 127–128.

_____. "A Testimony of the Truth Comes through Righteous Living." Conference Report, Oct. 1944, 43.

Lee, Harold B. "Address," Conference Report, Oct. 1967, 98.

_____. "Admonitions of the Priesthood." Conference Report, Oct. 1972, 123–124.

_____. "May the Kingdom of God Go Forth." Conference Report, Oct. 1972, 18–20.

_____. "Stand Ye in Holy Places." Conference Report, Apr. 8, 1973, 179.

_____. "A Tribute to Father, Mother and Wife." Conference Report, Apr. 6, 1941, 141.

McKay, David O. "Address." Conference Report, Oct. 1956, 91.

_____. "General Conference Address." Conference Report, Oct. 1951, 182–183.

_____. Conference Report, Apr. 1964, 5.

_____. "Responsibility of Leadership." Conference Report, Apr. 9, 1951, 157.

_____. "Simple Faith of a Child." Conference Report, Apr. 1912, 52.

_____. "Spirituality in Leading and Teaching the Gospel." Conference Report, Oct. 1968, 84–87.

_____. "The Transforming Power of Faith in Jesus Christ." Conference Report, Apr. 1951, 93.

Smith, George Albert. "Assurance of Eternal Life." Conference Report, Oct. 1948, 165–166.

_____. "Conversion through Book of Mormon." Conference Report, Oct. 1948, 6–7.

_____. "Early Life." Conference Report, Apr. 1949, 83–84.

_____. "The Gospel, a Panacea for the Ills of Mankind." Conference Report, Apr. 1925, 68.

_____. "Humble but Great Men." Conference Report, Apr. 1931, 31.

_____. "In This Building." Conference Report, Oct. 1934, 51.

_____. "Incidents from Missionary Life." Conference Report, Oct. 1945, 115–116.

_____. "Mother's Teachings." Conference Report, Oct. 1946, 150–151.

_____. "The Promise of Eternal Life Conditional." Conference Report, Oct. 1921, 42.

_____. "Responsibilities of a Bishop." Conference Report, Oct. 1948, 181.

Smith, Joseph F. "Continuous Communication with the Spirit of the Lord." Conference Report, Oct. 1918, 2.

_____. "Unnecessary Questions." Conference Report, Apr. 1915, 138.

Smith, Joseph Fielding. "Address." Conference Report, Apr. 1960, 73.

_____. "An Anchor to Our Souls." Conference Report, Apr. 1962, 44.

_____. "Born of Goodly Parents." Conference Report, Apr. 1930, 91.

Smith, Joseph Fielding. "Scriptural Promises to the Obedient." Conference Report, Oct. 1935, 12.

Snow, Lorenzo. "Opening Address." Conference Report, Apr. 5, 1901, 3.

_____. "Testimony that Joseph Was a Prophet." Conference Report, Oct. 7, 1900, 61.

Unpublished Manuscripts

Benson, Ezra Taft. Regional Representatives Seminar, April 2, 1982, Salt Lake City. Church History Library, Salt Lake City.

_____. "Temple Memories." Ogden Utah Temple Dedication, Jan. 18, 1972, Ogden, Utah. Church History Library, Salt Lake City.

McKay, David O. "Letter of David O. McKay to Dr. Obadiah H. Riggs," Dec. 9, 1900, ms. 668, box 1, in David Oman McKay Papers, Western Americana Special Collections, Marriott Library, University of Utah, Salt Lake City.

_____. "North British Missionary Meeting," March 1, 1961, in Clare Middlemiss notebooks, 1955–1980, ms. 9427, unpaginated, Church History Library, Salt Lake City.

_____. "Where Knowledge Is Absolute," Jan. 11, 1923, in Clare Middlemiss notebooks, 1955–1980, ms. 9427, unpaginated, Church History Library, Salt Lake City.

Simpson, Robert L. Interview in Oct. 1997, St. George, Utah, by Mary Jane Woodger, transcript, McKay Research Project, in author's possession.

Smith, George Albert. Journal, Feb. 24–25, 1909, George A. Smith Papers, ms. 36, box 73, book 6, fd. 5, 30, Marriott Library, University of Utah, Salt Lake City.

Smith, Joseph. History 1832, 1. Letter Book I, 1829–1835, Joseph Smith Collection, Church History Library, Salt Lake City.

_____. Letter to Emma Smith, March 21, 1839, Liberty Jail, Liberty, MO, Joseph Smith Collection, Church History Library, Salt Lake City.

Smith, Joseph F. Letter to Reed Smoot, April 9, 1904, Smoot Papers, L. Tom Perry Special Collections, Harold B. Lee Library, Brigham Young University, Provo, UT.

Woodruff, Wilford. Journal (1807–1898), July 25, 1887, typescript, Church History Library, Salt Lake City.

Young, Brigham. Journal (1801–1877), Nov. 26, 1842, typescript, Church History Library, Salt Lake City.

ENDNOTES

1. Spencer W. Kimball, "President Kimball Speaks Out on Profanity," *Ensign*, Feb. 1981, 3.

2. *Millennial Star*, Aug. 24, 1899, 532–533.

3. "Welfare and the Relief Society," *Relief Society Magazine*, April 1962, 238; Howard W. Hunter, "Welfare and the Relief Society," general Relief Society conference address, Sept. 28, 1961, in Williams, *Teachings of Howard W. Hunter*, 159.

4. Joseph Smith—History 1:5, 10.

5. Joseph Smith—History 1:11–12.

6. Joseph Smith—History 1:17, 19, 21, 25.

7. Joseph Smith—History 1:34.

8. Roberts, *Comprehensive History*, 2:349–350.

9. D&C 135:3.

10. Brigham Young, "March of Mormonism, etc.," in *Journal of Discourses*, 1:88.

11. Edward W. Tullidge, "Chapters from the Life of Pres. Brigham Young," *Millennial Star*, Apr. 9, 1877, 226.

12. Watson, *Manuscript History*, 17–18.

13. Watson, *Manuscript History*, 169.

14. Edward W. Tullidge, "Chapters from the Life of Pres. Brigham Young," *Millennial Star*, May 7, 1877, 291.

15. Smith, *History of the Church*, 7:233.

16. Smith, *History of the Church*, 7:256.

17. "History of Brigham Young," *Millennial Star*, July 11, 1863, 439.

18. Brigham Young, "The United Order, etc.," in *Journal of Discourses*, 18:355–356.

19. Roberts, *Life of John Taylor*, 38.

20. Roberts, *Life of John Taylor*, 48.

21. *Journal of Discourses*, 25:86.

22 Paul Hyde and Dennis Wright, "John Taylor," in *Presidents of the Church*, 65.

23. In *Journal of Discourses*, 26:156.

24. Roberts, *Life of John Taylor*, 47–48, 394.

25. Cowley, *Wilford Woodruff*, 18, 33–34.

26. Cowley, *Wilford Woodruff*, 109–110, 119.

27. Cowley, *Wilford Woodruff*, 204, 208.

28. Cowley, *Wilford Woodruff*, 346–347, 477.

29. Cowley, *Wilford Woodruff*, 506.

30. Cowley, *Wilford Woodruff*, 506, 560, 565.

31. Cowley, *Wilford Woodruff*, 570.

32. Jenson, *LDS Biographical Encyclopedia*, 1:26.

33. Romney, *Life of Lorenzo Snow*, 11.

34. Romney, *Life of Lorenzo Snow*, 15.

35. Gibbons, *Lorenzo Snow*, 10.

36. Snow, *Biography and Family Record of Lorenzo Snow*, 19.

37. *Teachings of Presidents of the Church: Lorenzo Snow*, xii.

38. Gibbons, *Lorenzo Snow*, 214–215.

39. Romney, *Life of Lorenzo Snow*, 425.

40. *Church News*, Jan. 20, 1934.

41. Romney, *Life of Lorenzo Snow*, 439.

42. Smith, *Life of Joseph F. Smith*, 124.

43. Smith, *Life of Joseph F. Smith*, 180–181.

44. Smith, *Life of Joseph F. Smith*, 227.

45. Joseph F. Smith to Reed Smoot, April 9, 1904, Smoot Papers.

46. Smith, *Life of Joseph F. Smith*, 433.

47. Heber J. Grant, "Gifts Promised and Bestowed," in Conference Report, Oct. 1919, 32.

48. Durham, *Gospel Standards*, 355.

49. Durham, *Gospel Standards*, 194.

50. Durham, *Gospel Standards*, 195–196.

51. James H. Wallis, "President Grant—Defender of the Word of Wisdom," *Improvement Era*, Nov. 1936, 698.

52. Heber J. Grant, "Criticism Shows Failure to Observe Law," in Conference Report, Apr. 1937, 13.

53. "President Heber J. Grant," *Improvement Era*, June 1945, 332.

54. Creed of George Albert Smith, in Bryant S. Hinckley, "Greatness in Men: Superintendent George Albert Smith," *Improvement Era*, Mar. 1932, 295.

55. George Albert Smith Journal, Feb. 24–25, 1909, George A. Smith Papers, ms. 36, box 73, book 6, fd. 5, 30.

56. George Albert Smith, "Your Good Name," *Improvement Era*, March 1947, 139.

57. Jeanette McKay Morrell, "Boyhood of President David O. McKay," *Relief Society Magazine*, Oct. 1953, 656; Terry W. Call, "David O. McKay," *Deseret News*, Sept. 25, 1993.

58. John Smith, Patriarch to the Church, in Preston Nibley, *The Presidents of the Church* (Deseret Book, 1974), 312.

59. David O. McKay, "Spirituality in Leading and Teaching the Gospel," in Conference Report, Oct. 1968, 84–87.

60. *Teachings of Presidents of the Church: David O. McKay* (2011), 49.

61. David O. McKay, "Highest of All Ideals," in Conference Report, Apr. 1951, 93.

62. Quoted from J. E. McCulloch, *Home: The Savior of Civilization* [1924], 42; in David O. McKay, "No Other Success Can Compensate for Failure in the Home," Conference Report, Apr. 1935, 115–116.

63. Joseph Fielding Smith, "Born of Goodly Parents," in Conference Report, April 1930, 91.

64. Bryant S. Hinckley, "Greatness in Men: Joseph Fielding Smith," *Improvement Era*, June 1932, 459.

65. Joseph Fielding Smith, "A Prophet's Blessing," *Ensign*, July 1972, 130.

66. *Presidents of the Church Student Manual*, 180.

67. "Harold Bingham Lee: Humility, Benevolence, Loyalty," *Ensign*, Feb. 1974, 90.

68. "President Harold B. Lee's Closing Remarks," *Ensign*, Jan. 1974, 129.

69. West, *Profiles of the Presidents*, 336.

70. *Presidents of the Church Student Manual*, 193.

71. Babzanne Park and Preston Heiselt, "President Spencer W. Kimball: The Arizona Years," *New Era*, Mar. 1978.

72. Kimball and Kimball, *Spencer W. Kimball*, 195.

73. Garr, Cannon, and Cowan, *Encyclopedia of Latter-day Saint History*, 94.

74. Garr, Cannon, and Cowan, *Encyclopedia of Latter-day Saint History*, 95.

75. Howard W. Hunter, "The Great Symbol of Our Worship," *Ensign*, Oct. 1994, 5.

76. Howard W. Hunter, "Exceeding Great and Precious Promises," *Ensign*, Nov. 1994, 7.

77. Gordon B. Hinckley, "A Prophet Polished and Refined," *Ensign*, Apr. 1995, 33.

78. J. M. Heslop, "Hard Work and Responsibility Bring Success," *Church News*, Feb. 8, 1975, 4.

79. Dew, *Go Forward with Faith*, 64.

80. "Gordon B. Hinckley," in *Presidents of the Church*, ed. Craig K. Manscill, Robert C. Freeman, Dennis A. Wright.

81. Jeffrey R. Holland, "President Thomas S. Monson: Man of Action, Man of Faith," *Ensign*, Feb. 1986, 17; see also Jeffrey R. Holland, "President Thomas S. Monson: In the Footsteps of the Master," *Ensign*, June 2008, 6.

82. Holland, "President Thomas S. Monson: Man of Action, Man of Faith," *Ensign*, Feb. 1986, 12.

83. Thomas S. Monson, "Looking Back and Moving Forward," in Conference Report, Apr. 2008.

84. Francis M. Gibbons, "President Thomas S. Monson," *Ensign*, July 1995, 10.

85. Swinton, *To the Rescue*, 1, 4.

ABOUT THE AUTHORS

DR. SUSAN EASTON BLACK JOINED the faculty of Brigham Young University in 1978, where she is a professor of Church history and doctrine. She is also past associate dean of General Education and Honors and director of Church History in the Religious Studies Center.

The recipient of numerous academic awards, she received the Karl G. Maeser Distinguished Faculty Lecturer Award in 2000, the highest award given a professor on the BYU–Provo campus. Dr. Black has authored, edited, and compiled more than 100 books and 250 articles. She and her husband, George Durrant, are currently serving a mission in Nauvoo, Illinois.

DR. MARY JANE WOODGER IS a professor of Church history and doctrine at Brigham Young University. After obtaining a master of education degree at Utah State University, she received a doctor of education degree from BYU in educational leadership, with a minor in Church history and doctrine.

She was honored by Kappa Omicron Nu with the Award of Excellence for her dissertation research on the educational ideals of President David O. McKay.

She is the author of several books and has also authored numerous articles on doctrinal, historical, and educational subjects that have appeared in various academic journals and religious publications. Dr. Woodger received the Best Article of the Year Award from the Utah Historical Society and has received the Brigham Young University Faculty Women's Association Teaching Award.